PLAINS INDIAN TRIBES
DURING THE PERIOD 1800-1860

The broken line encloses the true high Plains Indian
culture, c. 1820, generally defined as the nomadic-
horse-buffalo culture. To the east were the semi-
sedentary groups, and a detached group (Mandan,
Hidatsa, Arikara) on the upper Missouri.

Note. During this period a number of tribes were moved
from the east and relocated in this area. Principally
the Kickapoo, Shawnee, and Delaware from the
north-east and the Cherokee, Creek, Chickasaw,
Seminole, and Chocotaw from the south-east. *Adapted
from the original map by M. G. Johnson, Walsall.*

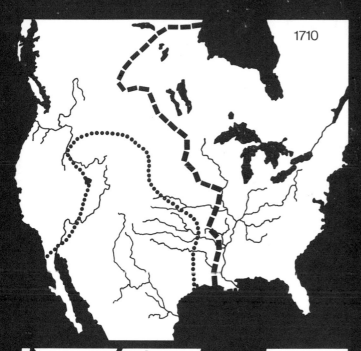

1710

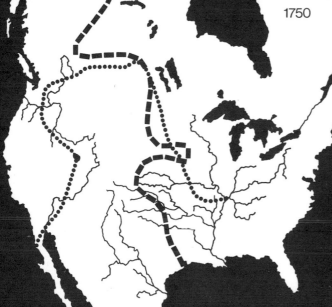

1750

■■■ Gun Frontier   ●●●●● Horse Frontier

The horse frontier moved north, and opened out —
finally encompassing the whole west. The gun frontier
moved west, inexorably. *Top,* North America in 1710
and, *bottom,* in 1750. *Based on information in
F. R. Secoy: CHANGING MILITARY PATTERNS
ON THE GREAT PLAINS. University of Washington
Press, 1953.*

The Warriors
of the Plains

Colin Taylor

HAMLYN

London · New York · Sydney · Toronto

Contents

16026

Published by
The Hamlyn Publishing Group Limited 1975
London · New York · Sydney · Toronto
Astronaut House, Hounslow Road, Feltham, Middlesex, England

© Copyright The Hamlyn Publishing Group Limited 1975

ISBN 0 600 36974 9

Printed in Spain by
Printer Industria Gráfica sa, Tuset 19
Barcelona, San Vicente dels Horts
Deposito Legàl B.38060–1974
Mohn-Gordon Ltd., London

Preface

I owe the idea for this book to Peter Watkins who, nearly a decade ago, asked me to undertake research for him on various aspects of North American Plains Indian culture and warfare.

Two people, friends of almost twenty-five years' standing, have particularly influenced me in my studies – Edward H. Blackmore, who for more than fifty years has lectured on the Plains Indians and championed their cause and J. C. Ewers, Senior Ethnologist of the Smithsonian Institution, Washington, D.C. The former has always kept me aware of the fact that the warriors of the Plains were human beings – The People – and not just objects to be studied dispassionately; the latter the importance of diligent and careful research together with a balanced interpretation of the facts.

It is not possible to do full justice to the many topics which I have attempted to cover in this book; the geography of the Great Plains and the many and varied facets of the way of life of its people are studies in themselves but I hope that the ethos of the old-time Plains Warrior comes through.

I have drawn on most of the published scientific writings of the Plains tribes and supplemented this with unpublished material, including my own research notes. The illustrations are from various sources and have been carefully selected to match the topics covered in the text. A large number have never been published before. Some are from private collections through the courtesy of the owners, and thus I hope the book will have appeal not only to the general reader, but also to the amateur and professional scholar.

Many friends have helped and advised with this book. Edward H. Blackmore and Ian West read the chapters on material culture while Barry Johnson, for many years editor of the *Brand Book* of The English Westerners' Society, read the chapters on the Indian wars, and I am most grateful for their invaluable advice and comments. The final text, however, is my own responsibility. Additionally Sam Cahoon, Paul Dyck, John Ewers, Paul Ewald, Norman Feder, Dick Frost, Mildred Goosman, Mike Griffiths, Michael G. Johnson, Dick Pohrt and Francis Taunton were generous with their advice and help, particularly with the illustrations.

My thanks to my family who helped with the text, editor Michael Stapleton who so efficiently smoothed the way, Richard Crossman who has tracked down the illustrations, and to my wife, Betty, who gave the whole thing its final polish.

We look back with nostalgia over the last fifteen years when, at various times, with British and American friends of equal enthusiasm – the Blackmores, Cahoons, Pohrts and Wests – we visited the reservations and battlefields, danced with the Sioux and Crow, hunted with the Gros Ventres, lodged with the Nez Percé, and visited the Mandan.

Together, in friendship, we recaptured the spirit of the old-time Warriors of the Plains.

Colin Taylor
Hastings, 1974.

The Land and the People

THE GREAT PLAINS, the primitive inhabitants of which are the main concern of this book, is that region within the heart of the North American continent covering a land area of almost one million square miles. Its boundaries are approximately defined by the Missouri-Mississippi valleys to the east and the Rocky Mountains to the west, the North Saskatchewan river in present-day Alberta and Saskatchewan and to the south by the Rio Grande River of Texas and New Mexico. It is a land of 'sun and wind and grass' (Wedel, 1961, p. 20).

To the traveller it can be a land of stark and sudden contrasts particularly of climate and terrain but the entire area exhibits at least two of the three features which scholars who have studied its anatomy in detail class as typical of a Great Plains environment. It is a level surface of great extent, is entirely unforested and largely devoid of trees while the limited rainfall produces a sub-humid climate. On the eastern low prairie plains however it is humid; on the western border it exhibits so-called 'bad land' topography and becomes arid, and only on the High Plains which run north to south across the slightly graded east-to-west slope, terminating at the foot of the Rocky Mountain front, does the region have all the three distinguishing characteristics.

This vast land, largely devoid of any natural barriers, gives free play to air currents and many areas experience ocean-like winds which blow from the northwest in winter and from the south in summer. The winds have in some ways compensated for the general scarcity of water, bringing unique weather features. The gentle, warm 'chinook', for example, which blows down from the eastern foot slope of the Rockies from Montana to Colorado, melts and evaporates the deep winter snow in an astonishingly short time. The artist-cowboy Charles Russell epitomized its character in one of his earliest paintings, showing a worn, half-frozen steer weathering the last of the winter blizzards with the caption 'Waiting for the Chinook'. The blizzard, often called 'the grizzly of the Plains', could cause the weather on the northern plains (where it was most prevalent) to deteriorate to Arctic conditions within the space of a few hours. A 'norther' appearing suddenly and sweeping down from the north, often accompanied by black clouds of frightening intensity, could cause the temperature to plummet, often by 50 degrees.

During summer an almost exact reverse of these conditions could occur, caused by narrow bands of excessively hot winds blowing across the High Plains with velocities varying from a gentle breeze to a gale. 'Everything goes before the furnace blast ... it is not uncommon for fine fields of dark green corn to be destroyed in two days ... these hot winds render people irritable and incite nervousness. The throat and respiratory organs become dry, the lips crack and the eyes smart and burn.' (Webb, 1931, pp. 23 & 24).

To describe the Plains in deficiency terms, however, would be to give an inaccurate characterization, for within this area there are islands of timber, deep valleys and high hills, lush grasslands and numerous picturesque streams and rivers. Such features enabled aboriginal man, responding to his environment, to formulate a balanced and effective life style. Like the later nomadic buffalo-hunting Plains Indian of less than a century ago, it appears that he lived well on the game which abounded in the region, often selecting only the young animals which were best for eating (Wedel, 1961, p. 59).

Across the Great Plains the natural vegetation was predominantly various grasses, the character of which was closely associated with the changing climatic conditions. To the east, on the humid prairie lands, the grass was tall and luxuriant with deep roots; moving west it gradually changed to a short grass variety including what was commonly termed 'buffalo grass' which grew quickly in the spring and then lay dormant during the summer. Cured by the hot sun it provided nutritious winter forage for the great varieties of grass-eating animals which inhabited the Plains region including the buffalo (*Bison americanus*) and the unique pronghorned antelope, the former especially roaming the region in immense herds. Farther west still, particularly in such areas as central and western Wyoming, there are extensive areas of a desert-like terrain where sagebrush and other shrubs abound.

Along the eastern border of the Great Plains runs the Missouri River, the region's most important water course. The Missouri is formed by the confluence of the Jefferson, Madison and Gallatin Rivers at Three Forks just northwest of present-day Bozeman, Montana. Here it widens into a mighty river as it winds its almost 2500-mile course to St Louis. There it joins the Mississippi which in turn empties into the Gulf of Mexico some 800 miles farther south. The Missouri is a river of incredible variety and erratic character and first impressions immediately confirm the aptness of its nickname 'The Big Muddy'. Plains rivers were once succinctly described as 'three miles wide and two inches deep' and in places this is almost true of the Missouri. At a time when the river was the main artery of travel the upper region could only be reached by flat-bottomed boats of shallow draught and often with great difficulty at that, having to negotiate numerous sandbars, submerged rocks and waterlogged trees whose fate was sealed seasons before when swirling water undercut the bank on which they stood. In other parts the water is deep and the swirling whirlpool-like currents make it especially dangerous. To swim in the Missouri is an experience neither to be forgotten nor repeated; even on the hottest day the murkiness of the water, the numbing coldness, the swift undercurrents, hidden crags and unstable jagged bottom detract from the pleasure; little wonder that even the water-loving beaver retreated to the more inviting tributaries, leaving the Missouri largely to the catfish and sturgeon. One of the main tributaries of the Missouri is the Yellowstone which, running north to southwest across present-day Montana, passes through some of the most picturesque country in the whole of North America. From the Yellowstone, in a direction running almost directly north-south, there are such water courses as the Bighorn, Tongue, and Powder Rivers producing a haven of unsurpassed beauty and natural wealth.

The great rivers of the world hold a special place in the history of nations and the Missouri is no exception. For thousands of years it carved and moulded the land but now modern man has tamed it with massive dams and in so doing has destroyed much of its original character. However, between Fort Benton and the Fort Peck Reservoir (in present-day Montana) there is a stretch of river nearly 200 miles long which has hardly changed in thousands of years. The area remains one of the least mapped in the whole of the United States and is rich in historic sites and spectacular scenery.

South of the Missouri, running approximately east to west from the city of Omaha, Nebraska, is another prominent water course. However, the Platte River never figured so prominently in the history of the Great Plains as did the Missouri. After a 300-odd mile journey the main artery splits, the north fork reaching Casper in Wyoming and Denver in Colorado. Geographically the Platte serves to divide the area conveniently into two regions – the Northern and Southern Plains, the latter region being characterized by sub-humid conditions, and the High Plains country becoming increasingly arid to the south.

The Great Plains country abounded with wild life. One student of the Plains has pointed out that many Plains animals exhibit certain common characteristics which were particularly signifi-

Buffalo – on which the whole life style of the Plains Indian depended. The largest mammal in North America, the male could weigh up to 2000 lb. and stand 6 feet or more at the shoulder. They have poor eyesight but a keen sense of smell and hearing. Both sexes have horns and although the cow was considerably smaller, both could be dangerous when cornered. A blue jay provides a free service as it hunts for ticks on the hump of the right-hand buffalo. Water colour by the Swiss artist, Rudolph Kurz, about 1852, from his original sketch book. Historische Museum, Berne.

cant since they 'indicate the nature of the country, serve as an index to the problems of the Plains and suggest with some definiteness the directions of institutional development.' (Webb, 1931, p. 33). All except the coyote and the wolf are grass-eaters; two different species, the antelope and jack-rabbit, are particularly noted for their speed – depending primarily on this for safety; all can survive an extended period without water (some, such as the jack-rabbit and prairie-dog, need none at all). All Plains animals are extremely shy, difficult to approach and difficult to kill. 'Any one of these

Early mode of hunting buffalo: model of a Pishkun or Buffalo Kill of the Blackfoot. Prior to the acquisition of the horse, the pedestrian nomads of the Plains commonly drove buffalo into V-shaped pounds which terminated at a circular enclosure or at a cliff edge as shown here. Such methods of hunting provided large quantities of meat and the early Plains dwellers fared well, often leaving the more inferior meat for the wolves. Archaeological evidence indicates that this method of hunting was early employed and it is still possible to locate the popular sites. Montana Historical Society, Helena, Montana.

Hunting buffalo under wolf-skins. Few animals frightened the buffalo, and dressed this way a skilful hunter could bring down a bull. Note the circular stance that the bulls are taking, probably protecting cows or calves in the middle. The immensity of the herds (which might approach millions) is clearly shown as are the virtually endless treeless plains. This painting is by George Catlin who visited the Great Plains in the 1830s. From his *North American Indian Portfolio*. Museum of Mankind, London.

animals is liable to run for a quarter of a mile though his heart be split as with a knife.' (Dodge, 1877, p. 112). Their extreme vitality is exemplified by the pronghorned antelope, the purest type of Plains animal; its sense of sight enables it to detect danger over immense distances, it is amongst the swiftest four-legged animals in the world, 'and so far as is known there is nothing but a blooded race-horse that can outrun it on a mile'. (Seton, 1913, p. 85). It is exceptionally cautious but at the same time curious of unusual objects, surviving so well because it is further endowed with a built-in signal system which enables communication of danger at great distances to be achieved. When interested or frightened the antelope contracts his muscles and the white patch on his rump 'becomes a flare of white'. (Webb, 1931, p. 35). This white disc 'which shines in the sun and shows afar as a bright white spot' (Seton, 1913, p. 85) has been described as the antelope's heliograph and is suggestive of the equally tenacious historic Plains Indians' system of sign language which was probably originally developed for communicating over great distances for 'on the Plains the eye far outruns the ear in its range'. (Webb, 1931, p. 73).

The most important of all Plains animals was the buffalo; although not entirely indigenous to the Great Plains – in early days it was found as far east as North Carolina and Virginia and in the Great Lakes area, as confirmed by the early 17th and 18th century explorers – it was only here that it appeared in large numbers. By 1850 they were to be found roaming in immense herds west of the Missouri but virtually extinct east of it. The naturalist, William Hornaday, who made a special study of the buffalo, estimated that at this period the herds were at least 4,000,000 in number and might even total 12,000,000. On this unique, vir-

tually inexhaustible, supply of big game, pivoted the whole economy of primitive man on the Great Plains – from the pedestrian prehistoric to the equestrian historic nomads. It provided food, shelter and garments and when eventually the buffalo passed away so did the wild and free Plains Indian.

The anthropology of the American Indian presents considerable difficulties. It is generally contended that the Indian, as he was known when the first white man made contact with him in the 16th century, was of Old World Mongolian stock. The considerable physical differences between many of the various groups was attributed to the extended time period over which the migrations took place. These migrations were by way of Asia to North America in the vicinity of the present-day Bering Strait. During each glacial age it is known that the ocean level decreases as the water freezes within the continental ice sheets and it has been estimated by geologists that a drop of 180 feet 'would lay bare a broad strip of relatively flat land connecting Siberia and Alaska . . . appearing as a gently rolling plain, perhaps sprinkled with lakes and ponds, intersected by small streams, and clothed with lush prairie grasses that would have provided abundant pasturage for mammoths, bison, horses and other large grazing animals of the time.' (Wedel, 1961, pp. 46 & 47).

The time scale is still conjectural; conservative estimates suggest that primitive man had established himself in the southern part of the United States at least four thousand miles from the Bering Strait between twelve to twenty-five thousand years ago. Some anthropologists have even suggested that other non-Mongolian people preceded the Indian in America and that perhaps it was peopled as far back as forty to sixty thousand years ago. A convenient designation 'Paleo-Indian' refers to the early big-game hunters who hunted both elephants and later buffalo on the Great Plains some 10,000 years ago. The comparatively limited amount of archaeological work which has been carried out on the Great Plains, particularly within the last 50 years or so, further suggests that the life style between say AD 500 and 1400 on the Central Plains was probably in many ways similar to that of the later pedestrian nomads described by the Spaniards in 1541 (based on Wedel, 1961, pp. 46–102) and that possibly this period saw an attempt by corn-growing sedentary Indians to become Plains people by making the transition from a 'food producing to a primarily bison-hunting Plains subsistence economy'.

The famous Coronado expedition was the first ever made by white men to the Great Plains. The rich hordes of gold which they had been led to believe were to be found in settled villages to the northeast proved to be a myth and in this respect the expedition was a failure. The chronicles of the expedition however provide us with a rich first-hand narrative of both the pedestrian, nomadic and sedentary Indians of the Great Plains.

The expedition made a rendezvous at Compostela on the Pacific coast west of present-day Mexico City. They left on 23 February 1540 and travelled north to the Rio Grande valley. Here they ransacked the permanent dwellings of the Pueblo Indians of Zuni and Tiguex and finding no gold decided to push on farther to the northeast. The Plains subjected the Spaniards to some alarming new experiences. 'The country is so level that men became lost when they went off half a league. One horseman was lost, who never reappeared, and two horses, all saddled and bridled, which they never saw again. No track was left of where they went, and on this account it was necessary to mark the road by which they went with cow dung, so as to return, since there were no stones or anything else.' (Winship, 1896, p. 543).

After a month's travel the expedition was in an exhausted state and most returned to Tiguex. Coronado however pushed on with thirty well mounted horsemen and in July 1541 he arrived at the Indian settlements which Coronado designated as the province of Quivira in what is now central Kansas. Here Coronado spent more than three weeks exploring the area. He found people who lived in permanent settlements, raised some corn but depended mainly on the buffalo. These Indians have since been identified as Wichitas who lived in grass-covered houses in contrast to their cousins the Pawnee of Nebraska (who the Spaniards also met in 1541) who lived in more permanent earth lodges. That there were completely nomadic hunters roaming the Plains to the west of these villages there can be no doubt, for on their journey across the Plains to Quivira the Spaniards met bands of Indians who were well at home on the Plains and had no permanent abode. The explorers give us the first description of the tipi*, 'buffalo skin covered frames with poles fastened at the top and spread apart at the bases'. Large dogs were used for transport, the unfortunate animals were

* Tipi is a Sioux word (strictly Teton Sioux dialect); *Ti* means dwelling and *pi* means 'used for'. It was early used by the Sioux. For example, when the French explorer Hennepin visited the Sioux in 1680 in what is now present-day Minnesota, he noticed that they 'pitched tents of skin' – probably referring to the conical tipi.

loaded 'like beasts of burden and [they] make light pack saddles for them like ours, cinching them with leather straps . . . the dogs go about with sores on their backs like pack animals'. The first mention of a makeshift travois (a simple device consisting of two poles joined by a frame – the frame carried the load and the poles were harnessed to the dog which dragged the weight over the ground) was also made in the reports 'in addition to what they carry on their backs, they transport the poles for the tents, dragging them fastened to their saddles. A load may be from thirty to fifty pounds, depending on the dog.' (Bolton, 1916, p. 233). They also refer to the use of sign language, buckskin clothing, shields of buffalo hide, pemmican and the bow and arrow. Two separate linguistic groups were recognized, the Querechos and Teya, probably Plains Apache and Comanche, the latter tribe roaming across an immense area of the Plains stretching from present-day southern Montana to northern Mexico. Thus the Apache and Comanche are amongst the oldest of the nomadic Plains tribes and whilst it was to be at least a century before they acquired the horse, the Spanish descriptions clearly indicate that an economy and a nomadic life-style based on the buffalo was well established by the mid-sixteenth century.

We can only infer that this was also the case for the central and northern Plains as well for we have no comparable early descriptions for this region. However, when the Hudson's Bay Company's fur trader, Henry Kelsey, visited the great Plains of western Canada in 1691, he met nomadic pedestrian Indians (Assiniboin and Cree) who were skilled buffalo hunters and well adapted to the Plains life. To the west of the Assiniboin were a particularly warlike tribe of whom Kelsey wrote '[they] knew not the use of canoes and were resolved to go to wars'. (Kelsey, 1929, p. 16). They were probably Piegan, the most westerly of the Blackfoot confederacy, who even though still pedestrian were expanding their territory into the Plains country, leaving their ancient wooded habitat north of the Saskatchewan river and forcing

Indians hunting buffalo in snow. This painting done by the Swiss artist P. Rindisbacher about 1820 shows Cree hunters of the Canadian plains. The hunters are pursuing the animals early in spring – a favourite time for hunting by these people when the snow is sufficiently frozen to bear men – but not the buffalo, which break through and cannot run.
Public Archives of Canada.

Earth Lodge of Mandan Indians, Upper Missouri. Such dwellings were used by many semi-sedentary village tribes of the Missouri river, including the Arikara and Hidatsa in the north and the Pawnee and Omaha in the south. Styles varied – the entrance passage generally projecting ten to fifteen feet beyond the door with the southern groups. Varying between twenty to sixty feet in diameter (ceremonial lodges could be even larger), they could accomodate entire families including the favourite horses. Slant Village, North Dakota.

the Kutenai, Flathead and Shoshone tribes of the Plains in present-day Alberta and Montana to seek refuge in the foothills and plateaux of the Rocky Mountains. The early life style of these latter pedestrian nomads is not difficult to reconstruct; in many ways it probably resembled that of the numerous Cree bands who occupied the plains of Saskatchewan from early times until the late 19th century. Such small bands lacked cohesion and any well-developed political and social organization. Further, they were probably the constant prey of the unified predatory Blackfoot tribes, who frequently ventured from their woodland homelands to hunt on the northern Plains.

The principal beast of burden was the dog, the strongest of which was probably capable of 'packing a load of approximately 50 pounds or dragging 75 pounds on a travois'. (Ewers, 1955, p. 306). One early observer described the Plains Indian dog as 'nothing more than [a] domesticated wolf. In wandering through the prairies I have often mistaken wolves for Indian dogs. The larger kind has long curly hair, and resembles the shepherd dog. There is the same diversity amongst the wolves of this country. They may be more properly said to howl, than bark.' (Brackenbridge, 1816, pp. 141–142). A systematic study of the Indian dog was made by Glover M. Allen, who published an extended essay on that animal in 1920.

Buffalo hide tipis would have been small, since long poles would be impossible to drag, but as early traditions suggest, other forms of portable dwellings might well have been employed. For example, in 1913 Buffalo-bird-woman, an elderly Hidatsa informant, described to the ethnologist, Gilbert Wilson, a hunting trip on which dogs alone were used. Although this hunt occurred about 1870, Wilson was of the opinion that it could 'be taken as typical of prehistoric days, before the horse and gun were known'. (Wilson, 1924, p. 231).

The narrative refers to the use of shared dwellings where poles were cut each time camp was made, and each woman contributed at least one large rectangular piece of hide for the cover. Such makeshift dwellings were shaped like tipis and might hold up to six couples. The same woman referred to the use of a shelter employing as a frame three dog travois joined together at their tops and covered with a tent skin. 'Two persons could be accommodated very well in such a shelter.' (Wilson, 1924, p. 224).

Movement with dogs as the only means of transport would be somewhat restricted, possessions reduced to essentials and the aged or infirm would have to be abandoned when times became particularly hard. When camp was made the portable dwellings would probably have been pitched in two parallel lines since this formation was best suited for repelling slow-moving infantry style war-parties. In later years a circular formation was adopted when the enemy would be well mounted and surprise attacks a reality; further, horses could be corralled and protected within a camp circle.

The immense herds of buffalo provided both food and clothing. Virtually impossible to kill with the bow and arrow on foot, the buffalo were driven or lured into V-shaped pounds. The termination of the pound might be a cliff edge or large circular enclosure in which the animals could be killed. As late as 1949 a large number of the remains of these buffalo drive sites were still observable on the plains of Alberta and Montana. 'A bison drive site generally is now recognized by low piles of rocks, placed at intervals of several feet in two lines extending for hundreds of yards over flat or gently rolling plains in a great V shape, converging at the top of a cliff.' (Ewers, 1949, p. 355). In the mid-nineteenth century a fur trader, Edwin Denig, sketched the layout of such a bison drive and the Canadian artist Paul Kane painted a small one at about the same time. They were commonly used by Cree and Assiniboin tribes who were poor in horses.

Such drives required a combined band effort and were not without a considerable degree of hunting ceremonial, which probably acted as a seasonal unifying factor. According to Denig a 'divining man of known repute, who is believed to have the power of making the buffalo come in to his enchantments' (Denig, 1930, p. 532) planted a pole in the centre of the pound; to the top of this pole was attached a strip of scarlet cloth, some tobacco and a cow's horn. This was a sacrifice to the wind. At the foot of the pole were placed buffalo skulls painted red and decorated with feathers and coloured cloth; these were a gift to the buffalo spirits. The medicine man then performed certain rites with another painted buffalo skull 'painted and decked very gaudily ... and placed in the lodge of the master, who smokes and invokes it, at times singing the Bull song, which he accompanies with a rattle nearly all night, and prophesies as to their appearance of success in the morning.' (Denig, 1930, p. 533).

On the appearance of the herd another man disguised as a buffalo imitated the bleating of a buffalo calf, enticing the herd leaders well into the gigantic V pound; hunters, previously concealed behind the three-foot-high piles of earth, now made their appearance, stampeding the terrified creatures into the ever-narrowing channel and over the cliff edge. 'The whole herd plunges madly down the precipice, one on top of the other breaking their legs and necks in the fall. Into the pen they tumble, those in front having no power to stop ... when all have passed into the pen the work of slaughter commences, with guns and bows firing as long as any appearance of life remains.' (Denig, 1930, pp. 532–533). Many thousands of buffalo were killed annually by this method, often apparently producing a surplus of food, for in December 1809 the fur trader, Alexander Henry, observed of a Blackfoot pound on the Vermilion River, in present-day Alberta, 'The bulls were mostly entire, none but the good cows having been cut up.' (Henry and Thompson, 1897, pp. 576–577). This statement is interesting in the light of recent archaeological evidence which suggests that even the earliest inhabitants of the Plains were well enough provided for: they could afford to discriminate and leave the inferior meat to the wolves.

Little archaeological work has been carried out in the Canadian prairie provinces and the actual outline of the prehistoric cultures, especially those on the fringe of the mixed prairie-woodland region beyond the Saskatchewan river, still needs to be established (Wedel, 1961, p. 260). This area would be of particular interest since it was, as we have seen, the ancient habitat of the three powerful Blackfoot tribes who were later to dominate the northern Plains. It is possible that subsequent

Mandan moving to winter village using dogs for transport. Many earth lodge villages were built on high bluffs overlooking the Missouri and protected on one or two sides by the river. In winter such villages were abandoned and most effects were transferred to villages in the woodland areas along the Missouri which generally consisted of lodges of smaller dimensions. From an aquatint by Carl Bodmer, 1833. Joslyn Art Museum, Omaha, Nebraska.

research will reveal a culture in many ways similar to that described in considerable detail by the explorers who first visited the semi-sedentary tribes of the Upper Missouri region in the early 18th century. The first of these was the French fur trader, Pierre Gaultier de Verennes de la Vérendrye who visited the Mandan villages (located near the mouth of the Heart River in present-day North Dakota) in 1738. La Vérendrye described an economy virtually identical to Coronado's description of the Wichita almost two centuries earlier. The Mandan however lived in spacious earth-covered lodges, more permanent dwellings than the Wichita grass houses, and thus archaeologists have been able to document this tribe's culture at least as far back as Coronado's time and have concluded that the life style then differed little from that first described by Vérendrye and other travellers such as David Thompson of the Northwest Company (1797), Lewis and Clark (1804–1805) – the official explorers for the U.S. government after the Louisiana Purchase of 1803 – Alexander Henry (1806), George Catlin (1832) and Alexander Philip Maximilian, Prince of Wied Neuwied (1833). To the north of the Mandan lived the linguistically related Hidatsa and to the south the powerful Arikara but for centuries it was the Mandan villages which dominated as one of the most important centres in the aboriginal economic and cultural patterns on the Great Plains. So extensive were the Mandan villages that in historic times at least trade relations extended 'from the Pacific Northwest coast to the Great Lakes and into the southwest' (Wood, 1967, p. 167).

That the pedestrian nomads, probably Shoshone, to the west of the village Indians were

Plains Cree Indians, about 1890, with a dog travois. Even in horse days the Cree and Assiniboin were poor in horses and tended to make great use of the dog. Museum of the American Indian.

extremely warlike is suggested by the discovery of fortifications in the form of ditches and palisades surrounding the permanent village sites. The existence of plazas some 150 feet in diameter located in the very heart of the village also suggests that the intense ceremonialism and associated supernaturalism which so dominated later Plains culture was well developed.

There might well be something within the unique Great Plains environment which causes a people to live with such vivid intensity, awareness and wonder of the things around them. The Plains Indian was so much in daily association with nature, and so dependent upon it, that not only animals but plant life and even some inanimate objects were believed to have a spiritual existence. One scholar who made a special study of such associations amongst the Plains Indians in the historic period put it particularly well. 'The cedar, appearing to be withdrawn into lonely places, and standing dark and still, like an Indian with his robe drawn over his head in prayer and meditation, seemed to be in communion with the Higher Powers. The willow was always found along the water-courses, as though it had some duty or function in the world in connection with this element so imperatively and constantly needful to man and to all other living forms. The cottonwood they found in such diverse situations, appearing always so self-reliant, showing such prodigious fecundity, its lustrous young leaves in springtime by their sheen and by their restlessness reflecting the splendour of the sun like the dancing ripples of a lake, that to this tree also they ascribed mystery. This peculiarity of the foliage of the cottonwood is quite remarkable, so that it is said the air is never so still that there is not motion of the cottonwood leaves. Even in still summer afternoons and at night when all else was still, they could ever hear the rustling of cottonwood leaves by the passage of little vagrant currents of air. And the winds themselves were the paths of the Higher Powers, so they were constantly reminded of the mystic character of this tree.' (Gilmore, 1919, pp. 57 & 58). There was an awareness of a great force – the Sioux called it *wakan* – distinct from physical power which could act in different ways for good or evil and there were few Plains warriors who did not endeavour – often by great personal sacrifice – to possess and control at least part of it.

The great antiquity of these impulses amongst Plains Indians is confirmed by the symbolism associated with the ancient Cedar Pole of the Omaha which was kept in the Tent of War. The pole was said to represent a being; additionally it was a political symbol representing the authority of the chiefs of the tribe. Associated with the pole was the power to protect the people in warfare and bring success in the hunt. Its power was derived from the Thunder: 'The cedar tree was a favorite place for the Thunder birds to alight and according to the Legend attention was called to the tree from which the Sacred Pole was shaped by the Thunder

birds coming to it from the four directions and the mysterious burning which followed, all of which caused the Sacred Pole to stand in the minds of the people as endowed with supernatural power by the ancient Thunder gods.

'As a result' the legend says, 'the people began to pray to the Pole for courage and for trophies in war and their prayers were answered.' (Fletcher-La Flesche, 1905–1906, p. 229).

Very similar ideas must have been anciently associated with the sacred cedar which stood at the centre of the Mandan village plazas. Together with their great medicine pipe, it gave unity to tribal organization and ultimately led to an elaborate ceremonial known as the O-kee-pa. Performed in spring or early summer the O-kee-pa dramatized the story of creation and annually reinforced tribal unity by its complex four-day ceremonials. Eight warriors dressed to represent buffaloes performed the spectacular Bull Dance before the sacred cedar pole invoking its power to call the buffalo and assure success in the coming tribal buffalo hunt.

The fate of those who did not respect the sacred lore of the tribe or attempted to disrupt the ceremonials was demonstrated by the antics of O-ke-hee-de who approached the village plaza during the performance of the buffalo dance. This Evil Spirit represented powers which could bring death or other misfortune at the hands of the enemy if the buffalo dance was unsuccessful. Scantily dressed and grotesquely painted he carried in his hand a long staff to the end of which was a red ball symbolic of a human head (suggestive of early head-hunting days). This he slid along the ground before him as he ran. He wore an artificial penis carved from wood which extended below his knees. O-ke-hee-de, the gigantic penis now erect, first approached the women, who retreated in terror, but the power of the tribal medicine pipe was demonstrated when the Conductor of the Ceremonies thrust this before O-ke-hee-de. Ancient Mandan tradition states that such evils could always be subdued by the power of the pipe and at this point O-ke-hee-de acknowledged its superiority and directed his attention to the buffalo dancers whom he mounted – symbolic of the rutting season. Thus the obvious advantages of the Evil Spirit were turned to the advantage of the tribe and the annual 'creation of the Buffaloes' had symbolically taken place.

Exhausted and thus no longer a danger, O-ke-hee-de was mobbed by the women, his regalia removed and attached to a pole of the O-kee-pa medicine lodge. This is but one episode of a ceremony which also displayed the masochistic character of Plains Indian personality. Thus, young warriors seeking supernatural powers subjected themselves to tortures so incredibly cruel that when first described were not believed. Rawhide cords were attached by wooden skewers through the flesh of the chest or back and then the warrior was raised clear of the ground. Suspended from the central beams of the O-kee-pa lodge he

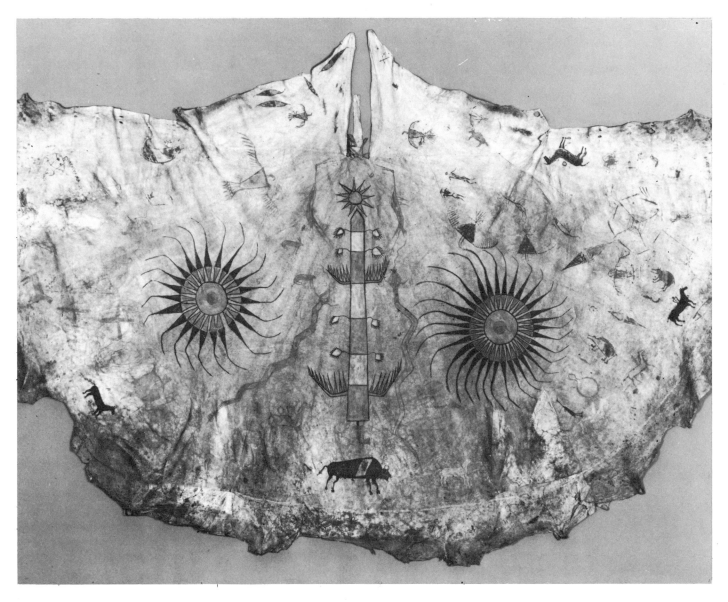

A small skin tipi (Sioux). Collected before 1850, this tipi is only about eight feet in diameter which was typical of the pre-horse period when the only beast of burden was the dog. The position of the smoke flaps indicate that the painting was on the inside of the tipi rather than the exterior, which adds weight to the suggestion that it was probably associated with religious ceremonies. Museum für Völkerkunde, Berlin.

eventually lost consciousness, during which period some were fortunate enough to communicate with the Great Spirit. 'It was believed that experiences with the supernatural when acquired at that time were the most genuine and richest ones.' (Bowers, 1950, p. 135).

It is probable that the O-kee-pa ceremonies contributed many ideas in the development of the better-known Sun Dance which was to become such a spectacular feature of the nomadic Plains Indians' religion during the historic period.

That intertribal warfare was a common practice of the pedestrian Plains warrior there can be no doubt, and although war honours undoubtedly ranked a man highly, warfare, as in the historic period, was more motivated by the forces of economics (perhaps in early days more imaginary than real) than those of personal glory. Thus the semi-sedentary Plains village tribes, whose economy pattern was one of trading, were less prone to the waging of offensive warfare and had to contend with repeated attacks from their more aggressive westerly nomadic neighbours, hence the formidable fortifications which we know from both historical and archaeological evidence commonly surrounded the earth lodge villages.

Early explorers in the eastern part of North America repeatedly mentioned the common custom of trading female slaves who had been captured as spoils of war. Father Marquette, who visited the Illinois Indians in 1673, wrote 'They are warlike, and make themselves dreaded by the Distant tribes to the south and west, whither they go to procure Slaves; these they barter, selling them at a high price to other Nations, in exchange for other Wares.' (Kenton, 1956, p. 351).

Likewise, scalping was a common practice and represented more than simply a trophy of war. Thus, amongst the 'Nations of Louisiana', the war chiefs bestowed names upon warriors according to their conduct in battle. 'To deserve the title of a great man-slayer, it is necessary to have taken 10 slaves or to have carried off 20 scalps.' (In Kenton, 1956, p. 417). The scalps represented those of the enemy whose souls would be slaves to the slayer

11

in the next world; symbolically, scalping was an insurance for the good life hereafter, and captured the soul of the warrior who, alive, would be more than useless.

We can only speculate as to whether early pedestrian Plains nomads held a similar philosophy. However, elements of these religious concepts are to be found in the tales of an aged Piegan chief, who was actually Cree by birth, by the name of Saukamappee (The Boy) who related them to the explorer David Thompson in 1787. Saukamappee, who could clearly remember life in pre-horse days, told of the case of a successful war party which had returned with more than fifty scalps. There was much discussion as to the significance of those taken from the enemy who were found dead under their shields 'as not one could say he had actually slain the enemy whose scalp he held'. However, there was no doubt about others; 'those who had taken the trophy from the head of an enemy who they had killed, said the Souls of the enemy that each of us has slain belongs to us and we have given them to our relations in the other world to be their slaves, and we are contented.' (Thompson, 1787, p. 332).

When white fur traders first visited the northern Plains Indians in the mid-18th century they observed that raiding for female slaves was an established custom; considering their vital economic value amongst which must be counted both their

Mandan buffalo dancer, Fort Clark, Upper Missouri 1833. Buffalo societies were perhaps the most widespread in the Plains, being especially favoured by the Upper Missouri village tribes. Belonging to a series of age-graded societies, they were predominantly military in character. Catlin observed such dancers during the O-kee-pa ceremony in 1832 and noted that O-ke-hee-de mounted each, symbolic of the buffalo in rutting. The dancer shown here – one of two leaders, distinguished by the complete buffalo-horned headdress – was painted by Carl Bodmer. Joslyn Art Museum, Omaha, Nebraska.

burden-carrying and child-bearing capacity, there seems little doubt that in common with their eastern cousins this was a motive for warfare and had been practised for centuries by pedestrian Plains tribes. Later, it was to receive further impetus after the coming of the fur traders when women captives were sold to them. 'In these war expeditions many female slaves were taken, who are sold to the Canadian traders and taken down to Canada.' (Umfreville, 1790, p. 177).

Northern pedestrian Plains Indian warfare tactics took two major forms both of which depended on numerical strength and good organization. Hence, in those pre-horse days, effective centralized leadership was pivotal to success and the war chief evidently held a paramount position within the tribe. This leader tended to confine himself exclusively to war matters, leaving the social organization to the civil chief, who according to one early observer of the Piegan, he viewed 'with indifference as a garrulous old man more fit for talking than for anything else' (Thompson, 1787, pp. 332–333).

In the battles for loot – principally women – the favourite method was to locate a small isolated village of perhaps ten to thirty tents which had separated from the main body for hunting purposes and by a massive overwhelming force destroy the male inhabitants. The armaments at this time consisted of shock weapons, such as stone-headed war clubs and lances, with bows at least five feet in length and stone-tipped arrows. Large shields were carried which were perhaps three feet or more in diameter, these being particularly well suited to the needs of the second style of tactic employed, which occurred when warring tribes met on more equal numerical terms – perhaps in a dispute over territory. Here the emphasis was on infantry-style warfare. Saukamappee described such a battle which he witnessed as a boy of sixteen and which occurred about 1725 in the vicinity of the Eagle Hills (in present-day Saskatchewan). At this time the Piegan, the frontier tribe of the Blackfoot confederacy, were beginning to push out onto the Plains displacing the ancient pedestrian occupants, in this case the Shoshone. The Piegan had some 350 warriors, the Shoshone perhaps considerably more, both parties making great show of their numbers.

'After some singing and dancing, they sat down on the ground, and placed their large shields before them, which covered them. We did the same, but our shields were not so many, and some of our shields had to shelter two men. Theirs were all placed touching each other; their Bows were not so long as ours, but of better wood, and the back covered with the sinews of the Bisons which made them very elastic, and their arrows went a long way and whizzed about us as balls do from guns. They were all headed with a sharp, smooth, black stone (flint) which broke when it struck anything. Our iron headed arrows did not go through their shields, but stuck in them; on both sides several

Ark of the First Man. Mandan village of Mi-ti-was-kos, Upper Missouri, 1833. This sacred altar stood at the centre of the village plaza where the O-kee-pa ceremony traditionally took place in the spring or summer. The eight or nine feet high palisade surrounded a sacred cedar post which symbolized the body of Nu-mohk-muck-a-nah or First Man, a mythological figure who brought the Medicine Pipe to the Mandan which became central to all the O-kee-pa ceremonies. Sacred wild sage was used to wrap up ceremonial accoutrements and these were presented to the Ark at the close of the O-kee-pa; it is thus possible to locate where the shrine stood by the concentration of the plant at that spot. In recent years the shrine has been reconstructed on a remote part of the reservation in North Dakota. From Maximilians *Travels in the Interior of North America.* London, 1841.

were wounded, but none lay on the ground; and the night put an end to the battle, without a scalp being taken on either side, and in those days such was the result, unless one party was more numerous than the other.' (Tyrrell, 1916, Vol. 12, pp. 328–329). When this occurred the foot soldiers attempted to extend their infantry line as long as possible, the outer warriors gradually moving ahead so that a concave line was presented to the smaller party of opposing enemy who within a very short time found themselves virtually surrounded and were subsequently slaughtered to a man. Such a battle (probably between Plains Apache and Wichita Indians) was witnessed by the members of the Oñate expedition to the southern plains in 1601. They described a body of more than fifteen hundred Apache in a semi-circle formation and referred to massive showers of arrows raining down on the opposing side. (Secoy, 1953, p. 12).

While the shield was evidently of great utility in this form of warfare, body armour was also commonly worn by the pedestrian nomads throughout the Plains region and beyond. In 1775 the explorer, Peter Pond, described such protective clothing used by Yankton Sioux warriors. They wore a 'Garment like an Outside Vest with Sleeves that Cum down to thare Elboes Made of Soft Skins and Several thicknesses that will turn an arrow at a distans.' Possibly the early inhabitants of the Plains such as the Shoshone and Apache were the prime users of this form of protective clothing, which was copied and used for a comparatively short period by such tribes as the Blackfoot after they took up more permanent residence on the Plains. So useful was it found to be that members of the Coronado expedition adopted

it in preference to their own armour and more than two centuries later 'Spanish soldiers of Sonora still wore knee-length sleeveless jackets of six or eight layers of well cured deerskins as armour against their Apache enemies.' (Pfefferkorn, 1949, p. 155). Armour was not altogether abandoned with the introduction of the horse, but it was somewhat modified in order to give mobility and when the gun and horse frontier met it rapidly fell into disuse. Symbolically, however, it was retained in the form of a single layered garment – the so called 'war-shirt' – which traditionally could only be worn by men of military distinction.

By 1740 a number of guns were at the disposal of the Piegan through their allies the Cree and Assiniboin who had acquired them from the Hudson's Bay fur traders, and although by now the Shoshone had a few horses (but no guns) they failed to employ what might have been effective cavalry tactics against their pedestrian enemies. The effect of the gun on the traditional infantry-style warfare was to suddenly transform it into a bloody encounter and to cause consternation amongst the gunless Shoshone. Again Saukamappee graphically relates such an encounter.

'When we came to meet each other, as usual, each displayed their numbers, weapons and shields, in all of which they were superior to us, except our guns were not shown, but kept in their

Mandan pole shrines, 1833. As with most Missouri River tribes, the Mandan had a rich mythology. The skin of a white buffalo cow was considered powerful 'medicine' by many tribes. According to Maximilian he who possesses such a hide amongst the Mandan generally offers it to the Lord of Life. 'He collects, perhaps, in the course of a whole twelve-month, various articles of value, and then hangs them up all together on a high pole in the open prairie, generally in the neighbourhood of the burying place, or in the village before his hut.' The Mandan restored to them when they wished to achieve some goal 'and sometimes lament for days and weeks together'. From an engraving by Carl Bodmer, Fort Clark, 1833. Smithsonian Institution, Bureau of American Ethnology.

Pedestrian warriors from a northern Plains pictograph. At this period the emphasis was on infantry-style warfare where the shield was of great importance. Weapons were stone-headed war clubs, lances, and bows at least five feet in length. Warring sides opposed one another in long lines, each attempting to surround the enemy by moving ahead at the extremity, thus the more men the better. The forces sometimes numbered more than a thousand. Efficient co-ordination was vital and war chiefs held a paramount place in the tribal organization.

leathern cases, and if we had shown (them) they would have taken them for long clubs. For a long time they held us in suspense; a tall chief was forming a strong party to make an attack on our centre, and the others to enter into combat with those opposite to them; we prepared for the battle the best we could. Those of us who had guns stood in the front line and each of us (had) two balls in his mouth, and a load of powder in his left hand to reload. We noticed that they had a great many short stone clubs for close combat, which is a dangerous weapon, and had they made a bold attack on us, we must have been defeated as they were more numerous and better armed than we were, for we could have fired our guns no more

Cree pedestrian hunters and warriors, Fort Union (Assiniboin territory), Upper Missouri. Sketched from life by Rudolph Kurz, September 1851. Both warriors carry the famed Northwest gun. The effect of the gun on traditional pedestrian warfare was to suddenly transform it into a bloody encounter. Historische Museum, Berne.

than twice; and we were at a loss what to do on the wide plain, and each Chief encouraged his men to stand firm. Our eyes were all on the tall Chief and his motions, which appeared to be contrary to the advice of several old Chiefs, all this time we were about the strong flight of an arrow from each other. At length the tall Chief retired and they formed their long usual line by placing their shields on the ground to touch each other, the shield having a breadth of full three feet or more. We sat down opposite to them and most of us waited for the night to make a hasty retreat. The War Chief was close to us, anxious to see the effect of our guns. The lines were too far asunder for us to make a sure shot, and we requested him to close the line to about sixty yards, which was gradually done, and lying flat on the ground behind the shields, we watched our opportunity when they drew their bows to shoot at us, their bodies were then exposed and each of us, as opportunity offered, fired with deadly aim, and either killed or severely wounded, every one we aimed at.

'The War Chief was highly pleased, and the Snake Indians finding so many killed and wounded kept themselves behind their shields; the War Chief then desired we would spread ourselves by twos throughout the line which we did, and our shots caused consternation and dismay along their whole line. The battle had begun about Noon, and the Sun was not yet half down, when we perceived some of them had crawled away from their shields and were taking to flight. The War Chief seeing this went along the line and spoke to every Chief to keep his Men ready for a charge of the whole line of the enemy, of which he would give the signal; this was done by himself stepping in front with his Spear, and calling on them to follow him as he rushed on their line, and in an instant the whole of us followed him, the greater part of the enemy took to flight, but some fought bravely and we lost more than ten killed and many wounded. Part of us pursued and killed a few, but the chase was soon to be given over, for at the body of every Snake Indian killed, there were five or six of us trying to get his scalp, or part of his clothing, his weapons, or something as a trophy of the battle. As there were only three of us, and seven of our friends, the Stone Indians, we did not interfere, and got nothing.' (Thompson, 1787, pp. 330–332).

The gun not only tended to make infantry-type warfare on the Northern Plains a more bloody affair, it also upset the balance of power in the eastern woodlands. In 1650 the Teton Sioux, who lived a largely sedentary horticultural existence in what is now Minnesota and Wisconsin, acquired a few guns from Huron and Ottawa refugees who had been forced west by the Iroquois. Already a numerically powerful group and exceptionally warlike, their aggressive activities expanded to be felt more decisively by tribes to the east and northeast such as the Chippewa and Cree, and the Miami, Fox, Potawatomi and Illinois to the southeast. By 1670 however the Cree (who allied them-

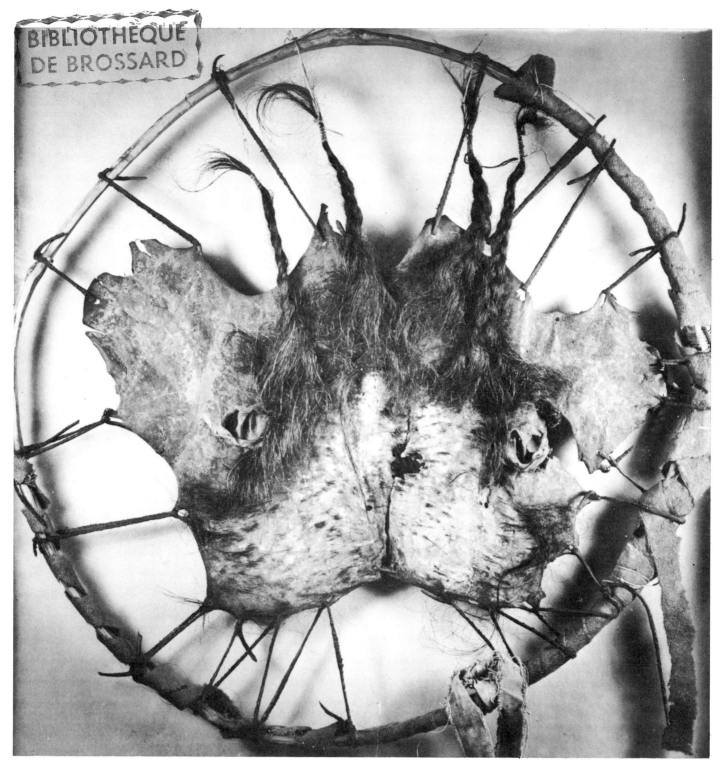

Head scalp, complete with ears and cheeks. Sioux, 1836. Scalps were valuable war trophies particularly before the introduction of the horse; symbolically they captured the soul of the warrior, and enslaved it in the spirit world to the relatives of the slayer. Large scalps were usually stretched on a wooden hoop (the one shown here is over twenty inches in diameter). This particular scalp is that of Crow Feathers, a great warrior of the Ojibwa, who was killed by the Sioux in the battle of Crow

Wing in 1836. The Ojibwa chief, Hole-In-The-Day, ransomed this scalp from the Sioux during the peace council of 1837. Crow Feathers wore a most unusual style of face and head decoration. The top of his head was shaved and painted red; four hair braids hung over his face which was painted blue-green. The fatal wound can be seen clearly on top of his head. Paul Dyck Collection, Paul Dyck Foundation, Arizona.

selves with the Assiniboin) began to acquire a steady supply of guns from the Hudson's Bay traders and these in turn filtered down to the Chippewa groups to the east of the Sioux. Intent on revenge, the Chippewa now waged constant war against the Sioux, who themselves had no direct access to the supply of firearms and under this pressure they gradually moved west.

By 1700 the foremost bands such as the Brulé

and Oglala hunted as far as the valley of the James River in present-day North and South Dakota, and by 1760 they had drifted southward, crossed the James River and reached the Coteau du Missouri. In their wake were to follow the Miniconjou, Sans Arcs, Hunkpapa and Blackfoot Sioux. This move was hardly an invasion and presented little danger to the massive fortified Mandan and Arikara villages which were strung along the banks of the

15

Missouri River. The Mandan were ancient occupants of this area; the Arikara – a Caddoan speaking tribe related to the Pawnee and sometimes in fact called 'Black Pawnees' – were more recent arrivals having been earlier driven west by aggressive eastern tribes. George E. Hyde, one of the foremost authorities on the Sioux, described the situation as follows: 'They were no conquerors, but poor people afoot in the vast plains . . . we may therefore picture the little Teton camps about the year 1760 coming in on foot, with their little tipi poles tied in bundles to the sides of their big dogs, and their women and little girls loaded with packs, to visit at the villages, to beg for corn, dried pumpkins and native tobacco, and also obtaining a *few horses* from the friendly people.' (Hyde, 1937, pp. 16 & 18).

In their migrations west the Sioux retained their mode of warfare which was essentially woodland in character; rather than act in a body and move forward in an infantry-type formation with shields touching, as was so common on the Northern Plains, immediately they met the enemy they tended to 'scatter their forces so that the individual warriors could take advantage of the best nearby cover and still effectively support each other by fire'. (Secoy, 1953, p. 68).

War parties were generally large and well organized – perhaps several hundred men at least; a description of a battle between a small band of Sioux and a large war party of Cree which occurred in the 1730s may serve to illustrate what was typically Eastern Woodland style warfare adapted to the Plains environment. '500 Cree after twenty

days' march in the prairies came within sight of the smoke of the village which they wished to attack at sunrise . . . when their rearguard was attacked by 30 Sioux who had crossed their track and who took them for Assiniboin not on the warpath. The assailants killed four, when the whole party came on them. The Sioux, surprised at the number of enemy, took flight, abandoning a portion of their arms, in order to reach an isolated wood in the midst of the prairie, where the fight went on until nightfall, the Cree in the open like brave men, the Sioux hiding behind trees.' (In Burpee, 1927, p. 136).

Few guns were to be found in the possession of the Plains tribes west of the Missouri prior to 1750. The Spanish settlements which might have been a source of supply to the southern Indians were prevented from developing such a trade by a Spanish government order which forbade the sale of firearms to Indians. These settlements, however, became a source for the supply of horses, which rapidly became an essential part of Plains life.

The movement of many other tribes – who later became typically equestrian nomads – is essentially the same. The Cheyenne, Arapaho, Hidatsa and Crow all migrated to the Plains region from the northeast under the relentless pressure of gun-armed Woodland tribes. In 1680, for example, the Cheyenne were roaming as far south as present-day Peoria, Illinois over 100 miles east of the Mississippi; by 1700 they were to be found near the bend of the Cheyenne River in present-day southeastern North Dakota more than 500 miles northwest of their original habitat. They were possibly preceded by the Sutaio, a people speaking a similar language and with whom they eventually made an alliance. The Cheyenne at this time occupied a permanent village consisting of about seventy earth lodges where they probably led a dual life of nomadic hunting during the summer months and returned to their permanent village in the winter. They apparently warred with the Chippewa who about 1770 attacked with a force of some 150 gun-armed men and burnt the village to the ground. This battle was described in some detail in 1790 to the explorer David Thompson by a Chippewa chief and his descriptions of the site have since been confirmed by archaeological evidence. The Chippewa chief also stated that there were horses in the village when they attacked it, indeed many of the occupants 'had just gone out hunting on horses' (Jablow, 1950, p. 8).

Comanche Warrior. Although sketched in the 1830s, this is probably a very fair representation of a typical Plains pedestrian warrior who roamed the southern Plains in Coronado's time (1540). He is armed with a large rawhide shield and a bow and lance. He wears moccasins and fringed buckskin leggings and a horned headdress –favourite regalia of distinguished Comanche warriors. From a sketch by Lino Sanchez y Tapia after the original by Jean Berlandier. Thomas Gilcrease Institute, Tulsa, Oklahoma.

Assiniboin warrior painted by Carl Bodmer, 1833. This man is probably a good representation of a pedestrian warrior on the northern Plains before the introduction of the horse, although his shield would have been somewhat larger. He wears a large buckskin shirt which never found such favour farther south. Such garments might be multi-layered, acting as an effective protection against stone-headed arrows. The weapon he carries is a combined bow and lance which in later years, after its abandonment as a weapon, was adopted by many societies as symbolic regalia. From an aquatint in Maximilian's *Atlas*. Museum of Mankind, London.

The Coming of the Horse

*Saukees, be cautious; you live in the woods . . . you will only
have time to discharge your guns, before, on horseback, their
spears will spill your blood . . . As you have seen the whirlwind
break and scatter the trees of your woods, so will your warriors
bend before them on horseback.*

Agent, B. O'Fallon, E. W. T. Vol. XIV, c. 1850

WHILE THE FRONTIER of the gun moved into the Plains area from the east and northeast, the horse frontier moved through it from the southwest. By 1790 these frontiers had met. That fusion produced the Plains Indian and ultimately a formidable barrier to western expansion. The Plains tribes did not of course all simultaneously acquire the horse. Centred predominantly in the south, the introduction was a gradual and ever-broadening process following at least four different routes and probably more. The tribes of the southern Plains such as the Ute, Kiowa, Apache and Caddo had the horse considerably earlier than did the central Plains tribes such as the Sioux, Cheyenne and Crow, and, at least some of the Blackfoot appear to have acquired the horse from another source before the central tribes. Mathew Cocking, trader for the Hudson's Bay Company, travelled to the northern Plains in 1772 and afterwards wrote that the tribes of that region – Piegan, Blood, Blackfoot, Sarsi and Gros Ventres – were 'all Equestrian Indians' (Cocking, 1908, pp. 110–111).

For many years it was erroneously contended that the first horses acquired by the Plains Indians were animals which were lost or abandoned by the Spanish exploratory expeditions led by De Soto and Coronado in 1541. On analysing this theory in depth Haines, Ewers and others have found that little credence could be attached to it. Arthur Aiton, who published Coronado's Compostela muster roll, commented 'Five hundred and fifty-eight horses, two of them mares, are accounted for in the muster. The presence and separate listing of only two mares suggest that we may have been credulous in the belief that stray horses from the Coronado expedition stocked the western plains with their first horses.' (Ewers, 1955, p. 2).

By the early 17th century, Spanish stock-raising settlements in the region of Santa Fe, which traded directly with Indians, were probably the principal centres from which the southern tribes acquired their first horses. By 1705 Comanche raids on the New Mexico settlements were becoming a fairly common way of acquiring horses. Tradition has it that the Comanche in turn traded them to their linguistically related kinsmen, the Shoshone, who distributed them to the more northern Plateau tribes. Certainly by 1805 most Plains tribes were equestrian.

Horses exercised a tremendous influence on the Plains Indians and indeed the liberty which it gave these people to rove at will produced a culture which was not only a gigantic magnification of pre-horse days but changed their very character. The people were transformed from more or less stationary groups dwelling in the wooded areas and devoting their energies to hunting and food supply, to dynamic tribes whose way of life turned on intertribal warfare, and whose personal ambitions focussed on glory and riches from warlike pursuits.

When and how the Plains Indians came to acquire the horse has been well documented and studied by advanced students of Plains culture and the mass of statistics, maps and scientific data which have been so ably accumulated leave very little room for further constructive speculation. It is a fact that most tribes considered the horse as something sacred; the Sioux, for example, called it *Shonka Wakan* or 'Medicine Dog' and its origin was explained in mythological terms. Thus in the late 19th century Wolf Calf (a Piegan over one hundred years old), related how the horse came to the Blackfeet. 'Long ago, when I was young, just getting big enough to use a bow, we used arrowpoints of stone. Then the knives were made of flint. Not long after this, arrowpoints of sheet iron began to come into use. After we used the stone knives, we began to get white men's knives. The first of these that we had were made of a strip of tin. This was set into a bone, so that only a narrow edge of the tin protruded, and this was sharpened and used for skinning.

'Before that time the Piegans had no horses, when they moved their camp they packed their lodges on dogs.

'The first horses we ever saw came from west of the mountains. A band of the Piegans were camped on Belly River, at a place that we call "Smash the Heads", where we jumped buffalo. They had been driving buffalo over the cliff here, so that they had plenty of meat.

'There had come over the mountains to hunt buffalo a Kutenai who had some horses, and he was running buffalo, but for some reasons he had no luck. He could kill nothing. He had seen from far off the Piegan Camp, but he did not go near it, for the Piegans and the Kutenais were enemies.

'This Kutenai could not kill anything and he and his family had nothing to eat and were starving. At last he made up his mind that he would go into the camp of his enemies and give himself up,

Warrior on horseback. Mandan pictograph on a buffalo robe, c. 1800. The acquisition of the horse by the Plains Indians was a gradual and ever-broadening process, following at least four different routes. The Indian pony was of North African ancestry, introduced into Spain during the 8th century and crossed with native stock. The Spaniards in turn introduced them to North America and such settlements as San Antonio and Santa Fé were the primary centres for diffusion to the Great Plains. This is a pictograph from a Mandan robe collected on the Lewis and Clark expedition and sent by them in April 1805 to the Peale Museum in Philadelphia. Peabody Museum, Harvard University.

for he said "I might as well be killed at once as die of hunger." So with his wife and children he rode away from his camp up in the mountains, leaving his lodge standing and his horses feeding about it, all except those which his woman and his three children were riding and started for the camp of the Piegans.

'They had just made a big drive and had run a great lot of buffalo over the cliff. There were many dead in the piskun, and the men were killing those that were left alive, when suddenly the Kutenai, on his horse, followed by his wife and children on their's rode over a hill near by. When they saw him, all the Piegans were astonished and wondered what this could be. None of them had seen anything like it and they were afraid. They thought it was something mysterious. The chief of the Piegan called out to his people: "This is something very strange. I have heard of wonderful things that have happened from the earliest times until now, but I never heard of anything like this. This thing must have come from above (i.e. from the sun) or else it must have come out of the hill (i.e. from the earth). Do not do anything to it; be still and wait. If we try to hurt it, maybe it will ride into that hill again, or maybe something bad will happen. Let us wait."

'As it drew nearer, they could see it was a man coming, and that he was on some strange animal. The Piegans wanted their chief to go toward him and speak to him. The chief did not wish to do this; he was afraid; but at last he started to go to meet the Kutenai who was coming. When he got near to him, the Kutenai made signs that he was friendly and the Kutenais rode into the camp and were received as friends, and food was given them and they ate, and their hunger was satisfied.

'The Kutenai stayed with these Piegans for some time, and the Kutenai man told the chief that he had more horses at his camp up in the mountains and that beyond the mountains there were plenty of horses. The Piegan said "I have never heard of a man riding an animal like this." He asked the Kutenai to bring in the rest of his horses; and one night he started out, and the next day came back driving all his horses before him and they came to the camp, and all the people saw them and looked at them and wondered.

'Some time after this the Kutenai said to the Piegan chief "My friend, why not come across the mountains to my country and visit me? Bring with you those of your people who wish to come. My people will give you many horses."' (Grinnell, 1896, p. 232–5).

When the horse arrived the change in the limited culture of the pedestrian nomad was rapid: the earlier way of life underwent both magnification and modification. The dog had been the beast of burden and in consequence what tipis were employed at that period were small and of little use for family living. The horse made it possible to transport much larger dwellings.

Many Plains tribes traditionally state that 'in the earliest times there was no war' and one can accept that broadly speaking this was true; there was limited motive for war, the land was so vast, natural barriers so insurmountable, the people so few and the spoils so meagre. But the horse changed all that. For example, although the Blackfoot had acquired the gun before their enemies, the

Plains Indian dress, probably Cree, c. 1830. Such costumes were traditionally worn by eastern Indians and are probably good representations of styles formerly utilized by those Plains tribes which abandoned the sedentary life after they acquired the horse. The move west tended to cause a development of more flamboyant styles; headdresses acquired extended tails and shirts and leggings took on a more untailored form. Glasgow City Museum, Scotland.

Six Indian Chiefs. An oil painting by the Canadian artist, Paul Kane, about 1850. The celebrated Blackfoot chief, Big Snake, stands at the centre holding a spear and carrying a shield. To his right stands 'Wahnistow' or White Buffalo, principal chief of the Sarcee tribe. Although Kane describes the warriors as wearing 'full war costume' it is extremely unlikely that such elaborate regalia was actually worn in battle; but it served to designate the warrior in council and parades. Note the similarity between these costumes and that in the previous figure, although here the outfit is far more tailored. Royal Ontario Museum, Toronto.

Shoshone, the latter had a good supply of horses and had obliged the Blackfoot to adopt defensive tactics: during the summer months the Blackfoot tended to assemble in large camps. With the acquisition of horses, and armed with the gun, a new world opened up before them and this was true of a number of the tribes who were edging into the Plains from the east and north.

Costume became more flamboyant to match the new dynamic personalities and way of life of these wandering people. For example, headdresses now acquired tails of feathers, shirts and leggings took on an untailored form, the original shape of the hide being deliberately maintained. In this society man related strongly to animals and nature; he recognized the vitality and power of the eagle, buffalo, antelope and bear and thus incorporated the feathers, horns and claws within the symbolic lore of the tribe and wore these as a mark of distinction. He recognized the forces of nature – the Sun, Moon, Wind, Thunder and Lightning, and adopted them into his mythology to a degree hardly matched anywhere in the world. He did indeed become, as one anthropologist has described him, the 'make-believe Indian'.

Broadly speaking, linguistically related groups united, acquired a previously undreamed of mobility, became aggressive and dynamic hunters and warriors and started to expand their territory.

Fierce struggles occurred and the weaker tribes were forced to occupy inferior, less desirable territory. The powerful Blackfoot drove the Shoshone to the south, the Kutenai and Flathead from their traditional hunting grounds on the plains of Montana to the west, and caused the withdrawal of the Cree tribes to the east. By 1790 the Sioux were sweeping westward, equipped with both horses and guns, and with no resistance from the Arikara, after a massive smallpox epidemic which all but exterminated that tribe, they forced the Kiowa from the Black Hills south to the region of the Arkansas river and the Crow westward to the region of the Yellowstone valley. On the southern plains, the Comanche who split from the Shoshone migrated southwards and under Sioux and other tribal pressure they forced the Apache west and allied themselves with the newly-arrived Kiowa. Thus, by the mid-19th century, three major military tribal powers dominated the Great Plains. In the south were the Comanche, supported by the Kiowa and Kiowa Apache; in the north the Blackfoot, supported by the Sarsi and Gros Ventres, and on the central plains the Sioux, supported at various times by the more northerly branches of the Cheyenne and Arapaho.

At least a decade before the Louisiana Purchase of 1803 the Plains area, using the geographical term in its wider sense, was inhabited by a score or so tribes more than half of which were completely nomadic.

The stage was set and for more than a century the Great Plains were to become host to one of the most captivating races of people the world has ever seen. For convenience, anthropologists have grouped the Indians of the Great Plains according to their geographical position:

1. *The Northern Tribes*

Assiniboin*	Plains-Cree
Blackfoot*	Plains-Ojibwa
Crow*	Sarsi
Gros Ventres*	
Teton Sioux*	

2. *The Southern Tribes*

Arapaho*	Kiowa Apache
Cheyenne*	
Comanche*	
Kiowa*	

3. *The Village or Eastern Tribes*

Arikara	Omaha
Hidatsa	Osage
Iowa	Oto
Kansa	Pawnee
Mandan	Ponca
Missouri	Eastern Dakota
Wichita	

4. *The Plateau or Western Tribes*

Bannock	Northern Shoshone
Nez Percé	Ute
Wind River Shoshone	

(After Clark Wissler, 1920).

Of these, those starred in the table were completely nomadic and are generally considered typical Plains Indian tribes in every sense. The other tribes listed shared many common cultural traits with the nomads. A number were related linguistically, representing most of the major language groups found in North America. Thus the Blackfoot, Cheyenne, Arapaho and Gros Ventres were Algonquians; the Kiowa Apache and Sarsi were Athapaskan; the Pawnee, Arikara and Wichita were Caddoan; the Mandan, Hidatsa, Sioux and Crow were Siouan; the Comanche and Northern Shoshone were Uto-Aztecan, whilst the Nez Percé were Shahaptian. Such groupings tell us much about the original locations of the tribes with tracings perhaps back to Asia. When I was on the Nez Percé reservation in 1969, for example, I was told on good authority that over eighty cognates had been found in Nez Percé and ancient Tibetan as spoken more than 10,000 years ago.

Physically, they were generally a tall people. The Sioux for example *averaged* just over five feet seven inches whilst the Cheyenne – the tallest – averaged almost five feet nine inches (twenty per cent of the sample taken were almost six feet three inches). Their build tended to be lithe rather than muscular although in some tribes – such as the Pawnee and Omaha – there was a tendency towards corpulence. One recent writer has described the Arapaho as a 'handsome people, their full blood men tall, gaunt and muscular, usually about five feet eight inches to six feet in height . . . because of their prominent Roman nose, they are known to the Osage as Big Nose People' (Trenholm, 1970, p. 4). Facially, there were some marked differences, the Crow were broader faced and in general strikingly handsome; the Pawnee tended towards heavier features whilst the Blackfoot were 'rather rounded and delicate' (Wissler, 1920, p. 144).

The blood grouping, in common with that of other American Indians, was predominantly group 'O', and although no detailed studies have yet been made on their full physical characteristics Clark Wissler, one of the outstanding authorities on the Plains Indians, was of the opinion that when closely considered they tended to form a distinct group, physically different from the tribes of other

Horned headdress from the region of the Great Lakes, c. 1750. There is remarkable similarity between this headdress and the so-called Issiwun or Sacred Medicine Hat of the Cheyenne. However, before 1790 the Cheyenne were a horticultural tribe who formerly lived to the east of the Great Plains. Although abandoning agriculture for the chase after the acquisition of the horse, they obviously remembered much of their earlier life and this became part of tribal lore. The sacred Issiwun and the associated Medicine Bundles acted as a powerful unifying factor within the tribe. Musée de l'Homme.

areas. Certainly it is quite safe to suggest that early travellers recognized a definite type when they first made contact with the Plains Indian. Apart from the obvious world of plumed warriors, mounted on spotted ponies in picturesque cavalcades, with a fierce independence and pride of race, it was recognized that this vigorous way of life produced tense, creative and rich personalities with strong and positive attitudes which at least one anthropologist has classed as 'Dionysian' – where emotions were played out to the full. There was an ethos which gave powerful recognition to a competitive life style and where all men had definite goals – where *coups* and heroics counted and, displayed in warfare, placed a man high on the social scale.

The Plains Indians' emphasis on an autonomous way of life was reflected in their attitude towards child rearing, where an offspring was treated as a person with definite rights. His security was deeply rooted in social rather than material values and grandparents often raised their grandchildren which probably 'strengthened emotional bonds with the tribal past' (Devereaux, 1969, p. 97). The Plains Indian ethos was further demonstrated by the fact that most tribes referred to themselves as *The People* – the Kiowa going so far as to describe themselves as *The Principal People*.

Plains Indian society was a complex one. It involved an understanding of the division of

Ojibwa village, Rainy River. From a water colour by Verner, 1882. These tipi-shaped bark wigwams were used extensively by eastern Indians. When some tribes moved out on the Plains after the acquisition of the horse they retained the style but instead of using bark as covering employed the more easily obtained and transported tanned buffalo skins.

Comanche village on the headwaters of Red River in western Texas, southern Plains. Sketched by George Catlin in 1836. The Comanche early adopted the horse. By the first quarter of the 18th century most bands were completely nomadic. This scene is a typical equestrian Plains Indian village and gives a wealth of ethnological data. The women are shown tanning buffalo hides which are both pegged out on the ground and stretched on a wooden frame. Meat is drying on racks. While the women work, the men play a game of chance, ride about camp or rest by their tipis. A group of wolf-like dogs are shown to the right – a feature of most Plains villages. From Catlin's *Albums Unique*, 1841. Museum of Mankind, London.

labour between sexes, the obligations to their own relatives and to the tribe as a whole, an understanding of the way of life which was imposed upon them for economic reasons (for example the splitting up into small units or sub-bands during winter months), their genealogical and kinship systems, their highly developed system of fraternities and finally their religion. Only then could an outsider begin to appreciate the motivations of war, their warfare tactics and the associated attitudes and obligations. The old time Plains Indian was frequently completely misunderstood by early white explorers, by the fur traders and, ultimately, by the United States soldier.

The structure of a semi-sedentary tribe consisted of a politically autonomous and linguistically related unit which tended to be concentrated within one or two villages. For example, in 1830 the Mandan, who lived on the banks of the Upper Missouri in the present state of North Dakota, occupied the villages of Mi-ti-was-kos and Ruhptare, about two miles apart; thus it was comparatively easy for them to develop a system where definite leaders moderated by a tribal council could hold sway.

In the 1830s both Catlin and Bodmer mentioned Wolf Chief as first and Four Bears as second chief of the Mandan. The latter was, however, 'the most popular man in the nation' and had an outstanding war record. As a broad generalization such a system could be said to exist for most of the eastern semi-sedentary village tribes such as the Pawnee, Omaha, Hidatsa and Arikara. Moving west, however, to the more nomadic tribes, we find a considerable variation and independence which can best be illustrated by specific examples.

Although often referred to as Blackfoot, these people actually consisted of three distinct tribes – the Piegan, Blood and Blackfoot proper, all linguistically related and ranging over a territory of

120,000 square miles or more. The Sioux likewise were divided into sub-tribes, at least seven distinct divisions being recognized, and two of the most warlike, the Oglala and Hunkpapa, traditionally occupied territory at least 200 miles apart. Similarly in the 1850s the Assiniboin were classified into at least seven separate bands. 'These 520 lodges form the nation, with the exception of those in the north whom they never visit. The bands named are distinct and usually encamped in different sections of country, though they mingle for a short time when circumstances require it, such as the scarcity of buffalo in some part of their lands or an approach of some numerous enemy. When these causes for combination cease they separate and occupy their customary grounds severally within three or four days travel of one another.' (Denig, 1930, p. 431).

Elderly Piegan informants recalled that during the winter months the bands would be spread out at distances of several miles apart, from 'near the junction of Cut Bank and Two Medicine Creeks forming the Marias to the big bend of the Marias' (Ewers, 1955, p. 125). The Cheyenne seemed to have stronger ties than many of the other nomadic tribes and attempted at one time to stick together 'during the cold season, but they very nearly perished in consequence' (Lowie, 1954, p. 87).

Turning to the southern Plains we find that the powerful Comanche were divided into at least thirteen different bands or sub-tribes who in the mid-19th century wandered over an area of about 120,000 square miles, bounded by the Arkansas River in the north, the Pecos River to the west and extending southwards almost to the junction of the Rio Grande and Pecos rivers – a region comprising much of present-day Texas and parts of New Mexico, Oklahoma, Colorado and Kansas. In 1846 Charles Bent – a well-informed trader amongst these people – estimated their population at about 2,500 lodges or 12,000 people, giving an astounding population density of one Comanche per ten square miles. (In Parker, 1856, p. 231). There were no distinct boundaries between the band territories, and any Comanche or family was free and welcome to settle, or hunt, or move through the regions of other bands, whatever his own affiliation might be. There were no restrictions to prevent a change of residence from one band to another at any time, and no formal ceremony was required. In general, in the large bands, relatives tended to camp together and thus the camp pattern retained a degree of regularity. Although the various bands had very similar cultures, each band did have certain peculiarities which served to identify its members in any company. Each had its favourite dance.

One band habitually made clothing from antelope skins; the others preferred deer skins. One made no pemmican, another made it without berries, and a third always added berries. There were also slight differences in speech. The more southerly Comanche pronounced their words slower than the Antelope band of the Staked Plains. The famed Quanah Parker, one of the last great war chiefs to surrender to the United States authorities, was chief of this band.

During the 19th century there were five outstanding divisions, the largest being the Penatzke or Honey-eaters who were the most southerly group, whilst the Yamparika occupied the most northerly portion of Comanche territory some 400 miles distant. (Wallace and Hoebel, 1952, pp. 22–27).

In short, while all Blackfoot, Teton Sioux, Cheyenne, Comanche and others felt a sense of tribal solidarity, each group within the main tribe tended to be independant and treaties or allegiances made by one tribe, say the Oglala, were not necessarily binding on or recognized by another such as the Hunkpapa. It was often this fundamental lack of understanding of social organization by white people which led to considerable bitterness during the period of the Plains wars of 1860–1890. At that time, government agents or army men would frequently appoint a chief to act on behalf of the whole *nation*, which in reality, as we have seen, consisted of a large number of independent groups, who had their own ideas of the required qualities of a head chief. Even today on the Sioux and Nez Percé reservations one can observe this group independence – an inheritance of traditions going back generations.

Within each of the bands there would be men who would bear the rank of chief. This man was far from an autocrat – his powers were considerably limited by public opinion or council – but he did have ability, commanded respect and could speak for his band as a whole. As the trader, Edwin Denig wrote in the middle of the last century 'There is, as observed before, but one nominal chief to each band, and it is he who leads it. Yet this position does not destroy nor militate against the will of several others in the same band whose voices are as much entitled to a hearing and sometimes more so than his. No man's rule over them is absolute; their government is pure democracy. Their consent to be governed or led by any man is voluntarily given and likewise withdrawn at the discretion of the person. But their existence as a people depends on forming themselves into bodies capable of defense. These bodies must have leaders and these leaders must be brave, respected, followed and supported. In case of a treaty either with whites or with Indians of other nations, the leading chief's voice would have no additional weight because he was in that position. He would be allowed to state his opinion with others of the same standing as men in the same band but nothing more.' (Denig, 1930, p. 435).

When the Comanche were asked 'How did you *select* your headmen?' answers were vague. As one informant put it 'No one made him such; he just got that way.' (Wallace and Hoebel, 1954, p. 211).

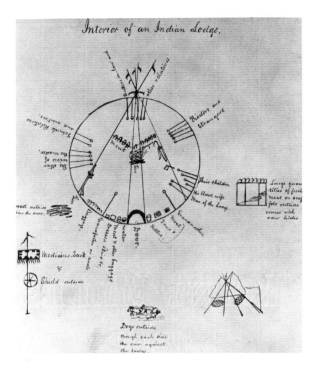

Interior of an Indian Lodge. Probably Assiniboin, this sketch was done by the fur trader, Edwin Denig, at Fort Union about 1852. Tipis were made of buffalo hides – one, some 16 feet in diameter, required 14 skins and weighed about 100 lbs. Such a tipi could sleep a family of about eight, but good interior organization was essential. This unique sketch shows the typical central fireplace, baggage, dressed meat, kettles, pans and water near the door, and weapons hanging on the supporting poles. Meat is drying on racks above the fire and the position of the various occupants is clearly designated. Outside is shown (on the right), a travois with the characteristic netted support, while the medicine bundle and shield of the owner is supported on a pole to the left. Smithonian Institution, National Anthropological Archives, Washington.

From these bands there would emerge from time to time men of outstanding ability, capable of gaining a large following and whose opinions would be carefully weighed in council; head and shoulders above others, proven in battle, of powerful perception, balanced in judgement, they were keenly opposed to losing their free and democratic way of life. Good examples in the post-1850 period were such leaders as Sitting Bull and Red Cloud (both of whom appeared to have occupied a unique position in the Sioux nation).

The Plains people must be seen as many separate groups varying appreciably in size, perhaps averaging some 300 people (although that figure could have a very high percentage tolerance) with continual shifts from one group to another; sedentary for up to five months in a year (November to March), becoming progressively more active, mobile and united in spring, culminating in annual get-togethers from June to August to perform the religious ceremonies typical of that nation. 'This summer season was the only time of the year when all the bands of the tribe camped together in one great village. In this tribal encampment friendships between individuals of the different bands were formed, renewed, and strengthened, the men's societies held their ceremonies and men competed against one another in games and races, young men courted girls of other bands, horses

Piegan encampment on Brulé Flats, Upper Missouri
(in present-day Montana), August 1833. The German
explorer, Maximilian, together with the artist,
Carl Bodmer, stayed at nearby Fort McKenzie and daily
visited this large village of Piegan who came to trade
at the Fort. To the right, women are transporting goods,
one utilizing a burden strap which loops around the
forehead to give support to a massive load. Wolf-like
dogs abound and warriors exchange gossip; the horses
look more like spirited thoroughbreds than Indian ponies,
possibly due to the influence of the European artists who
later – but under Bodmer's supervision – engraved the
plate for this scene. From Maximilian's *Atlas*,
Museum of Mankind, London.

were bartered, painted lodges and sacred bundles were ceremonially transferred, successful warriors were honored, visitors from friendly tribes were feasted and showered with gifts, and the chiefs and headmen of the tribe met in council to discuss the economic, political and military problems of the entire tribe and to make plans for the future. All these varied activities helped to strengthen feelings of tribal unity and solidarity among members of hunting bands who might not even see each other from one summer to the next.' (Ewers, 1958, p. 91).

While somewhat modified (because of the imposed sedentary life), this latter pattern still exists amongst present-day Plains Indians. On my visits to the Sioux Sun Dance celebrations at Pine Ridge, South Dakota, I have met representatives of not only the host Oglala but Hunkpapa, Blackfoot Sioux, Yankton and Brulé, many of whom had travelled perhaps two hundred or more miles from the more eastern or northern reservations. Likewise at the Crow Agency in Montana at one time I noted not only Crow from remote parts of the reservation but Blackfoot, Kiowa, Sioux, Cheyenne, Nez Percé, Kutenai and Yakima, underlining the age-old tradition of the Plains (and Plateau) Indians and their love of an annual 'get together'.

A large camp, such as that assembled after the winter division, would be moderated by a leading chief who would be responsible for assembling councils, the location of the camp site, the positioning of the council lodge, policy on trade, and further he would advise on the formation of war or hunting parties. His final policies and decisions, however, would be determined by the council who would be drawn from the ranks of the headmen or chiefs of the smaller bands; in fact, Plains Indian society was generally so democratic that it would be more correct to say that the leading chief acted as no more than a spokesman through whom the general concensus of opinion of the people could be brought to bear.

In a well organized village the council's decision was enforced by an effective 'police force' drawn from one of the numerous societies – in particular at the time of the assembly for the Sun Dance festival and annual summer buffalo hunt, it was important that 'things were done right'. Individuals who attempted to hunt buffalo alone could startle the herd, with serious repercussions all round. In general, the considerable powers extended to camp police were seldom used – since the policy followed was that of the majority anyway and social status could stand or fall on public gossip. The recruitment of such camp police varied from tribe to tribe but powerful military societies figured prominently in most. It was particularly well developed by the Sioux and appeared in similar forms (to a lesser extent with such people as the Comanche) amongst all the Plains people. (See next chapter 'War Ceremonial' for more details).

In his classic study of the societies of the Oglala Sioux, Clark Wissler enumerated six – what he termed – *Akicita* societies, the members of which were particularly concerned with the duties of camp police. These societies have often been described as 'soldier' or 'warrior' societies but in fact, while one important function could be warfare, another of primary importance was the enforcing of tribal law especially at times of the annual summer gatherings which we have already discussed. Indeed the very word *Akicita* means 'police' or 'guard' rather than soldier, or warrior.

It was the custom of the tribal council (traditionally there were four members, called in Sioux

– strictly the Lakota dialect – *Wakicunza*, 'thinkers') to select four *Akicita* headmen from one particular society and these men in turn chose assistants from the same society. In consequence in one particular year that society performed the duties of camp police. In subsequent years other societies would be selected to perform the same duties so that a rotation of responsibility was accorded. Members of *Akicita* societies wore distinctive regalia or carried society emblems. For example, Fox society members wore a kit-fox skin around the neck, the Crow owners carried a Crow skin in a rawhide parfleche and the Stronghearts carried a feather banner.

One decided advantage of the horse, the new servant, was its ability to transport larger tipis. All nomadic Plains tribes exclusively utilized this conical shaped dwelling – it was uniquely adapted to their way of life. The true tipi was 'a tilted cone, steeper at the back with the smoke hole extending some distance down the more gently sloping side, or front of the tent, and with two flaps – called smoke flaps, ears or wings – flanking the smoke hole and supported by movable outside poles to regulate the draft, ventilate the tent, and carry off the smoke' (Laubin, 1957, pp. 3 & 4).

Styles varied considerably. Classification has broadly been done on the basis of either a three or four-pole foundation around which the remainder of the poles were stacked including those for the smoke flap. Perhaps up to twenty would be needed for a good-sized tipi. The Cheyenne, Teton Sioux, Assiniboin, Kiowa, Arapaho, Mandan, Pawnee, Arikara, Ponca and Wichita, commonly employed the three-pole base while the Blackfoot, Crow, Sarsi, Omaha, Comanche, Hidatsa, Flathead and Kutenai were 'four pole people'. As one student put it 'it seems to us that the four-pole people were mainly those who live in the northwest, in or close to the mountains, which would be one explanation why they retained this method. The winds in those regions are not quite so strong as farther out on the open prairies' (Laubin, 1957, p. 124).

The case of the Nez Percé – a tribe which exhibited a number of Plains traits – is a point of dispute. Reliable authorities mention that either a three-pole or four-pole base was employed, whilst my own work in the field amongst the Nez Percé on the western portion of their reservation in Idaho would suggest that traditionally these people employed three poles. An experienced Plainsman could often tell at a glance which was a three-pole or four-pole tipi. 'In the early days it was an advantage to be able to recognize these

Structure of the Sioux Nation.

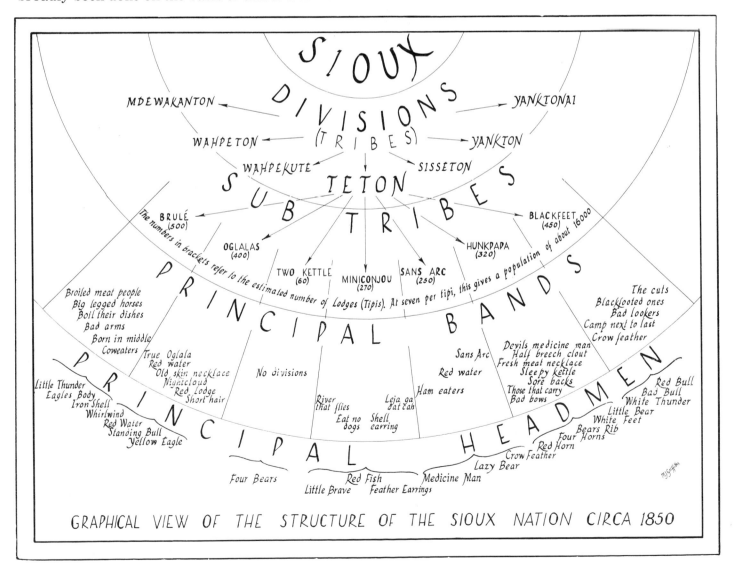

GRAPHICAL VIEW OF THE STRUCTURE OF THE SIOUX NATION CIRCA 1850

25

differences, for on approaching a strange camp, one could tell at a glance whether it was friendly or hostile. During the late Indian wars, Crows were friendly to the white people, Blackfeet at least not openly hostile. They were four-pole people. The heaviest fighting was against the Sioux, Cheyenne, Arapaho, Kiowa and Comanche, all three-pole tribes except the Comanche who used a four-pole base, though a very peculiar one that actually looks like three poles.' (Laubin, 1957, p. 122).

Pine, tamarack and white cedar were used for the poles but in particular, in the region of the foothills of the Rocky Mountains, a special pine – called 'lodge pole pine' – was highly prized and commonly employed. The Crow, in whose country some of the best pines can be found, commonly employed such long poles that when the tipi was pitched they presented the appearance of a huge hourglass, being over thirty feet long. Even today the Crow, who have always had the most elegant and finest of tipis, often use the poles but once during their summer encampments on the Little Big Horn River and then have 'give-aways' of these poles to visiting tribes who have less ready access to them in their own country. Crow informants told me that 'this had always been their tradition'. By comparison the Hunkpapa at Little Eagle, South Dakota, with whom we camped in the summer of 1966, had few tipis erected, mostly employing canvas wall tents. These people had not got ready access to 'lodge pole' country – the Black Hills, their original source of supply, having been lost during the period of the Indian wars of the 1870s.

The skins for the cover were finely dressed, cut out, and made up by a guild of women. Since at best a hide tipi did not last longer than about three years, it was a full time job keeping them all in good repair. The discarded covers were not wasted but employed to make various articles of clothing such as moccasins and leggings.

Entrance was made in a stooping posture, moving forward in this way to the designated seat. Tipi etiquette was well developed. There were traditional designated places of honour and definite locations for relatives and guests. On entering a man moved to the right, a woman to her left. On moving around the tipi, it was considered more 'proper to walk behind a seated person, the seated one leaning forward, if necessary' (Laubin, 1957, p. 92).

In the mid-1850s, Edwin Denig, chief factor at Fort Union which at that time was in Assiniboin country, described and sketched a typical Plains Indian lodge and its surroundings. Some students of Plains ethnology could perhaps criticize the placement of some of the tipi's occupants, but Denig is such a reliable authority that one must conclude that tribal variations were inevitable and that to make broad generalizations can at times be a gross distortion of the facts. Such cases have arisen in Wissler's, Lowie's and others' con-clusions based on central and northern Plains fieldworks leading to generalizations about the southern Plains which were erroneous, and are only now being re-examined by contemporary ethnologists.

Except when employed as 'burial tipi', the lodge was never vacated and left standing. The cover was carefully folded up and transported on a pack horse, while the poles were divided into bundles of five or six and tied to either side of the saddle employing a special 'lodge pole hitch'. The butt of the poles dragged along the ground, appreciably increasing the horse's difficulty in pulling the load. Since a tipi had something like eighteen or twenty poles it 'required two horses to transport the poles of an average lodge' (Ewers, 1955, p. 133). Thus the possession of a large number of horses was a good criterion of wealth among people for unlike the country squire who could own a mansion but ride a bicycle, the nomadic Plains Indian greatly depended upon his mobility – measured in terms of the horses he possessed – for the size of his common lodge.

Crow Indians did not generally paint the exterior surface of their tipis, preferring to keep them a plain white. The Teton Sioux, however, frequently painted their tipis as did their semi-sedentary cousins, the Yankton, farther east. A series of Dakota (eastern Sioux) tipis were copied from a decorated robe collected about the middle of the last century and is now in the Speyer collection in Germany. Both geometrical and live designs are displayed. Warriors commonly decorated their lodges with exploit feats or with designs representing visions and sacred dreams and additionally most large summer camps would have more than one warrior society tipi which was decorated in a symbolic manner. Customs varied considerably, however, throughout the Plains and Plateau region. Traditionally, among the Southern Plains Kiowa, every fourth tipi was painted; although the designs on some Kiowa tipis were merely heraldic, others were painted with the warlike exploits of their owners. (Laubin, 1957, p. 147). An old hide tipi, which one of my Nez Percé informants told me was owned by their tribe, was not painted, which perhaps reflects the influence of the Crow from whom most of the best tipis came. At least two students of the Cheyenne have commented that these people commonly painted their tipis, the term 'medicine lodge' frequently being employed to designate a painted tipi.

Of all the Plains tribes perhaps the Blackfoot should be considered the most outstanding in the ability they displayed in the decoration of their tipis. When Walter McClintock visited a great Blackfoot encampment just before the turn of the last century he estimated that in a camp of 350 lodges there were 35 painted tipis. (McClintock, 1910, p. 217). This is probably above average for a typical Plains village of the 19th century. These imposing painted tipis of the Blackfoot decorated with pictographs of beasts and birds, were mentioned by the fur trader, Alexander Henry, in the first decade of the 19th century. While in general the live designs on Sioux tipis illustrated the exploits of the owner, the designs on Blackfoot tipis were considered to be of a far more sacred character. The designs were believed to secure for their owners and families protection against sickness and misfortune, they were acquired in dreams after long fasting and communion with nature and were thus the exclusive property of the owner. A worn out painted tipi could be duplicated by the owner 'but the owner must destroy the original, sacrificing it to the Sun by spreading it upon a lake and sinking it beneath the water' (McClintock, 1910, p. 212).

Every painted tipi had a 'medicine bundle' attributed to it. These were usually in the form of wrapped objects – beads, bones, stuffed animal skins, pipes, arrows and the like – which were said to have some mysterious property or power associated with them. The medicine bundle was very much an integral part of the Plains Indian religion and is discussed in more detail in Chapter III. The bundles demanded elaborate ceremonies which had to be carried out from time to time and which had to be strictly observed and followed should the owner of a painted tipi decide to transfer it to some other person. If these ceremonies were not observed it was believed that sickness or loss of property would be the penalty.

The transfer of tipis to white men was forbidden. Thus, at the turn of the century, McClintock spent several years of repeated failure in trying to purchase a painted tipi. 'I was made to realize the force of the rigid customs governing their ownership, the religious barriers of ceremonial requirements and the strict secrecy of the owners. I finally secured an otter tipi from an Indian, but only because of unusual circumstances that he believed it had lost its protective power, his wife and children having died.' (McClintock, 1910, p. 212). Strong religious beliefs still influence these Blackfoot people.

Because of the particular religious significance of Blackfoot decorated tipis, a reluctance to any change of style is very apparent. Figures representing otters, eagles, deer and buffalo exhibited on a model Blood tipi, now in the collections of the British Museum, are probably typical of pictographs used for over a hundred years by these people. Ewers was led to conclude that the animal figures were generally 'stylized and decorative'. Usually the body is of one solid colour, either black, red or yellow. A characteristically elaborate device on most of them was the representation of the throat, heart and kidneys of the animal which was believed to have been the source of its power.

While on the Blackfoot reservation in the summer of 1969, I found amongst some of the younger people there a marked reluctance to decorate their tipis as their fancy took them. Dolores Magee told me that she and her husband had been advised to consult Jim White Calf, an elderly member of the tribe, for advice on painting the cover.

A well-designed lodge could be a comfortable habitation if pitched correctly and maintained in good condition. When rapid travelling was demanded the lodge could be packed within the space of twenty minutes. Large camps could take longer – John Mix Stanley mentions that a Piegan village, which he accompanied in the fall of 1853, consisting of ninety tipis, took less than an hour to pack and get underway. (Stanley, 1855, p. 448).

Heavy buckskin shirt decorated with pony beadwork. Crow, or possibly Hidatsa. This is society regalia and obviously related to the attenuated form of multilayered hide armour which was utilized in early days by equestrian warriors. With the introduction of accurate and powerful rifles it rapidly fell into disuse but was retained as ceremonial dress. Collected before 1860 by Colonel V. Raaslϕff. Danish National Museum.

Within a given tribal territory, definite camp sites were well known for their facilities of protection and availability of such essentials as water, wood, and good grass pasture for the horses. It was frequently difficult to drive the smaller tent pegs into the hard ground or high winds tended to cast doubt on their holding powers and so large stones were often employed to weigh down the bottoms of the tipi covers. This tradition has, fortunately, resulted in pin-pointing some of the old camp sites on the western Plains and much work has been done on their distribution and function; this particular branch of Plains archaeology has proved to be fascinating. While in the vicinity of Fort McKenzie on the Upper Missouri (in early days the traditional territory of the powerful Blackfoot), Farmer Bob Lundy showed me an interesting set of 'tipi rings' on the prairie – never moved and now deeply embedded in the soil – as they had been left by nomadic Blackfoot when they had come to trade perhaps a century ago.

For more permanent settlement, say for the annual get-together for the Sun Dance celebrations or during winter, the tipis would be pitched in a circle or arc.

Earlier camp formations were described as being in parallel lines with an avenue between them (see Chapter I). With the coming of the horse, a circular formation was probably adopted to corral the horses within the camp circle and also to protect them from the surprise attacks of mounted war parties. Traditionally, each family and band had its designated place – for example the very name, Hunkpapa, a division of the Sioux, refers to their tradition of camping 'at the entrance' or at the 'head end of the camp circle'. Centrally placed would be the Sun Dance or ceremonial circle.

Once erected, tipis would be made comfortable. The interiors would often be lined with the so-called 'dew cloth' which was a curtain extending from the ground to about a third of the way up the poles. Traditionally, this was painted with geometric or realistic scenes representing the owner's exploits or experiences. In winter, the double lining so formed could be stuffed with hay, insulating the occupants from the severe cold outside. Back rests would be carefully set up and beds covered with buffalo robes. At the centre would be a small fire and the smoke flaps would be carefully adjusted to ensure that a good draught was created in order to carry the smoke through the smoke hole. This was an essential operation as anyone who has ever camped in a tipi will appreciate! Old-time Indians reduced this problem by burning the virtually smokeless 'buffalo chips', but on those broad prairies they had another advantage as well – they knew that the wind direction was generally from west to east so the tipi was invariably pitched with the door facing east. This not only faced the direction of the rising sun but enabled the smoke flaps to be set, deflecting the wind upwards and assisting the rising convection currents emerging from the tipi interior.

Plains tribes were early risers, especially in the spring and summer months, when the camp was frequently on the move. 'On the morning camp movement was to get underway women were up and bustling around at dawn. They prepared the family breakfast, finished packing and were on the move before eight o'clock. Most of the family belongings were packed the night before. They needed only to be tied in their assigned places on horses or travois. The principal task was that of taking down the lodge.' (Ewers, 1958, p. 92).

In the territory of the Plains Indians there were eleven tribes who exclusively employed the tipi as their mode of dwelling and who displayed all the characteristics which classified them as true Plains Indians; that is they were nomadic and non-agricultural and depended on the buffalo for their existence. Another score or so, dwelling on the periphery of the Plains to the east or west, shared many Plains' traits but they exhibited a number of characteristics which must identify them as transitional groups merging one culture with another. Thus the Mandan, Hidatsa and Arikara in the northeast and the Omaha, Pawnee and Wichita in the southeast lived in more permanent dwellings and only used the tipi on certain occasions, for example when going on hunting or trading expeditions. To the west lived the interesting Plateau tribes such as the Kutenai, Kalispel, Flathead, Nez Percé, Bannock, Shoshone and Ute and to the southwest lived the various Apache tribes, such as the Jicarilla and Mescaleros. All these groups commonly occupied dwellings other than the tipi, although like the tribes farther north employed it to a greater or lesser extent at times.

The eastern semi-sedentary people occupied magnificent 'earth lodges' which were circular dome-shaped structures with roofs covered with earth. Such dwellings could be up to fifty feet in diameter and not only comfortably house the

A buffalo pound, northern Plains (probably Cree) about 1850. Those tribes such as the Cree and Assiniboin who were comparatively poor in horses employed buffalo pounds which had been used for centuries by pedestrian Plains nomads. Painting by the Canadian artist, Paul Kane. Royal Ontario Museum, Toronto.

occupants but the family horses and 'bull' boats as well.

The Nez Percé occupied different types of dwellings; the tule tipi was fairly common but in Lewis and Clark's time some Nez Percé villages consisted of one long house only which was some 150 feet in length. It was constructed of sticks, mats and dried grass, could contain two dozen fires and house nearly fifty families. My Nez Percé informants emphasized that considerable differences could occur between various Nez Percé groups. For example, the Upper Nez Percé band, which occupied the upper Clearwater and the Salmon River area employed the buffalo hide tipi at an earlier date and more frequently than the Lower Nez Percé bands, who lived farther to the south and west and were more remote from Plains contact. Some of the Upper Nez Percé frequented buffalo country so often, especially in the last quarter of the 19th century, that they were commonly referred to as 'Montana Nez Percé'. To this band belonged the famous chief, Looking Glass, who was tragically killed at Bear Paw Mountains in October 1877.

A typical Plains Indian village must have presented a lively, animated scene. Women would be busy dressing hides, the skin being either staked out on the ground or stretched on wooden frames, a laborious process which took many days to complete. The hide was first carefully washed of blood and was then staked or stretched out taut. The fleshy portions adhering to the raw side were removed by use of a fleshing tool which in early days consisted of a large bone with a chisel-like edge which was finely notched, but which was later modified employing parts of weighted metal gun barrels shaped in a similar manner. A large hide

Hunting buffalo on horseback. With the introduction of the horse, buffalo hunting took on a new dimension; although still generally under band control it reduced the interdependence of large numbers of individuals so necessary in the case of hunting by means of the buffalo pound. Success now depended on the skill of the individual and wealthier hunters had special buffalo-running horses. Hunting buffalo in this way – often referred to as 'the chase' to distinguish it from the far less popular method of 'surround' – was a dangerous occupation and men were not infrequently maimed or even killed especially if their horse was poorly trained or inept in the skills of buffalo running. From a painting by Rosa Bonheur. Glenbow-Alberta Institute, Calgary, Alberta.

could be cleaned by an experienced woman within two or so hours. The hair could be removed if necessary by use of an adze-shaped tool which was made from a large elk antler and the hide reduced to an even thickness using the same tool. The inner surface of the hide was then rubbed with a mixture of one part of brains to two parts of liver with a little fat added, the whole mixture having been thoroughly boiled. The hide was treated this way two or three times over a period of the same number of days, and then it was thoroughly washed in a stream. Finally it was softened and dried by pulling it back and forth over a short sinew rope loop attached to a pole or tree.

Similar techniques were adopted for smaller skins, such as those of the widespread pronghorn antelope and the western mountain goat and sheep. My own studies suggest that slight variations in techniques of dressing skins by different tribes led to definite types of finish which were not entirely characteristic of the animal from which it came. Broadly speaking, northern tribes smoked the hides over fires and dressed them so that they tended to be rather heavy, the Crow tanned to produce some of the finest heavy soft white buckskin, the Sioux generally not so soft and often considerably thinner whilst the southern tribes' finish was soft, thick and generally stained with yellow or green earth. Studies based on the known distribution of animals and finished hide textures could be helpful in the identification of specimens. However, because there are always many exceptions to a generalization of this nature, it must be emphasized that given specimens, such as hide shirts or leggings or women's dresses, must be examined in a broader context for tribal identification. Not very much hide tanning is now done on the reservations in the United States, except by a few isolated vigorous elderly women, and good hand-prepared buckskins are rapidly becoming a thing of the past. Dennis Lessard, experienced trader amongst the Sioux at Rosebud, South Dakota, told me during discussions on the Pineridge Reservation in 1969 that he now has to travel north into Canada in order to obtain good buckskin, while Mylie Lawyer, a reliable Nez Percé informant at Lapwai, Idaho, said that their last aged hide dresser died in 1968 although she herself was hoping to finish off the half-completed hides which she had inherited.

Polygamy was common amongst the Plains people; this served two purposes. It produced additional labour to enable a man to amass property and it took care of the surplus of women. In general, due to the dangers of war and the chase, men were considerably outnumbered: it has been estimated that there was an almost 'three to one preponderance of women over men which was a "normal" condition in the nineteenth century' (Lewis, 1942, p. 49). Earlier, there had been a far more even balance; now women captured in warfare were generally adopted into the tribe. The situation was acutely summed up by one observer of the mid-19th century Plains Indians. 'To support several women, of course, requires greater exertions on the part of the man in hunting, but this is more than compensated for by their labour in dressing skins, which enables him to purchase horses, guns, and other means to hunt with greater facility. When buffalo are plenty, anyone can kill. The rawhide of the animal has no value. It is the labour of putting it in the form of a robe or skin fit for sale or use which makes it worth. Women therefore are the greatest wealth an Indian possesses next to his horses. Often they are of primary consideration as after war by their labour is the only way he could acquire horses, the only standard of their wealth.' (Denig, 1930, p. 506).

In addition to the above, women would be expected to pitch the tipi, prepare the food and organize supplies for the winter. Buffalo meat was a staple diet of these people, supplemented with deer, elk and other smaller animals when available. Additionally, considerable quantities of wild fruit and plants were used. During the summer and fall fresh meat was prepared by roasting, boiling and stewing. A particularly popular preparation was to boil the ribs and joints with the marrow in them producing a delicious soup. According to

Catlin, salt was not used by the Plains tribes when he travelled amongst them in the 1830s. However, Alice Marriott's field work amongst the Kiowa indicates that before salt was procured from traders it was obtained from salt beds. 'The salt came from salt beds, where it was on the surface of the ground, or from salt springs where it was dissolved in water. When the salt was dry, the Indians dissolved it in water and then boiled it until the water had evaporated to be sure it would be clean. A deposit of salt was left on the hide or kettle where the water had been boiled. The women scraped up the dried salt, pounded it fine, and then put it away in little buckskin bags to use when she needed it. This salt was grayish in colour, and rather coarse in texture, but it was certainly better than no salt at all. Water from the salt springs was also boiled, and the salt it had contained was saved in the same way. Sometimes if a woman had used up all her salt, she might use finely powdered pecan or hickory ashes to season meat.' (Marriott, 1948, p. 80).

Great quantities of dried meat were and still are prepared for the winter months. Indeed the Plains tribes were past-masters at the technique of dehydration for the storage and preservation of food. Squashes, turnips and most types of wild fruits were dried for later 'out-of-season use'. Strips of meat about half an inch in thickness were hung up in the sun on poles and allowed to slowly dry. The strips were then flattened and placed into rawhide containers. The dried meat, or 'jerky' as it was commonly called, could be prepared in a number of different ways. Pemmican was particularly popular.

The best pemmican was made from buffalo meat and often mixed with pounded cherries or grapes. It was widely used and also became an item of trade, especially with the Red River half-breeds who dealt in this commodity extensively; west to the Plateau region it was traded to such tribes as the Flathead, Shoshone, Kutenai, Coeur d' Alêne and Nez Percé. While on the Nez Percé Reservation in 1969, one informant told me that she preferred the Sioux variety of pemmican to that of her own tribe 'as the Sioux tend to use more choke-cherries which make it taste better'. White women apparently did not share such a sentiment about pemmican. Thus Narcissa Whitman, who journeyed to Nez Percé country in 1836, wrote 'Meat and tea in the morn, tea and meat at noon' was their regular fare. The meat was always buffalo meat and while the Whitmans relished it, it made Mrs Spalding very ill. When they entered the mountains, however, even fresh buffalo meat was no longer available and they were forced to subsist on the same substance as dried by the Indians. The squaws were by no means careful about sanitation in the preparation and preservation of this pemmican and the otherwise stout-hearted and strong-stomached Narcissa Whitman was greatly pleased at the occasional rations of rice and the one batch of trapper-cooked, saltless, fried cakes that they were able to obtain. In her journal the best thing she could say about the dried buffalo meat was that 'it kept us alive' (Whitman, 1893).

Women also manufactured moccasins, leggings, shirts, dresses and the like, frequently garnishing them with artistic designs worked in porcupine quills and beads. Cradles would be manufactured for expected additions to the family, the style varying considerably from an oval shaped board in the north to a rectangular unit on the central and southern plains. An interesting point emerged in the discussion of the style of decoration for male or female children, in that the Nez Percé commonly left the final decoration on a cradle until the child was born and then finished the work according to the sex. Thus the niece of Mylie Lawyer, who had asked a Nez Percé woman to make her a cradle in the 'old style', could not get it completed until after the child was born. It would not seem unreasonable to assume that a similar custom existed amongst other tribes.

Men provided the meat and hides for the family, protected them from aggressors, made their own implements for the chase and warfare, guarded their horses, trapped fur-bearing creatures for trading and attended councils and ceremonials and only in hunting did the labours of both men and women over-lap when – if buffalo were killed near camp – women would help with the butchering and skinning. It was hard work cutting up a dead buffalo but little of that animal was wasted. Sioux informants, (who had direct experience of butchering these animals) interviewed in the early years of this century, said that in removing a hide to be used for a tent they began on the under side of a front leg, cut to the centre of the breast, to the lip, then up to a point between the horns, and then from one horn to the other. A cut was made down the belly and the inside of the hind legs. The tail was also split. When removing a hide for use as a robe, they laid the animal on its belly with legs extended front and back. In this case the cut began on the upper lip and extended along the backbone to the tip of the tail. The hide of one side was folded back and spread on the ground, and the carcass was laid on that while the cuts were made along the belly as described above. When removing a hide they did not cut all the meat from the inner surface but left a layer of meat on the hide of the back, and a still thicker piece along the belly. This was later removed by the women and said to be very good to eat. After removing the hide it was the custom to take out the tongue, which was the part of the animal considered the greatest delicacy by the Sioux.

Beyond this point there were no established rules. White Hawk, a Sioux warrior, said however that the front quarters were usually removed first. He said there was a 'blanket of flesh' on the back and sides of the animal which was removed in one piece, but that before taking this off they 'worked up under it' and detached the front quarters. The hind quarters were removed at the hip joints. The hump was underneath the outer 'blanket of flesh'. It was composed of fat and was cut off at the backbone. Below the outer 'blanket of flesh' is the inner 'blanket' which was removed in two parts. One side of it was turned down exposing the ribs and the entrails. The carcass was then cut along the belly, up the shoulder and along the backbone. A fresh hoof was used as a hatchet, and in the old days a knife made of the shoulder blade was used in cutting up the animal. The ribs were removed in the form of a slab, and the kidneys, liver, and fat also were taken out, as were the brains. White Hawk said 'In the intestines there is a pocket-shaped piece about the size of a man's arm. This was turned wrong side out, fastened with a stick, and tied at one end. The brains were put into it, and the liver and hump were tied in a bundle with it. The paunch was turned wrong side out and the heart, kidneys and fat were put into it. The lower backbone was split and later would be chopped for boiling to extract the grease.' (Densmore, 1918, p. 444).

In addition to the meat for food and the hide for tents the buffalo supplied over eighty non-food uses. The ingenuity displayed by the Plains tribes in utilizing buffalo products was amazing. Some

Crow Indian, Fort Union, September 1851. This is possibly the prominent chief, Rotten Tail (not to be confused with the more famous chief Rotten Belly who was killed in a battle with the Blackfoot, August 1834). He rides an Indian pony which Kurz was more adept at sketching than his predecessors, Catlin and Bodmer. His leggings are decorated with fine quillwork in the so-called plaited technique and his weapons consist of a long lance and a bow and quiver carried in a case. On his left arm – the side generally presented towards the enemy in battle – he carries a rawhide shield decorated with a conventionalized eagle design and eagle feathers. This is an excellent field sketch and shows accurately the way a warrior looked as he rode into battle; possibly the leggings would be discarded. From the original sketch book of Rudolph Kurz. Historische Museum, Berne.

of the more common applications were its use for robes, parfleches, saddles, shields, moccasins, cradles, ropes, gun covers and quivers. From the thick part of the neck skin glue was obtained by boiling and then skimming off the floating layer. From the horns, fine spoons, cups and powder horns were made. Additionally these horns were employed on headdresses worn by certain privileged personnel. The brains and liver were used for tanning skins, the pericardium for pouches and at times for binding the bases of hair locks which decorated shirts and leggings. The paunch was used for carrying water or as a container for porcupine quills. Even the droppings of this animal – commonly referred to as 'buffalo chips' – were burnt to provide heat for the tipis. It is no exaggeration to say that 'the buffalo furnished them with all the necessities of life' (Webb, 1931, p. 52).

The buffalo pounds commonly employed in pre-horse days and described in Chapter I did not guarantee a continuous food supply – some years the migratory herds failed to appear and the tribes faced starvation. The horse changed this; it enabled entirely different buffalo-hunting tactics to be adopted. The Indians could now seek out the buffalo and, broadly speaking, rove with them.

Many observers in the 19th century commented that the soldier societies applied the strictest regulations to the hunting of buffalo. Individual hunting of buffalo within a reasonable range of the camp was forbidden, although deer, beaver, elk and other smaller animals could be hunted by individuals as these were of little consequence to the tribe as a whole. Here is a graphic account of a typical buffalo surround written nearly a century and a quarter ago.

'Their march is conducted in silence, with the wind in their faces, consequently blowing the scent away from the buffalo while they are coming near them. The animal is not quick sighted but very keen scented, and a man can, in passing across the wind blowing toward them, raise a herd at the distance of two or three miles, without their seeing him.

'The party proceeds in this order, taking every advantage of concealment the country affords in hills, coulees, bushes, long grass etc., endeavouring to get around them. As soon, however, as they are close and see a movement among the buffalo intimating flight, they push their horses at full speed and riding entirely round commence shooting the buffalo, which run in the direction of the footmen, these in turn shoot, and the animals are driven back toward the horses. In this way they are kept running nearly in a circle until very tired, and the greater part are killed. Those on horseback shoot arrows into all they can at the distance of from two to six paces, and the footmen load and fire as often as the animals come near them.

'A "surround" party of eighty to one hundred persons will in this way kill one hundred to five hundred buffalo in the course of an hour. As soon as possible the women get to work skinning and cutting up the animals. The tongue, hide, and four best pieces are the property of the one who has killed it, and the rest belongs to those who skin it. When the men have stopped killing and turned their horses loose to graze they commence with their women, and the work being divided among so many is soon gotten through with. If any disputes occur as to the right to the hides or meat, they are settled on the spot by the soldiers; but these disputes do not often occur, as they generally all have as many hides and as much meat as they can pack home. The meat is cut into long, thick slices, merely detaching it from the bones and leaving the carcass on the plains. It is packed home on their horses and dogs. Before leaving, however, they all make a hearty meal of raw liver, raw kidneys, raw stomach, and cow's nose, with other parts in the same state, and the blood being thus smeared all over their faces presents a savage appearance.' (Denig, 1930, p. 531).

With so much of their way of life dependent upon the horse, their riding ability and feats of horsemanship became legendary.

George A. Custer praised their individual daring, their tactics, and their horsemanship as the best in the world. Dr W. A. Bell, who travelled in western Kansas in the summer of 1867, wrote that 'the Buffalo Indians are probably the finest horsemen in the world. Accustomed from their childhood to chase the buffalo, they live half their time in the saddle.' (Bell, Vol. I, 1869, p. 58). In turn, the Indians themselves recognized the superior horsemanship of some tribes.

As Captain William Philo Clark of the United States Army wrote 'The Comanches and Utes are considered by many Indians the best horsemen, and the Nez Percé and Cayuses as having the best or fastest ponies. The Southern Indians perform more daring and difficult feats on horseback, and are more expert in the use of the lasso than the Northern.' (Clark, 1885, p. 319).

When George Catlin visited the great Comanche village in the summer of 1834, he described the 'Comanchees' as rather low in stature, often approaching corpulency and in their movements both heavy and ungraceful. He considered them 'one of the most unattractive and slovenly-looking races of Indians that I have ever seen'. The moment, however, they mounted their horses 'they seem at once metamorphosed, and surprise the spectator with the ease and elegance of their movements. A Comanchee on his feet is out of his element, and comparatively almost as awkward as a monkey on the ground, without a limb or a branch to cling to; but the moment he lays his hand upon his horse, his face, even, becomes handsome, and he gracefully flies away like a different being.' (Catlin, Vol. II; 1842, p. 75).

Children of Plains Indian tribes learnt to ride at an early age; Ewers' Blackfoot informants claimed that their children would have learnt to ride alone in their fifth year. Riding lessons were commonly given to young children initially by tying them to a woman's saddle on a gentle horse and then as they gained in experience and confidence, the horse was led at a swifter pace, and they were taught to use the reins and control their mount. (Ewers, 1955, p. 67). The method could be dangerous, especially if the horse bolted, but it was a widespread practice employed throughout the Plains region from an early period. For example, the trader, François Larocque, observed the method amongst the Crow as early as 1805. (Larocque, 1910, p. 64). By the age of six or seven years, Blackfoot children were good riders. Personal observations in the field amongst Sioux, Crow, Gros Ventres, Assiniboin, and Blackfoot within the last decade would indicate that this is still the case. It is not uncommon to see boys of perhaps eight years of age or more riding the 'big American horses' barebacked with astounding ease and expertise. Amongst less historically nomadic tribes such as the Mandan, Hidatsa and Arikara comparatively little horse-riding expertise now appears to exist.

Whilst Ewers has found that the majority of the styles of horsegear were probably suggested by white influence, Plains tribes nevertheless invented additions to their riding equipment which gave them distinctive characteristics, some of the bridle, martingale and crupper work being exquisitely decorated with quillwork. The finer work was generally done on a loom by Cree women, many of whom were wives of white and half-breed traders and trappers. For example, Rudolph Kurz sketched a magnificent quilled headstall while staying at Fort Union in the early years of the 1850s, and there is at the Royal Scottish Museum in Edinburgh a similar headstall which is said to be of 'Blackfoot or Crow' origin. Generally speaking, pad saddles were employed by men and the wood saddle with its characteristic high pommel and cantle by women. The former style was probably derived from the Spanish-Mexican pack saddle and had wide distribution. The women's wood saddle, however, was possibly of a more indigenous nature. (Ewers, 1955, p. 81–91).

Such then was broadly the picture of life on the Great Plains in the 19th century. In many ways an enviable, wild and free culture developing 'A powerful and warlike people, proud, haughty and defiant well over six feet in height strong muscular frames and very good horsemen, well dressed, principally dressed in skins and robes; rich in horses and lodges; have great abundance of meat; since buffalo, elk, antelope and deer abound in their country. They say they are *Indians* and do not wish to change their mode of living . . .' (In Blackmore, 1869, p. 303).

But perhaps George Dorsey, the outstanding anthropologist who contributed so much to our knowledge of the Cheyenne and other Plains tribes, should have the last word in this chapter. He once remarked of the Cheyenne – a typical nomadic Plains tribe in every sense:
'They defy description
As do all the wonders of nature
Which move the soul to gladness.'

War Ceremonial

I will give my flesh and blood that I may conquer my enemies!

Sun Dance vow. Tokala-luta, Teton.
Sioux warrior, c. 1870

WAR AND ITS ASSOCIATED CEREMONIES was an important cultural facet of most North American Indian tribes, acting as a powerful unifying force within the tribal organization.

Apart from the expansion of territory conflicts which occurred early in the history of the Indians of the Plains, the two major reasons which led to the formation of a war party were the desire for scalps and the desire for horses. The Scalp Raid was without question, anciently at least, dominated by religious and social obligations which were triggered by the death of a close relative, friend, or in some cases the death of a respected leader of the tribe. The Horse Raid on the other hand, although still retaining a number of essentially religious elements, was more dominated by economic factors ante-dated by the raid for slaves which we know was a widespread custom in pre-horse days. These two modes of warfare were then essentially very different and as will be shown this difference existed not only in spirit but also in the pattern of organization.

Although Plains Indian culture was dominated by a martial spirit, continual warfare leading

Warriors dressed and mounted as for a scalp raid, probably Blackfoot. This unusual photograph shows the wolf skin headdress generally worn by the prominent members of the war party; wolves were war fetishes since the life of a warrior was said to be like that of the wolf. The skin also gave practical camouflage when scouting. The leader carries a pipe which would be regularly smoked, symbolically communicating with the higher powers to whom the warriors appealed for success. The utilization of the pipe this way was a widespread custom and was often used to identify the leader on pictographic war records—particularly by the tribes of the Upper Missouri. British Museum.

to extermination of a weaker group hardly finds a place in the annals of these warrior people. Their concept of the warpath – and this seems universally recognized – could be likened 'to a piece of string which is doubled so that its ends meet again' the point of conflict being marked at the bend of the string and whether success or failure was the outcome the homeward journey was immediately commenced and on return the force was disbanded. Seldom, if ever, did the war party continue on its way to attack another enemy encampment. Clearly the mercenary concept is not meaningful in describing Plains Indian warfare.

The history of Plains Indian intertribal warfare is one of dynamic change. In early days, the spirit of the widespread Scalp Raid prevailed but then as the horse increasingly dominated the culture, the Horse Raid became progressively popular and the desire to organize Scalp Raids decreased; in a word, the Plains Indian became more materialistic but now he could demonstrate in a very positive way – by the gift of horses – his generosity.

The ceremonies associated with warfare were embedded within the ancient lore of the tribes and we can learn much of this lore, and appreciate its form amongst the completely nomadic tribes, by reference to groups who remained semi-sedentary – there the rate of change was decidedly slower, even after the introduction of the horse.

The Omaha, for example, gave recognition to the tribally disintegrating effect of aggressive warfare which might be waged by the schemes of ambitious and selfish men. Thus the concept of war was allied 'to the cosmic forces and under their control'. These forces were manifested in the destructive power of the lightning and the 'roar of the thunder' (Fletcher and La Flesche, 1911, p. 403). A violation of the will of the God of War could bring his wrath to bear on the offending individual. Traditionally, all Omaha infant males were consecrated to the God of War and taught that it was this god who decreed death or otherwise on the battlefield. This philosophy thus modified the character of warfare in the Omaha mind for success pivoted on the benevolence of the supernatural powers and brought a dignity to the brutality of war. At the same time the necessity of observing strict rituals before the commencement of aggression was an 'effective means of establishing and maintaining tribal control over warfare'.

The Cheyenne, who in historic times were counted as amongst the most powerful warlike tribes on the plains, recognized their tribal solidarity through the four Sacred Arrows and the Medicine-Arrow ceremony, claimed to have been performed 'thousands of years ago'. Tribal mythology records them as being the gift of Maheo the 'All Father' to the Cheyenne culture hero 'Sweet Medicine'. Two of these arrows possessed power over men, the remaining two over buffalo and other animals. The former pair, called the 'man-arrows', were pointed towards the enemy and always ensured great success in battle. The story is told of a Keeper who made a mistake in performing pre-battle ceremonies and the arrows were captured by the Pawnee (c. 1830). Eventually two were returned to the Cheyenne and two re-made. To this day they are considered of a most sacred character and essential to the continued unity of the Cheyenne people, and few white men have observed the elaborate ceremonies. In recent years, the Roman Catholic priest, Father Peter J. Powell, has won the respect of the elders of the tribe and in July 1960 was invited to witness the entire Medicine Arrow ceremonial and was moved to record: 'Sweet Medicine himself told the Cheyennes that they would renew the Arrow shafts four times, then they would disappear as a people.' (Powell, 1969, p. 577).

Aggressive warfare was called by the Omaha *nuatathishon* meaning 'war with men' thus ancient custom at least decreed that neither women nor children were to be killed in intertribal battles. While the above specifically refers to the Omaha many of the fundamental ideas are to be found in the lore of other tribes and the warriors' best efforts were naturally directed at harnessing the power of the War God.

The Omaha Sacred War Pack (which I examined at the Peabody Museum of Harvard University in 1969) was traditionally kept in the Tent of War. The contents of the Pack were sacred, they consisted in part of the skins of various birds which were considered to be the special messengers of the God of War. Thus the birds of the air – the swallow, hawk, eagle and crow – acted as a connection between the War God (which was thought to reside in the storm clouds) and the earthbound warriors who so earnestly sought the sanction of this supernatural power. Traditionally, a prospective leader of a war party approached the keeper of the Sacred Pack and invited him to attend a feast; this was repeated four times and at the end of the last feast the Pack was opened, the leader was initiated into the rituals to be observed and practical advice on tactics was given. Some of the contents of the Sacred Pack might be loaned to the leader for the duration of the expedition so that before going into battle each man could be given a charm which acted as his protective medicine power.

During the time of the annual buffalo hunts the tribe recognized the importance of preparing for defensive warfare. Semi-sedentary tribes, in parti-

Tattooed Hidatsa warrior, 1850. Tattooing was common amongst the tribes of the Missouri river, particularly the Hidatsa and Omaha. It indicated high rank and success in warfare and amongst the Omaha the keeper of the packs of war was traditionally tattooed as a mark of distinction. This form of decoration was less common amongst the completely nomadic western tribes although it was used by the Assiniboin and others to signify that they had struck their first enemy. From the original sketch book of Rudolph Kurz. Historische Museum, Berne.

cular, would be leaving the protective confines of their pallisaded villages, moving west in search of the buffalo herds and probably into territory occupied by the fierce Plains nomads. Then the binding power of the war pipes was evoked, where their ceremonial smoking by each man was an act 'equivalent to taking an oath to do ones duty even at the risk of life'. It is possible that the unusual pipe sketched by George Catlin when he visited the Mandan in the summer of 1832, and which was tribal property and kept in the Medicine Lodge, was used in similar ceremonies. As will be seen, the War Pipe concept and its association with the thunder was widely recognized although modified from tribe to tribe.

Traditionally, Omaha war parties performed a dance before commencing on the war trail. It was of a sacred character, the steps and rhythm being imitative of a wolf whom they associated with war. The dance 'was an appeal to the wolf that the men might partake of his predatory character, of his ability to roam and not be homesick'. (Fletcher and La Flesche, 1905–1906, p. 416). Uninitiated white men, who described war dances in blood lust terms, obviously completely failed to grasp the significance of what they were observing and the deep-seated cultural ethos of The People in which these ceremonies were embedded.

When tribes who hugged their periphery moved out on to the Plains after the acquisition of the horse, their nomadic life demanded modification of the War Ceremonials and in time warfare too took on a different slant. The power of the war

Omaha warriors in dance regalia. Photographed about eighty years ago. In common with most Plains Indian tribes the Omaha traditionally performed a dance before a scalp raid. Warfare waged to suit the schemes of ambitious men was recognized as evil; thus strict tribally controlled rituals were associated with the scalp raid. The steps and rhythm often imitated the wolf, and both warriors wear the 'Crow' which was said to represent the field after the battle was over. Crows were generally first on the battlefield and the feathers on the pendants represent the dropping of feathers from them and other birds fighting over the slain bodies. Only men who had gained high war honours were entitled to wear this ornament. Smithsonian Institution National Anthropological Archives, Washington.

chief, as exemplified by the Keeper of the War Pack, amongst such tribes as the Omaha, and the powerful individuals who led the massive infantry formations during the period of expansion onto the plains progressively declined. The move to nomadism in most cases brought about a marked decentralization and an emphasis on individualism. The important events in the life of a warrior however still pivoted on ceremonial and religion. Indeed, religious doctrine permeated every aspect of the life cycle of the 19th-century Plains Indian, not least of all in warfare, and even many of the predominantly secular societies seldom lacked some supernatural association. As with their forbears, beliefs were tied in with the works of nature with a definite hierarchy of deities. The recognition of 'God' as a supreme power was more positively perceived by old time Plains Indians than it was by the average white man; investigations by observers in the field, however, indicate that concepts varied considerably from tribe to tribe. Amongst the Sioux – for which there is much data – there was recognition of an all-pervading force referred to as *Wakan Tanka*, the nearest translation being 'Great Mysterious'. *Wakan Tanka* was manifested through a great many deities in ascending order of power – the sun being considered

supreme whilst the moon, stars, lightning, and thunder were of lesser rank. Comanche informants were uncertain of the relationship existing between the Great Mysterious and the Sun. 'Sometimes the two were closely associated, while at other times a distinction was made between them.' (Wallace and Hoebel, 1954, p. 194). Early Crow religion pivoted on the concept of a supreme being which they called *Eehtreshbohedish* meaning 'Starter of all things' or 'First Worker', and it was First Worker who bestowed power to the lesser deities. (Wildschut, 1960, p. 2).

Many things were *wakan* or 'mysterious' to the Sioux; the horse was *wakan shonka* or mysterious dog; a dragonfly, turtle, lizard and gun were also *wakan* – they all were considered to have certain powers or qualities which were difficult to explain. Small pouches containing a child's umbilical cord were frequently in the form of lizards – creatures who had a remarkable tenacity for life and were not easily killed. As we shall see, Plains Indians frequently employed symbolic representations of *wakan* in their warfare activities and tended to be much less dependent on a tribally owned Sacred War Pack.

A brief view of their religion again demonstrates their independent and democratic spirit for, except in the annual ceremonies of the Sun Dance or comparable religious tribal festivals (such as the O-kee-pa), Plains Indian religion was in many senses a very personal thing. It did not have or need the complexities of a priestly sect or religious organization and there were certainly no preachers. Each man had his own personal *wakan* which he obtained in early adolescence by going on a vision quest. During a period of fasting and abstinence away from camp and usually on some high hill top, the boy would pray to First Worker to reveal to him a particular spirit which would henceforth be a guiding destiny. The spirit could be in the form of some animal, the sun, or something less tangible such as the thunder or lightning. It would direct the visionary as to the contents of his 'medicine bundle' and state the obligations associated with it which, if violated (even innocently), could bring catastrophe. Dreams or visions of thunderbirds were considered the greatest honour by the Sioux and brought the most obligations. It is interesting to note the widespread association with the thunder. Blackfoot medicine pipes for example (of which the explorer David Thompson wrote in 1787 were owned by 'each respectable man') were considered by them as a gift from the thunder. 'Thunder is a man who was very wicked and troublesome to the Indians, killing men and beasts in great numbers. But many years ago he made peace with the Blackfoot and gave them a pipe stem in token of his friendship, since which period he has been harmless.' (Henry and Thompson, Vol. II, 1897, p. 366).

Some of these medicine pipes were considered powerful war medicine and their owners could command high privileges for their services. In

The O-kee-pa ceremony of the Mandan.
Intense ceremonialism associated with hunting and
warfare tended to act as a unifying force within the
semi-sedentary villages on the eastern Plains.
Recent excavations in the Mandan villages have located
plazas, at sites which date from at least the 15th century,
where religious festivals were enacted. Perhaps the
O-kee-pa was the most spectacular and pre-dated the Sun
Dance of the nomadic Plains tribes. *Left*, the mythical
figure of O-ke-hee-de, the Owl or Evil Spirit, who
according to Catlin enters the Mandan village from the
prairies of the west, at noon, on the fourth day of the
O-kee-pa. From under the bunch of buffalo hair
covering the pelvis was an artificial penis carved in
wood which extended somewhat below his knees.
Right, the power of the Medicine Pipe. O-ke-hee-de at
his moment of assault upon the woman is held in check
by the sacred pipe carried by O-kee-pa-ka-see-ka,
the Master of the Ceremonies. This scene was observed by
George Catlin at the Mandan village in 1832.
'I stood within some 20 or 30 feet of this group, and
had the view exactly, here given, perfectly stationary
for 15, or 20 minutes.' He was subsequently forced to
describe such scenes in pseudo-Latin and never published
his sketches in their entirety. They have only recently
been discovered in the British Museum where they were
deposited by George Witt in 1865.
Museum of Mankind, London.

August 1833 on Brulé Flats near Fort McKenzie (an area which incidentally is still virtually unchanged), Carl Bodmer, the talented Swiss artist, painted Hotokaneh-hoh carrying his magnificent medicine pipe.

There was a definite grading of visions in the quest for supernatural guidance and often vivid dreams were considered as good; indeed both could give the desired effect – the acquisition of supernatural power – and with the emphasis on individualism, sacred bundles now became the property of individuals rather than the tribe. Among the Crow, for example, where the system of supernatural acquisition of power was particularly well developed, there were ten different categories of medicine bundles and at least six of them were concerned with war. Referring to War Medicine Bundles, Wildschut, a student of the Crow, says 'These sacred bundles were employed to bring success in warfare and in horse stealing. They contain the material representations of the original maker's visions and are therefore of many varieties. Of these, the hoop medicines and arrow medicines might be considered sub-classes.' Other interesting bundles in the series were Love Medicine Bundles. 'These bundles contain sacred objects which were credited with the power to attract such members of the opposite sex as their owners desired.' (Wildschut, 1950, p. 16–17).

My own examinations of medicine bundles now preserved in private and museum collections reveals a remarkable variety of objects. The following is extracted from notes made at the time of examining a Crow bundle, (from the Pohrt Collection in Michigan). 'Wrapped in seven layers of trade cloth, silk, calico and paisley cloth are: (i) medicine pipe stem length 31 ins. with Mallard duck head; (ii) five brown eagle tail feathers; (iii) one bunch of owl plumes; (iv) two owl feathers; (v) one bunch of braided sweet grass; (vi) one hank of red dyed horse hair; (vii) small pieces of trade tobacco; (viii) one rattle; (ix) one stick of choke cherry wood; (x) one stick with an ear of corn wrapped with buffalo wool and decorated with a small fluff.'

Additionally, various types of headgear, shields, shirts, and other apparel might become associated with, or be part of, a medicine bundle and were believed to bring success in war to the owner. The concept was widespread throughout the Plains; for example, some such regalia is shown in the unique self portrait which was drawn by a Comanche warrior in the 1860s which I located at the Musée de l'Homme in Paris a few years ago. To the average white man, the contents of medicine bundles would be classed as a strange mixture of meaningless feathers, beads, stuffed animals and botanical objects. To the Indian they were very real expressions of their traditional religious beliefs – they might almost be called the Plains Indian reliquary and at least part would be carried on war expeditions.

The Blackfoot warrior, Rides-at-the-door, ex-

Medicine Man invoking supernatural powers for success in battle. War ceremonial gave great emphasis to seeking the aid of the supernatural powers, and it was particularly the thunder which was viewed as the god of war. Vows were generally taken with the right hand raised to the sky as shown here: *'Wakan Tanka!* I will give you my blood that I might conquer my enemies!' From a painting by Will Crawford, about 1900.

plained the use of his own war medicine: 'When I went to the enemy to steal horses, I carried my war medicine in a small cylindrical rawhide case. This medicine could never be put down. In a lodge it always had to be hung up. When my party got near the enemy camp, I made a little fire, took charcoal and sweetgrass and made a smudge. I sang the song given me with my medicine and prayed before donning my medicine plume. In my prayers I asked first for horses, to get away safely and not to have to return on foot. Sometimes I prayed to the sun, "See me. The rain is holy and the wind is holy." Then it was bound to blow, and the sleeping enemy would not hear us when we went into their camp and took their horses.' (Ewers, 1955, p. 180).

A war medicine bundle which had brought success to its owner (or owners if transferred) became valuable property and if under some circumstances proved ineffectual warriors were prepared to make excuses for it, blaming the rash action or lack of observance of some obligations by the owner.

The situation was somewhat different with newly acquired medicine bundles which a young warrior would be anxious to try out. If on his first expedition he was successful recognition was given to the bundle's power, and confidence in this increased with every new success; a warrior could ascend through the ranks by virtue of his war medicine power. The power of his bundle was assessed in terms of the success it brought, and other less fortunate warriors would pay handsome prices for duplicate bundles or the complete transfer of it to them (see Chapter IV – Rotten Belly's Shield). The Crow woman, Root Digger, who owned a skull medicine bundle – believed to be powerful war medicine – received many presents from warriors who requested that the skull be consulted on their behalf (Wildschut, 1960, p. 79). This augury function of a sacred object seems both old and widespread. The Omaha, for example, employed a wolf skin from a Sacred War Pack not only to learn of future success but also to ascertain conditions in hostile territory. The Winnebago, and probably their close neighbours the Iowa, Oto and Missouri, used an otter skin. The skin was wrapped around the throat of a volunteer within the war-party so as to render him unconscious. In this state he was supposed to be able to predict the future (Fletcher and La Flesche, 1911, p. 415). On the other hand those new bundles which failed to bring success were soon discarded.

The war medicine bundle of Two Leggings, chief of the River Crow, gives a good insight into the full significance of the medicine bundle to the Plains Indian. The bundle case was made of rawhide and measured eighteen inches by ten. A painting of a black horse on the case depicted the vision of Weasel Moccasin, one of the former owners of the bundle, who said that his vision had been of the black horse standing in the sky which had been struck by lightning – represented by red zig-zag lines painted on the case. The bundle contained

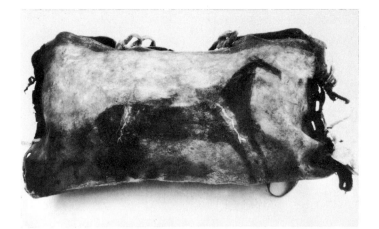

Case and contents of Two Leggings' War Medicine Bundle. Crow. The bundle originally belonged to Weasel Moccasin and was acquired by Two Leggings when he wished to go to war and had no war medicine of his own. Weasel Moccasin had claimed that it was a gift to him by the Thunderbird as represented by the eagle head. Each article in the bundle was thought to bestow desirable qualities for success on the war trail to the owner or his horse. For example Two Leggings said that the swallow 'is significant of the power of that bird to fly speedily through a great flock of its kind without touching one; the owner of the medicine ascribes this power to himself and his horse in being able to evade a number of enemies without mishap'. The symbolism of the other contents is discussed in the text.
Collected by William Wildschut, Crow Reservation, Montana, 1922. Museum of the American Indian, Heye Foundation.

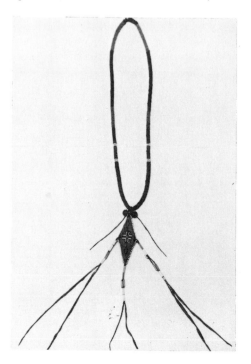

A navel amulet in the shape of a lizard. Probably southern Plains. These small pouches contained the umbilical cord of the child and were carried by the wearer, often to the grave. They were symbolic of long life and protection against danger. The Sioux believed that lizards had *wakan* powers – they were difficult to capture and kill. John Datlen Collection, Dover.

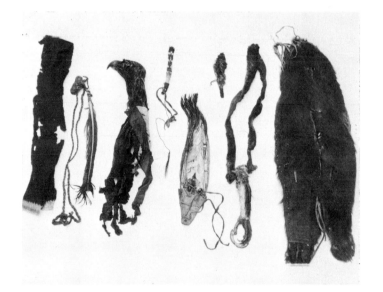

eleven items which had symbolic meaning. A feather necklace which was to be tied around the horse's neck, and by its power make the horse feel as light as a feather and hence able to run faster and easier: an eagle plume combined with a hawk feather was to be attached to the horse's tail, producing the same result as the necklace. To renew the horse's strength there was a small bag of herbs, a pinch of which was placed inside the horse's mouth and nostrils at the appropriate time. The bear claws and hair were to be fixed around the horse's neck to ensure that it would remain in prime condition. A small swallow skin was significant of the power of that bird to fly speedily through a great flock of its kind without touching one. Such power was ascribed to the medicine bundle owner so that he and his horse would be

Top. Contents of Joe Assiniboin's (also known as 'Assiniboin Boy') war bundle. Gros Ventres. This is a personal war bundle carried by Assiniboin Boy in the last battle the Gros Ventres fought. Such bundles had their origins in so called war packs which were in the care of some tribally elected keeper. Before waging war its services were sought, in this way tribal control was maintained over warfare. With the change to nomadism the influence of central control decreased, and many warriors owned their own war bundles, of the type shown here. Acquired at Fort Belknap Reservation, Montana by the collector Richard Pohrt in 1937.

Above. The story tellers. Painting by Charles M. Russell. Although somewhat romanticized, this painting gives a wealth of detail and captures the continuing spirit of the Plains Indian as an aged Grandfather relates lore and legend of the tribe to the attentive youngsters. Possessing no written language the history of the tribe was this way perpetuated during the long winter months. During winter, tipis were permanently pitched and made comfortable and warm by use of a lining which extended part way up the poles as shown here. This so-called 'dew cloth' was often elaborately decorated with geometrical designs or the war and hunting record of the warrior owner. Back rests made of slender willow rods, the central fire-place and a child holding a doll (a common toy) are also shown in this thoughtful study. Whitney Art Gallery of Western Art, Cody, Wyoming.

Bull Lodge's Shield. Gros Ventres. Montana. Before the introduction of powerful and accurate rifles the shield was an important part of military costume. In pre-horse days it could be up to three feet in diameter, affording considerable protection to pedestrian warriors. The protective power of a shield was considered to lie more in the medicine power of the painted designs than the mechanical protection it afforded. Designs were generally painted on a buckskin cover over which in turn was another covering of plain buckskin. The Crow generally acquired the designs for their shields in visions, shields often being inherited. This shield is made of buffalo hide and is about twenty inches in diameter. It is decorated with two small medicine bundles and a profusion of eagle feathers attached to a red strip of cloth around its circumference. Purchased from Phillip Powder Face at Hays, Montana, by the collector Richard Pohrt.

able to evade a number of enemies without mishap. A piece of blue cloth was to represent good luck in general. A strip of otter skin with an eagle claw attached to it was used as a necklace. This necklace was worn over the left shoulder and under the right arm. The eagle claw was symbolic of the lightning striking the horse as described in the vision, as well as of the power of the eagle to pounce upon its enemy, a power which is thereby given to the owner of the bundle. A horse's hoof was thought to impart the power to make easy the capture of enemy horses. An eagle's head in the bundle was to be carried by the owner when he went into battle. At the time of tying this on he was to repeat the songs and prayers related with the bundle, thus the flight of the eagle was symbolized, imparting to the owner all the desired attributes of that mighty bird – keen vision and noiseless but swift approach. Coloured ribbons were attached to the eagle's head, being an emblem of the sky as seen in the vision and another eagle feather which was attached to the back of the owner's head was said to have the same symbolism as the eagle's head itself (adapted from Wildschut, 1960, p. 52).

Both types of Plains warfare are catered for in

Hotokaneh-hoh, a Blackfoot warrior, with his medicine pipe. Such pipes together with their associated bundles were considered to have powerful influence in warfare. This one is decorated with eagle feathers the quills of which are garnished with rawhide strips wrapped with porcupine quills. At intervals on the stem are tied what appear to be woodpecker bills which a number of tribes consider synonymous with the thunder. As early as 1787 the fur trader David Thompson noted that each 'respectable man' owned a medicine pipe. Blackfoot tradition states that the stems were copied after one given to them by the thunder as a token of friendship. Privileged owners could command high prices for their services to others evoking the power of the pipe. From an original water colour by Carl Bodmer, Fort McKenzie, August 1833. Northern Natural Gas Company Collection, Joslyn Art Museum, Omaha, Nebraska.

this bundle. Thus, the eagle medicine imparts the ability to pounce and kill – a 'Scalp Raid' – whilst the horse's hoof endows a power to capture many enemies' horses – a 'Horse Raid'.

Military Societies

Mention has already been made of the importance of societies in the social organization of the Plains tribes. The tendency was for the people to scatter into small groups during the winter but with the coming of spring the camp circle was reformed and its government organized. Amongst the Sioux this was initiated by the selection of the *Wakicun* – four men who were responsible for both the civil and economic affairs of the tribe and acted for the Chiefs' Society. In turn they delegated responsibility to the *Akicita* societies who acted as a kind of police or marshal force during the summer months and made for smooth running of camp life especially at times of the buffalo hunts. However, additional to the *Akicita* societies there were others of a more specialist nature which were not concerned with the primary *Akicita* duties – these were dream societies and war societies, and were common to many tribes.

The former consisted of men who banded together because during their fasting visions they had seen the same animal. Buffalo societies were the most widespread and were most highly developed by the Upper Missouri village tribes. In this region, however, membership was by right of age rather than because of some vision, being part of an age-graded series. Age societies, as they became known, were particularly well developed by the Mandan, Hidatsa, Blackfoot, Gros Ventres and Arapaho. Men progressed from one to the next. According to Mandan informants, the sequence of age societies amongst them was White, Fox, Dog, Black Mouth, Buffalo (or Bull), and Horse, while the very old men were said to belong to the Coarse Hair Society (Densmore, 1923, p. 108). They were predominantly military in character, *Akicita* type duties being of secondary importance and less well defined. Characteristic costume was worn by members.

Thus, Maximilian, Prince of Wied Neuwied, in describing the Mandan Bull society dance tells us 'they wear the skin of the upper part of the head, the mane of the buffalo, with its horns, on their heads; but two select individuals, the bravest of all, who thence-forward never dare to fly from the enemy, wear a perfect imitation of the buffalo's head, with the horns, which they set on their heads, and in which there are holes left for the eyes, which are surrounded by an iron or tin ring . . . they have a woman, who during the dance, goes round with a dish of water, to refresh the dancers, but she must give this water only to the bravest, who wear the whole buffalo's head. . . . The men have a piece of red cloth fastened behind, and a figure representing a buffalo's tail; they also carry arms in their hands. The men with the buffalo heads always keep in the dance at the outside of the group, imitate all the motions and voice of this animal, as it timidly and cautiously retreats, looking around in all directions.' Such buffalo dances were ancient – an 18th-century painted robe now preserved in the collections of the Musée de l'Homme in Paris represents what is probably the earliest pictorial record of the dance.

Leaders in the Bull (Buffalo) society of the Blackfoot dressed differently. Characteristically, they wore a vertical style of headdress at the front of which was attached an arrow. In later years the regalia of the Bull society was adopted by the Horns society and there is some evidence to suggest that the arrow was replaced by a 'hackle plume' decoration on the front of the bonnet, thus distinguishing the wearer as a member of that society.

According to Clark Wissler the Miwatani Society, one of the most important amongst the Sioux, consisted of:

2 Leaders	1 Drum Bearer
2 Sash Bearers or Bonnet men	8 Singers
2 Whip Bearers	1 Herald
1 Food Passer	Lay members
	(Wissler, 1912, p. 42).

According to Charging Thunder, a member of this society, 'Each member pledged himself to sacrifice his own life in defence of a wounded member, if such a sacrifice became necessary on the warpath.' (Densmore, 1918, p. 327).

The term 'Dog Soldier' was commonly employed to describe many of the societies which concerned themselves with warlike activities. In particular it was, during the period of the Indian–White confrontation, applied to Cheyenne warriors on the southern plains, many of whom gained considerable reputation under Tall Bull who was an outstanding leader of the society known as the 'Dogs', one of six associated with the Southern Cheyenne.

Most Plains military societies included at least one which had the rendering Fox, Wolf or Dog. Traditionally, as with the semi-sedentary tribes, wolves were considered war fetishes – at least ten common war songs of the Sioux being referred to as wolf songs and sung before the departure of a war party. 'The life of a warrior was said to be like that of a wolf and a number of these songs mention the wolf.' (Densmore, 1918, p. 333).

Sumḱa iśmala	Lone wolf
miyélo ća	I am
maká óka wiṅhya	in different places
omá wani	I roam
kon	but
hećíya	there
tamoṅka sni yeló	I am tired out.
	(Densmore, 1918, p. 337).

The Raid for Scalps

One distinguishing feature of the expeditions organized for the purpose of scalping and revenge was that the raiders invariably started out on horseback whilst traditionally the raid for horses was on foot, since it was so much easier to conceal themselves this way and stealth was of prime im-

portance in such raids. Further, unlike the horse raid which tended to be a spontaneously organized project, the raids organized for revenge were carefully planned and prior to 1850 they commonly involved a large number of mounted warriors. Ewers' analysis of large-scale battles in which Blackfoot participated in the period 1808–1870 indicates that between 1500 and just under 70 warriors figured in the various campaigns (see Ewers, 1955, p. 195). Certainly many times the numbers used in horse-raid expeditions. Such large war parties were led by one distinguished war chief who had sent invitations to other bands or friendly

Comanche warrior, c. 1860. His shield, warbonnet and warpaint probably has association with his war medicine bundle, bringing protection and success in warfare. There is a wealth of ethnological data in this sketch. The bridle is probably a Spanish chileno which had long iron fringes and jingled with the slightest movement of the horse. The dark legs on the horse may be paint– Comanches commonly painted their horses for battle. The peculiar hook-like feet represent horse tracks– uniquely, of all animals the Plains Indians encountered, only the horse had a single toe! The horned headdress was commonly worn by Comanches in this period–it was not until the reservation period that the flowing feathered warbonnet was worn. The shield is characteristically decorated with a fringe of feathers around its perimeter and near the centre is the *pouhahante* or 'medicine'– a small dried or stuffed animal which had powerful protective powers for the owner.
Musée de l'Homme, Paris.

tribes. Thus in the summer of 1848 a combined force of 1500 Blackfoot, Blood, Piegan, Gros Ventres and Sarsi warriors attacked a Cree camp consisting of 90 lodges encamped on the Canadian plains. More than 19 Crees lost their lives and 10 Blackfoot died (Kane, 1925, pp. 303–305). Such attacks had tended to perpetuate the pattern of large-scale battles throughout the 18th and well into the 19th centuries. They were organized to maintain tribal ties and this type of warfare was vital to the early social organization of the pedestrian and early equestrian nomads. With increased mobility they declined in importance.

Closely associated were the smaller scalp raids which were often instigated by a warrior after the loss of a friend or relative 'saddened and angered by sorrow' (Clarke, 1885, p. 263). Thus the warpath also served as a socially recognized emotional outlet. As one anthropologist put it 'there was a definite connection between mourning and war. The emotions of grief, anger and shame which the former excited were allayed by social recognition of success in the latter.' (Smith, 1938, p. 461).

Earlier we saw that ancient traditions associated the act of scalp-taking with deep-seated religious meanings and while in later years scalps taken on horse raids were probably looked upon purely as war trophies, there continued to be a strong association between the hair and life-blood of a warrior. As well as the well-known hair-fringed shirt worn by a few distinguished Sioux warriors, the Cheyenne also had a tradition that should any member of their warrior societies distinguish himself in battle he would be allowed thereafter to wear 'as a badge of distinction' (Dorsey, 1905, p. 15), a buckskin coat adorned with a fringe of enemy hair.

The prelude to large-scale scalp raids enabled the Plains Indian to display his love of ceremonial. There was full public involvement, with a great deal of debate, feasting and private consultation taking place 'with sacrifices by the chiefs and soldiers, and also by many of the warriors to the several supernatural powers' (Denig, 1930, p. 548). Tokála-lúta was more graphic: 'Just before we started there was a Sun Dance in the village, and the leaders said, "If anyone wants to be successful in war let him come and join the Sun Dance." There were a hundred men standing abreast in the circle. We were asked "What offer will you make to the great sun shining over your head? Will you give him tobacco? Will you give him your flesh and blood?" When the Intercessor came to me and asked these questions, I said in reply "I will give my flesh and blood that I may conquer my enemies." I fulfilled this vow at a Sun Dance when I returned victorious from war.' (Densmore, 1915, p. 375).

The main parade was the so-called 'horseback' or 'big' dance which seems to have been widespread and varied in form. Thus amongst the Comanche 'the captain and the warriors of the tribe, bedecked with feathers and covered with their war ornaments, mount their horses and form two lines, in which formation they make a tour of the camps of those who have already arrived, singing as they go. They promise to distinguish themselves in the coming war and to supply all possible succour to those who are exposed to too great danger. The host tribe replies to this visit with a ceremony of the same sort, and this scene is repeated at the camp of each tribe that has come to join the two plaintiffs on the warpath. These meetings sometimes take place some two or three hundred leagues distant from the enemy.' (Berlandier, 1969, p. 73). The Blackfoot warriors, on the other hand, traditionally rode into the village not in two lines but four, converging from the cardinal directions dressed in their finest regalia, painted and bedecked and riding their favourite war horses. 'As a number of old men and women stood in the centre of the camp beating drums and singing a song with a lively rhythm, the warriors encircled the camp on horseback. Then they shouted, dismounted and danced on foot imitating the prancing of their horses, which stepped along beside them to the beating of their drums.' (Ewers, 1955, p. 196).

The Sioux referred to these prelude ceremonials as *uci tapi* or charge-around-camp. It was a time for the display of fine costume, of society parades, of pageantry, of Indian cavalcades. War parties consisted of groups of individuals of varying backgrounds and status and although – as in all societies – there was a degree of stratification, no individual was excluded from the right to lead, or join, a war party. In these prelude cavalcades warriors of distinction stood out by the splendour and value of their costumes. Thus in the mid-19th century the dress of a mounted Assiniboin warrior as worn in such parades was listed (and valued) as follows:

Mounted Warrior's Dress

Buffalo robe painted with battle scenes and garnished with porcupine quills; best; 6 robes	$18.00
Skin shirt and leggings garnished with human hair and porcupine quills, valued at 1 horse or 10 robes	$30.00
Feathers of the war eagle on shield, price, 2 horses 10 robes each	$60.00
Necklace of bear's claws wrought on otter skin, 6 robes	$18.00
Feathers of the war eagle on shield, lance, and horse, 10 robes	$30.00
Garnished moccasins, 1 robe	$3.00
Shell ear ornaments, 4 robes	$12.00

(Denig, 1930, p. 589).

Members of the various warrior societies could also be distinguished by their distinctive costume or regalia, particularly that which brought with it an obligation to fight in a particular, sometimes spectacular, way. Thus a widespread custom amongst many military societies such as the Sioux 'Strong Hearts', the Cheyenne 'Contrary Ones', the Crow 'Crazy Dogs Wishing To Die', and the Comanche 'Pukutsi' to name a few, was the wearing of a sash a foot or so in width which was slit near one end so as to pass over the head and shoulder and long enough to drag on the ground. In battle the wearer was obliged to pin the free end to the ground and there take a stand:

kolá	friends
túwa	whoever
napé cinahan	runs away
ópa kte śni ye	shall not be admitted

(Densmore, 1918, p. 322).

A more spectacular, and undoubtedly original, version of the no-retreat ritual was that of the Pawnee Crazy Dogs who, dispensing with the sash would take a stake and a rope, plant the stake before the enemy and tie a string to the rope – the other end of which was attached to the warrior's penis; hence the 'Tied Penis Society' (Murie, 1916, p. 580).

Distinctive headdresses were also worn by members of these societies, frequently decorated with buffalo horns which had been shaved almost paper thin and attached either side of the cap; additionally the headdress might be trimmed with eagle or owl feathers and fringed with weasel skins. Such insignia were highly valued for with them went the status of a high ranking warrior who was expected to adhere to the severe obligations which went with it. For example, Teton Sioux warriors who related customs of the *Canté Tinźa* (Strong Hearts) said 'Each member had one of these headdresses, which he wore only when going on the warpath or in actual battle. If a man had been uniformly successful and had never shown any signs of cowardice, he might be buried with this bonnet on his head; but if he showed cowardice on the warpath, he was punished on his return by being severely reprimanded in the presence of all of the members, his headdress was taken away, and he was expelled from the society.' (Densmore, 1918, p. 320).

With the passing of the large, tribally-involved scalp raid, the horseback dance continued to be performed into the reservation period – among the Blackfoot at least – during the Sun Dance festivals; the original concept as a means of arousing 'courage and enthusiasm for war' (Wissler, 1913, p. 456) now having largely lost its significance. Two aged Blackfoot informants expressed the wish to the ethnologist, John Ewers, that 'this picturesque and exciting dance might be revived [so] that younger Indians might learn the splendor of their tribal past' (Ewers, 1955, p. 196). The Crows of present-day Montana have retained it over the years and today it is probably one of the most picturesque Indian cavalcades to be seen in North America; but few who now witness it would be aware that traditionally it was the prelude to warfare and part of a complex ceremony which served to unify the tribe. The gradual passing of the ritual scalp raid, and its replacement by the materialism of the horse raid, tended to put more emphasis on individualism, weakening the old religious concepts and their tribally-bound obligations in the field of warfare. This gift from the Thunder to The People brought in its wake many changes.

Raiding for horses
Below a certain threshold of horse ownership, neither the economic nor survival security of a Plains Indian family could be taken for granted. The average Kiowa family consisting of some five adults 'owned approximately ten pack animals, five riding animals and two to five buffalo horses. With such a herd a family possessed the prerequisites for economic security and could easily satisfy all its needs.' (Miskin, 1940, p. 20).

By 1850 many individuals owned large herds of horses and although the Southern tribes, such as

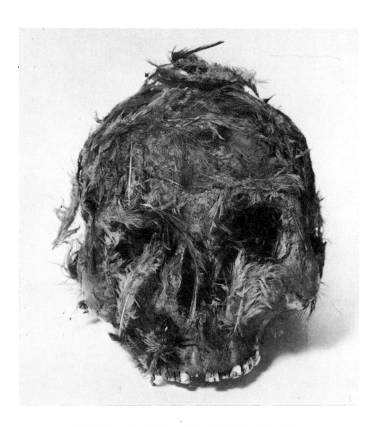

Skull from the White Child Medicine Bundle. Collected by W. Wildschut at the Crow Reservation, Montana, March 1923. Some medicine bundles were believed to possess augural powers. The owner of this bundle was Root Digger, the younger sister of White Child. A tradition occasionally evoked was the preservation of a skull of some near relative to help fill 'the void created by the departed' (Wildschut, 1960, p. 76). After acquiring her dead brother's skull Root Digger occasionally heard her brother's voice 'prophesying what was going to happen'. The Crows came to regard the skull as powerful war medicine, giving Root Digger many presents and requesting her to consult the skull on their behalf. The ethnologist J. C. Ewers describes the skull as being covered with numerous small feathers smeared with red sacred paint and having trade beads inserted in the eye sockets. Although rare such bundles are not unique. This grisly – but sacred to The People – bundle is now in the Museum of the American Indian.

the Kiowa and Comanche, were generally considered the wealthiest in horses some men of prominence amongst the Blackfoot for example 'owned from one hundred to three hundred and four hundred' (Schultz, 1907, p. 152). Amongst the completely nomadic tribes the horse became a standard of wealth and social status. Some individuals apparently developed an insatiable desire to acquire more and more. Thus an aged and respected Kiowa warrior became so obsessed with horses that it developed into kleptomania; he was however 'tolerated by his amused tribesmen!' (Miskin, 1940, p. 52).

The raids for horses were generally successful because the nomadic tribes never fortified their camps. Seldom did they post guards and although a favourite horse might be picketed near the tipi at night, it was not unusual for bands of horses to be 'driven to a secluded place and left for days without a guard' (Bradley, 1923, p. 286). Horse raiding parties, consisting of perhaps ten or twenty men, commonly returned with a hundred or more horses and such warfare became integral to the economy and ethos of Plains Indian culture.

'Running off the enemy's horses was both legitimate and honourable. As a measure of aggression or reprisal, it was doubly effective; it enriched the plunderer while it deprived the 'plundered' of property indispensable to his safety and well being. A robust, manly pastime, it was also splendid training in the Spartan virtues – patience, cunning, courage – and the young man who excelled in it became a popular hero.' (Smith, 1949, p. 93).

Any man could organize a horse raiding party but he had to be of good standing and his medicine power worthy of the risk. In practical terms it really meant that proven successful warriors would be more sure of acceptance as leaders but Plains Indian society was such that no individuals were excluded in attempting to form a war party. Plans were discussed amongst those who consented to join. Occasionally, the expedition would have to be abandoned or delayed if public opinion decided that it was unwise to pursue such activities at that time, but even then it was not unusual for some younger, more ambitious men to ignore the warnings and slip off quietly. In general success would nullify the misdemeanour and everyone rejoiced on the party's return, especially since successful horse-raiders tended to be more than generous during the widespread custom of tribal 'give aways'.

Some members planning to join horse-raiding parties sought the services of a horse medicine-man who was believed not only to possess the

The Big Soldier, Sioux, 1832. Successful warriors were justly proud of their right to wear elaborate regalia which generally signified to the world at large their successes in war. This man wears a hair-fringed shirt which is the mark of a high-ranking warrior. Each fringe is bound at its base with coloured porcupine quills and the human hair appears to be interspersed with dyed horse hair – possibly significant of horses captured. The broad bands of quillwork on the arms and shoulders are edged with blue pony beads and he wears a 'pearl medal' medallion around his neck. The painted feathers in his hair undoubtedly have considerable significance but this was not recorded. Maximilian observed that this warrior stood motionless the whole day so that Bodmer could capture a 'capital likeness'.
From Maximilian's *Atlas*. British Museum.

ability to cure ailing horses or control their actions but could be influential in bringing about success on horse-raiding expeditions. Wolf Calf, (who was born about 1793 and died in 1899), is generally credited with the introduction of the horse medicine cult amongst the Piegan, but it was not limited to this tribe, having wide distribution amongst Plains Indians, although the emphasis on its controlling power varied. However, young Piegan warriors about to join a horse-raiding expedition used to consult Wolf Calf. If Wolf Calf accepted the man's pipe and gift when offered he gave him a plume from the ceremonial altar and explained 'If you can't get near the enemies horses take this dirt' (from the ceremonial altar) 'and mix it with water. Dip the plume in the mixture. It will rain, the enemy will stay inside their lodges and you will have no trouble taking their horses.' (Ewers, 1955, p. 272). Some of the songs employed by the members of the Teton Sioux Horse Society were used on the warpath to make a horse swift and sure; some hopefully predicted a successful raid:

| taté oü ýe tópa kin | the four winds are blowing |
| śunká wakan wańziǵźi aü welo | some horses are coming |

(Densmore, 1918, p. 301).

War ceremonial thus gave great emphasis to seeking the aid of supernatural powers to ensure success for the war party. Some warriors may have had visions or dreams which predicted success, even predicted the location of the enemy and the conditions which would be met with. Visions obtained during self-torture, as in the Sun Dance or O-kee-pa, were particularly taken note of and discussed in detail. Sitting Bull's vision after performing the Sun Dance some weeks prior to the Custer Battle in June 1876 predicted in a remarkable way the outcome and gave The People confidence in their stand.

Traditionally, a war-pipe would be carried by the leader, which was regularly smoked by the members of the expedition. The custom of smoking is ancient amongst North American Indians. Seldom, if ever, was a ceremony performed which did not involve the symbolic passing of the pipe – the tobacco, the pipe and smoke were often considered sacred. The famed *calumet*, or pipe of peace, was employed as a mark of friendship during treaties. The act of smoking was a communication with the higher powers to whom warriors could appeal, offer prayers for success and remind them of painful ceremonies undertaken as an appeal for success. Okí ćize-táwa (His Battle), a Sioux warrior, explained the pipe ceremonial he undertook before a successful war expedition.

With the bowl of the pipe in his left hand and the stem in his right hand he held the pipe upright in front of and close to his body, saying rapidly in a low tone, 'Wakan-tanka, behold this pipe, behold it. I ask you to smoke it. I do not want to kill any body, I only want to get good horses. I ask you to help me. That is why I speak to you with this pipe.' Changing the position of his hands and placing his left hand on the stem toward his left shoulder His Battle then said 'Now, wolf, behold this pipe. Smoke it and bring me many horses.' He then placed his right hand once more on the stem of the pipe and his left hand on the bowl, and pointing the stem upward and forward holding the pipe level with his face, he said 'Wakan-tanka, behold this pipe. I ask you to smoke it. I am holding it for you. Look also at me.'

After placing the stem of the unlighted pipe in his mouth again he said 'Wakan-tanka, I will now smoke this pipe in your honour. I ask that no bullet may harm me when I am in battle. I ask that I may get many horses.' He then again elevated the pipe, lighted and smoked it, holding it firmly in both hands. Then he said (referring to his participation in the Sun Dance), 'Wakan-tanka, behold this pipe and behold me. I have let my breast be pierced. I have shed much blood. I ask you to protect me from shedding more blood and to give me a long life.'

Such pipes were often decorated with a bunch of red horsehair which was traditionally said to be an emblem of the thunder horse. The hair signified the presence of 'the power of the thunder, as manifest in the horse, in all ceremonies connected with the pipe' (Wissler, Vol. 1, 1907, p. 48). When this ceremonial act was completed, His Battle filled another pipe, which was the one he commonly used, and smoked it. He said: 'It is the office of a certain pipe that it be smoked in making a request of Wakan-tanka. I always did what I have now enacted for you, and my blood was never shed after I took part in the Sun Dance. This was because I asked Wakan-tanka to give me success.' (Densmore, 1918, p. 390). The true Plains war-pipe

Horns Society headdress. Blackfoot, c. 1870. Military societies exerted powerful influence in warfare and its associated ceremonials. The predecessor of the Horns Society was that of the Bulls, the latter adopting much of the former's regalia. Straight-up headdresses of this type immediately distinguished the wearer during pre- or post-battle parades; but not all wearers were necessarily members of the Horns Society, rather they wore such a bonnet because of some dream or vision. American Museum of Natural History.

Sioux warshirt, about 1870. Such fine hair-fringed shirts could not only be worn by high-ranking warriors. Generally they were distinctively printed with a blue or green upper half and a yellow lower half. They signified tribal authority in the highly honoured position of *Wicasa* or 'Shirt Wearer' who acted as spokesman for the civil and economic affairs of the tribe under the direction of the Chiefs' Society. This shirt, which is credited as being the original property of the great warrior Crazy Horse, is decorated with bands of beadwork bearing typical southern Sioux rectangular fluted designs; the small crosses may signify the deed of rescuing friends in battle whilst under enemy fire. Nebraska State Historical Society.

differed considerably from that used everyday, the design being of considerable antiquity. In 1833, Maximilian, Prince of Wied Neuwied, observed 'The Indians on the Upper Missouri have another kind of tobacco pipe, the bowl of which is in the same line as the tube, and which they use only on their warlike expeditions. As the aperture of the pipe is more inclined downwards than usual, the fire can never be seen so as to betray the smoker, who lies on the ground, and holds the pipe on one side.' (Wied Neuwied, 1843, p. 196).

The pipes were constructed according to instructions received during a vision quest and were considered to be powerful war medicines.

Wakan ẏan	in a sacred manner
mícá kelo	he made for me
ćanoṅ pa wan tókeća	a *pipe* that is different
wakaṅ yan	in a sacred manner
mícá kelo	he made for me
nagi ksá pa wan	a wise spirit
maká hewaye	I met
wakaṅ yan	in a sacred manner
mícá kelo	he made (it) for me
kolá	friend
wanmá yanka yo	behold me

(Lakota Dream or Vision Quest Song, Densmore, 1918, p. 183).

Such a holy pipe, which had powerful war medicine, belonged to the Crow chief, Standing Bull, in the 1870s; it had a short stem made of willow about $\frac{5}{8}$ of an inch at its largest diameter and was $13\frac{1}{4}$ inches long. The bowl was a tubular one of red stone $6\frac{1}{2}$ inches long and 1 inch at its largest diameter. Seven small cup-like indentations were said to represent the Dipper. The incised lines near the front of the bowl represented the stars in

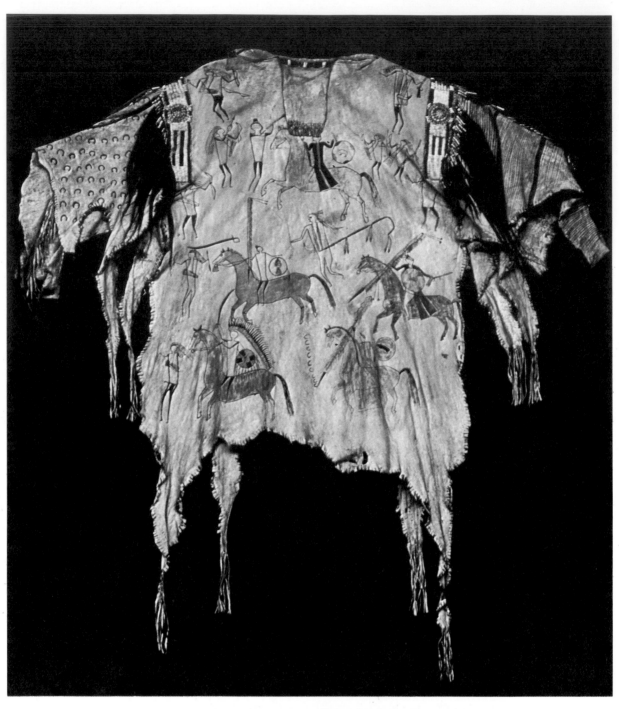

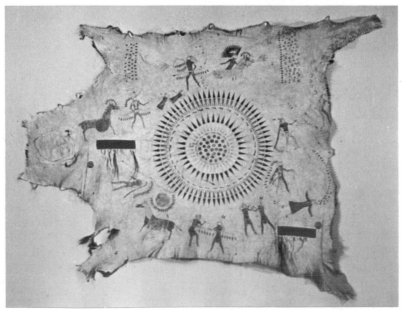

general and an incised zigzag line represented lightning. It was said that the pointing of this pipe toward the enemy by the leader of the Crow war party was thought to cause death just as surely as would a stroke of lightning.

In later years other types of pipe were employed. In fact the common T-shaped catlinite appears to have been used by the Sioux (Smith, 1948, p. 96) and the small elbow pipe by the Blackfoot, the archaic form being relegated to even more sacred status. 'Green-Grass-Bull regarded the straight pipe as a very holy object, used only in beaver bundle rituals but not those of the medicine pipe bundle. He also said that it was the straight pipe upon which the Blackfoot Indians used to take their oaths when they "swore by the pipe" that their testimony was true or their lives would be forfeited.

'Within the memories of my elderly informants, the straight pipe survived only in the form of ceremonial pipe bowls preserved in medicine bundles. It was smoked only at such times as those bundles were opened and ritually manipulated.' (Ewers, 1963, p. 36).

The war-pipe practice was widely recognized. Amongst the Comanches – the dominant military force on the southern Plains – the sacred pipe was formally smoked after the evening meal and after the usual offerings to the spiritual powers. It was passed to each warrior in turn. An accompanying ritual might consist of singing a spiritual song considered as a prayer to the guardian spirits for help and wisdom (Wallace and Hoebel, 1952, pp. 255–256).

The exploit robes of the Mandan Chief, Mato-tope, the Yankton (Sioux) warrior Monka-ush-ka, and the Teton Sioux, One Horn, whose robe is preserved in the British Museum, to mention but a few, show warriors engaged in warfare but apparently carrying pipes, testifying that not only was it an important part of the war ceremonial but that it was also a recognized way of designating the military leader.

A widespread and apparently ancient custom was the carrying of a war whistle. The Sioux (and it is probably true for most other tribes) sounded these in battle, the piercing sound symbolizing the cry of the eagle as 'a representative of the thunder-bird' (Wissler, 1907, p. 47), and as an appeal to the power of the thunder to rescue the hard-pressed warriors.

Such whistles were symbolically decorated with a zigzag line incised into the bone and filled with red paint which represented the thunder; the feathers of the woodpecker were attached to it, that bird being considered to have an association with the thunder, for when a storm approached the Sioux observed that the woodpecker gives a peculiar shrill call similar to the note of the whistle, so that the warrior was put in communication with the thunder (Wissler, Vol. 1, 1907, p. 48).

Such are the preliminaries to aggressive warfare amongst the Plains tribes. As one anthropologist once so rightly remarked, the 'Plains Indians were decidedly not a calm people' (Smith, 1938, p. 455). Thus war and its accompanying ceremonies became an essential fabric of their culture, and although the Plains Indian war game had a sound economic payoff it also served the important function of allowing pent-up violent emotions to be given free expression.

By the mid-19th century, however, the wind of change was blowing from the east as the white man extended his empire to new horizons: in its wake it was to bring many changes. No longer was the foe one who observed the war game rules which pivoted on give and take, but rather one who was to take, and occasionally – grudgingly – leave. Tribes small in numbers were trampled underfoot, and, to survive, the larger tribes drastically changed their warfare tactics. The emphasis was now on defence, and a degeneration of the war ceremonial followed.

Left, above. Sioux warshirt, about 1850. The shirt is painted with the deeds of valour of the original owner. The warriors on horseback are not riding side-saddle, rather it is a depiction of what the artist knew was there rather than what the eye actually perceived. At least one of the enemy is Crow or Hidatsa – note the distinctive hair ornament worn by the central pedestrian warrior who is being speared by the feathered lance. The tracks painted on the left-hand arm probably represent horses captured from the enemy. Musée de l'Homme, Paris.

Below. Mato-tope's buffalo robe. Mandan, c.1835. This is one of a number of robes which Mato-tope (Four Bears), a popular chief of the Mandan, painted. His style, which the ethnologist J. C. Ewers suggests was influenced by the white artists George Catlin and Carl Bodmer (the latter, particularly, encouraging the chief in his artistic endeavours) is sophisticated for Plains Indian painting of this period. The figures represent a number of the more outstanding war exploits of Mato-tope, the explanation of each being obtained by George Catlin while at the Mandan village of Mi-ti-was-kos in the summer of 1832. Mato-tope claimed to have killed five enemy chiefs and to have taken fourteen scalps. The exploit where he first received his name is shown at the top of the robe. The robe was taken to Switzerland by Lorens Alphonse Schock in 1842. Historisches Museum, Berne.

Weapons and Warpaint

In his war paint and his beads
Like a bison among the reeds
In ambush the Sitting Bull
Lay with three thousand braves

Longfellow

ALTHOUGH SOME INDIVIDUALS excelled in craft skills, for example in the manufacture of saddles, or warbonnets, just about every Plains warrior was a good craftsman in the field of weapon making where the necessity of being able to produce equipment for war and the hunt was paramount. The most important article was the bow, often regarded almost as a toy by the uninitiated but in fact a deadly and effective weapon in the hands of a skilled warrior.

The majority of bows were made from a single piece of wood; although compound bows of horn or antler were not unknown they were made by a few skilled men and seemed to reach their highest development amongst the Neź Percé who in turn traded them to their easterly Plains neighbours, in particular the Crow. The wooden bow was manufactured from a variety of woods although the geographical location of the tribe tended to dictate a predominant type. For example the common bow of the Comanche was generally made from Osage orange or bois d'arc. 'It was plentiful along the Arkansas and Canadian rivers and in the eastern fringe of the Comanche country southward into Texas. Bois d'arc is commonly recognised as one of the hardest, finest, and most durable of timbers.' (Wallace and Hoebel, 1952, p. 100). The Omaha referred to bois d'arc as yellow wood, other tribes (including the Blackfoot who sought it in trade) called the tree itself 'smooth bow' but 'bow dark' seems to have emerged as a universal terminology.

In the last quarter of the 19th century, William Philo Clark, a Captain in the Second Cavalry, observed that the difficulty of obtaining any forms of wood in the wide, virtually treeless expanse of the great plains resulted in the employment of practically any suitable seasoned wood for bows, and relates that while with a party of Indians one of them found an 'old broken ash wagon bow lying alongside of the road. It was taken into camp, greased, warmed by the camp fire, trimmed with their hunting knives, slowly, carefully, and skillfully bent into shape, and quite a shapely and serviceable article was the result.' (Clark, 1884, p. 76). Next to the bois d'arc, hickory was considered a very effective bow wood but ash, oak, willow, cherry, elm and cedar were all employed.

Having selected the wood for a bow, it was necessary to carefully season it for some months. Because green wood was generally easier to work

it was roughly cut to shape, care being taken to ensure that it was largely free from knots or any flaws which might weaken the final product. For this reason the wood was invariably cut from the straight grain section of a large tree. Every tipi housing a warrior of any worth would have a supply of bow and arrow wood hung up in the smoke well away from the flames, for while good bows might last for many years, the hazards of hunt and war could at any time result in a broken weapon.

The nomadic Plains Indian bow was notably short. Catlin, writing of observations made in the 1830s, states that the standard length of Crow and Blackfoot bows was about three feet – about the same as that of the Comanche, according to informants. (Wallace and Hoebel, 1952, pp. 98–99). A specimen in the British Museum, probably central Plains, dating from the mid-19th century, measures just over three feet and seven inches whilst Clark was of the opinion that the Sioux bow was 'generally four feet' long. For use on horseback in strategical and tactical movement a short, easily-handled weapon was of prime importance. In earlier pedestrian days (see Chapter I) bows had been considerably longer.

After seasoning, the wood was scraped and cut down with care. In section, Plains bows are elliptical, perhaps one and a half inches wide and an inch or so thick at the middle tapering down to half an inch or so at the extremities. Some bows had the appearance of a simple bowed lath while others – especially the compound horn ones – were gracefully curved outwards from the handle.

The Omaha had a definite criterion for well-fashioned bows: 'A good bow should be slightly curved at the middle of the back.' (Fletcher and La Flesche, 1905–1906, p. 449). Working hard with sandstone or file a warrior could fashion a serviceable bow within three days to a week while elegant, fancy ones could take up to a month. The work was done in stages. After seasoning and some working it was rubbed with fat to make it more pliable, heated in places where it was to be bent and at the same time permanently shaped by exerting pressure with the foot. In order to increase the strength and elastic properties it was frequently backed with animal sinew. Cut from the massive sinews that lie along the muscle adjacent to the backbone of the buffalo or elk from the shoulders to the tail, it was glued to the roughened back surface of the wood while still green and bound at the ends and handle. Left to dry after a further covering of glue and then carefully rubbed down and polished the final product resulted in a tough elastic stave surpassed only by the characteristic composite horn bow of the Plateau. Eastern Plains tribes were less inclined towards sinew backing – it was unusual for example amongst the Omaha of Nebraska. Theory has it that the idea was copied from the Plateau and Basin tribes who had developed the technique in conjunction with their compound bows.

The bowstring – a most important part of any bow – required skill in its making, derived from the heaviest sinews of the buffalo, deer or elk which was sub-divided longitudinally into fine threads. They were soaked in glue and water and while still wet twisted into a cord of circular section. One end of this string was attached permanently to the bow, the other was looped and slipped into notches when the bow was required for use. Thus the bow was always kept unstrung except in normal use so that the elastic properties were maintained at a maximum. Most warriors carried two strings, a spare one for emergencies.

One decided disadvantage of sinew-backed bows was that excessive humidity would temporarily

destroy their elastic properties. To reduce this possibility some tribes completely covered the bow with the skin of a rattlesnake – horn bows particularly were treated this way, the method having also been observed amongst Crow, Blackfoot and Gros Ventres. (Lowie, 1954, p. 75).

Arrows were long for the short bows, about twenty-five inches being the average. Specimens from widely different areas of the Plains which I have examined varied within only two inches or so. Tradition has it that Omaha arrows were longer than those employed by the Sioux for in the old days amongst the Omaha the standard for the length of the shaft was 'the distance from the inside of the elbow of the left arm to the tip of the middle finger of the left hand and from the tip of this finger over the back of the hand to the wrist bone'. The Sioux measurement however only added the distance from 'the wrist to the large knuckle of the third finger' to the forearm length. (Fletcher and La Flesche, 1904–1905, p. 450 and Densmore, 1918, p. 438). Arrows required considerable skill in their manufacture and were carefully handled. Much time was expended in searching for arrows which had been fired and failed to strike the quarry.

Wood for arrows had to be selected with particular care. It was important that they should be as straight as possible and combine strength with just the right amount of weight – a light shaft was deflected too easily from its intended path by air resistance whilst a heavy one would not carry the required distance. Experienced arrow makers seldom employed the ash shoots as they were far too soft and pithy. Preferred by the Comanche for high quality arrows was a hard, tough, straight-grained wood 'that of the young shoots of the dogwood were preferred because of their straightness and freedom from knots.' (Wallace and Hoebel, 1952, p. 102). Like the Sioux, they also employed various berry and currant woods although some of these required a good deal of time to straighten. After seasoning, the wood was examined carefully for any flaws, then straightened by rubbing with oil, heating over a fire, pulling through and simultaneously bending the shaft in the hole of an arrow straightener, which was a piece of horn or bone having a hole drilled in it just slightly larger than the arrow itself. Then the shaft was worked to a true roundness and given a slight taper by use of two slabs of whetstone. The Sioux said that such stone was found in the Black Hills. It was rather soft and easily worked. A groove perhaps six inches or so long was cut into the flat face of each whetstone; when brought together the channel so formed was of a diameter equal to that required for the arrow shaft, by placing the arrow into this channel and holding the whetstones together with one hand the other was used to pull the shaft back and forth until the desired dimension was obtained.

Most plains arrows were fletched with three feathers which were considerably longer and narrower than those used on the modern archery arrows of today, it not being unusual for them to

Hidatsa warriors carrying bows with combined bow cases and quivers. Upper Missouri, July 1851. The bow and arrow was a dangerous and effective weapon in the hands of a resolute man, even after the introduction of firearms warriors generally continued to carry a bow. This sketch done by the Swiss artist Rudolph Kurz is valuable for its detail – all too often artists dressed their subjects up and had them pose for a portrait. The bows are carried in a separate case attached to the quiver; note that they are probably no more than three and a half feet in length, which is typical of most Plains bows. The left-hand warrior's quiver is decorated with a painted hand which was a widely used motif signifying the counting of coup or the capturing of horses; the right-hand warrior has a wolf tail attached to his quiver probably signifying a successful war expedition. Historische Museum, Berne.

Quiver and bow case of the Mandan or Hidatsa. Maximilian expedition, June 1833. Unlike the previous sketch where the bow is carried in a separate case both bow and arrows are shown here in the same compartment. It is constructed of otter skin with worked discs of beadwork on the pendant. Note the great length of the arrows in comparison to the bow; typically Plains arrows were 20–25 inches long while bows were seldom more than four feet. Two bows are carried here; perhaps the shorter one was used for hunting buffalo on horseback where mobility rather than range was of prime importance. Examination of the original bows in the Maximilian collection at Stuttgart shows that the decorations at intervals on the bows are of braided porcupine quillwork wrapped over red trade cloth.

ably had two spiral or wavy grooves on one side and two straight grooves on the other while Lipan Apache arrows had four straight grooves. (See Wallace and Hoebel, 1952, p. 102). A wide variety of meanings have been given to these grooves. It is probable that many Plains Indians did it simply as a matter of convention, the origin of its function being as far removed from them as the wearing of a cravat is to the average Englishman. Tribes as distant as the Comanche and Omaha *believed* that the grooves prevented the shaft from warping. Still others say that it was to make the wounded animal bleed and hence easier to track. The Hunkpapa Sioux warrior, White Hawk, stated to Frances Densmore, and was supported by other old men of the tribe, that the 'function of the grooves was to make it' (the arrow) 'go straight.' (Densmore, 1918, p. 438). This latter statement is probably nearer to the original purpose than most. An experienced and noteworthy observer of the Plains Indian was moved to write 'as a matter of fact these grooves are merely a magic symbol representing lightning. They are believed to make the arrow more deadly – to give it some of the death-dealing power of the thunderbolt. Forty years ago, any middle-aged Crow or Sioux would tell you this.' (Decost Smith, 1948, pp. 43–44). Considering the awe with which the Plains tribes – Sioux, Crow and Blackfoot in particular – held the lightning, this latter explanation of a 'medicine' rather than a purely mechanical function is to my mind the most acceptable.

A notch was cut at the feathered end of the arrow to take the bow string. Invariably this was of a 'U' section while the shaft at this point was made bulbular to enable the arrow to be gripped more easily – an essential refinement since most Plains tribes released the arrow by holding the notch with the thumb and forefinger and pulling the string with the other three fingers.

The arrowhead was set into a slit cut in the end of the shaft, the shank of the head being bound in with sinew dampened with glue. The Omaha employed burnt mica to both whiten and dry the sinew. 'The arrow maker took great pride in finishing his work neatly and without soiling the sinew.' (Fletcher and La Flesche, 1904–1905, p. 451).

In early days arrow points were made of flint, and the sharp serrated edges of such arrow heads were said to be particularly wounding, worse than that of a metal arrowhead. White Hawk said that he knew of three kinds of arrow points. Those employed by his great-grandfather were of flint, by his father points of bone made 'from the outer thickness of ribs or marrow bones', while he himself used arrow points made of steel. He further stated that in his hunting days arrowheads were frequently cut 'from the thin frying pans sold by traders or used by the soldiers'. (Densmore, 1918, p. 438). Metal arrowheads were certainly employed at an early period. Catlin sketched those which he collected in the 1830s with long barbed metal points. While some were undoubtedly made by

extend one third the way down the shaft. According to Sioux informants, feathers employed on arrow shafts were not confined to any one kind. 'Some used feathers of the prairie hen, owl or chicken hawk that were large enough to split, while others used the smaller feathers of the eagle or buzzard. White Hawk said that after splitting a feather he held one end in his mouth and scratched it carefully with a knife to smooth it.' (Densmore, 1918, p. 438). Many Plains arrows which I have examined have the feathers bound at the ends only, the middle part being left free of the shaft. Other observers imply that the feathers were glued down. It appears that both techniques were in vogue and it is often difficult to generalize for a whole area. This point is well illustrated in the next step of the construction of a Plains arrow. Wavy lines are cut in the shaft from the lower point of attachment of the feathers and extending the whole length of the arrow. This was done using a bone containing a circular hole into which extended a small projection from the perimeter of the hole.

Hunkpapa Sioux arrows had first a straight line about an inch long then a wavy line, and finally about three inches from the arrow point a straight line. Comanche arrows on the other hand invari-

the Indians themselves, or perhaps by local blacksmiths, many were made in the east and became a very important trade item. 'Hundreds of thousands were manufactured yearly by eastern traders to be exchanged for furs. They were put in packages of one dozen each, cost the trader six cents a package and were the means for obtaining enormous profits. Usually one package was exchanged for a buffalo robe.' (Garretson, 1930, p. 180). They were also probably manufactured in England since they were early offered by the Hudson's Bay Company to the Canadian Indians (itemized, for example, on the York Factory Trade Goods list for 1813). Typically such arrowheads were triangular in shape, but long and narrow rather like a small spear point.

There was definite recognition of various arrow types although that described above predominated and were used for both war and the hunt. Small animals such as rabbits, squirrels and prairie chickens were often hunted with arrows which had no arrowhead as such but were simply sharpened. They were also employed in target practice. Other arrows with shafts knobbed at the foot were used to kill birds.

On firing, the bow was held on the slant and as buffalo were usually hunted at close range, there thus seems to be some justification in the suggestion that the plane of the arrowhead was set with definite reference to the bowstring so that the blade could pass easily through the vertical ribs of the running buffalo. Frequently, however, the hunter often aimed just *behind* the ribs, shooting in a forward direction so that it pierced the heart and lungs, as the paintings of Charles Russell illustrate. Certainly a spot check on a number of arrows bears this theory out. A set of four hunting arrows for example in my own collection all have the heads with planes at about thirty degrees to the cut of the notch so on normal use of the bow the plane would be vertical. It is said that war arrows had the plane set horizontally so as to easily pass through the ribs of a man. My own examination of arrows does not substantiate this and in fact Decost Smith was of the opinion that the only distinguishing feature of the war arrow of the Sioux was its longer blade and its better workmanship. 'The true war arrow of the Uncpapa' (Hunkpapa) 'had a blade four and a half to five inches long, or one to two inches longer than the ordinary arrow, and this they explained, gave it greater penetration. In actual practice the two types of arrow were used indiscriminately for both hunting and war.' (Decost Smith, 1948, p. 44).

For purposes of identification each man had a special mark for his arrows, while amongst the Omaha hunting arrows were commonly decorated in pairs. The Cheyenne were said to have decorated their arrows with stripes or employed wild turkey wing feathers for fletching. Some Comanche employed only two feathers and amongst the Ponca some societies painted their arrows a special way. While evidence is limited, it is highly probable that there were tribally distinguishing features, certainly there are area ones but a large number of factors need to be considered such as type of wood, feathering, the nature of channeling the arrowhead and finally the quality of finish.

The bow and arrow was a powerful weapon, superior to the old musket which, while of greater range, was difficult to load on horseback and lacked rapidity of fire. Clark illustrates the power of the bow thus: 'On one occasion I shot an arrow, while running, into a buffalo so that the point came out the opposite side, another arrow disappeared in the buffalo, not even the notch being visible. The power of the bow may be better understood when I tell you that the most powerful Colt's revolver will not send a ball through a buffalo. I have seen a bow throw an arrow five hundred yards and have myself often discharged one entirely through a board one inch thick. Once I found a man's skull transfixed to a tree by an arrow which had gone completely through the bones, and imbedded itself so deep in the wood as to sustain the weight of the head.' (Clark, 1884, p. 78).

While many Indians owned some type of gun prior to 1880 most still continued to carry the bow as well. It was contained in a combined bow case and quiver slung across the shoulders and hanging

(1) A bow lance (r) War and hunting arrows. The bow lance is an ancient weapon. The Omaha for example have a tradition that a blade was attached to one end of the bow—to be used like a bayonet for thrusting. This specimen was possibly the one carried by the Blackfoot medicine man painted by George Catlin about 1832. By then it was considered a purely ceremonial object having wide distribution and often designating society membership. For example the Cheyenne Bow-String society members traditionally carried an eight-foot long bow spear which was said to be a copy of one carried by the Great Prophet when he last visited the tribe. Peabody Museum, Harvard University. War hunting arrows. Left is a war arrow, possibly Sioux; right are three hunting arrows used for birds or small mammals and probably from the southern Plains. Most Plains arrows were fletched with three feathers and extended almost one quarter the way down the shaft as shown here.

almost horizontally behind. Some of these combined quiver and bow cases were magnificently decorated, reaching their peak amongst the Crow. Typical was the use of otter skin with long pendants decorated with bead or quill-work. Such styles are early. A specimen in the Historische Museum in Berne was collected by the Swiss merchant, Schoch, before 1840. Sioux quivers were less ornate and usually lacked the pendants.

When used the bow is removed and strung while the quiver is swung round under the left arm of the wearer so that the opening faces forward. To increase rapidity of fire two or three arrows may be held in the left hand together with the bow. Sioux quivers, on average, carried only ten arrows, accuracy and retrieval were thus important factors but not until a successful warrior obtained a repeating rifle with a ready access to ammunition did he dispense with this most typical of Indian weapons.

Mounted warriors additionally employed the lance as a shock weapon. Prior to the acquisition of the horse it appeared to have been traditionally used by northern tribes. In 1754 the fur trader, Hendry, referred to the Indians of the Saskatchewan Plains armed with 'bows and arrows and bone spears and darts' (Hendry, 1907, p. 335). It was apparently particularly popular with the Mandan

Pipe tomahawks from the Plains area. Both hatchet and spontoon types are represented here. This ingenious weapon—a combination of a pipe and a tomahawk— was probably invented by an Englishman well before the end of the 18th century, and became a valuable trade item. In early days a good many tomahawks were manufactured in England and France but later local blacksmiths made them, frequently utilizing old rifle barrels to produce the entire head from one piece of metal. The spontoon tomahawk was so called because the blade is similar in shape to the *esponton*, which was a polearm carried by 18th-century commissioned foot soldiers. It found special favour amongst the Crows. The hatchet type, especially with piercing, was favoured by the Sioux in the period 1860–1880.
Richard Pohrt Collection, Michigan.

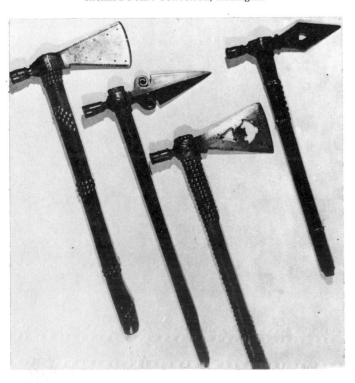

in early days for the explorer David Thompson wrote in the late 18th century 'They appear to have adopted the spear as a favorite weapon. It is a handle of about eight feet length, headed with a flat iron bayonet of nine to ten inches in length sharp pointed, from the point regularly enlarging to four inches in width both sides sharp edged, the broad end has a handle of iron of about four inches in length which is inserted in the handle and bound with small cords, it is a formidable weapon in the hands of a resolute man.' (Thompson, 1816, p. 228).

By the mid-19th century however it was predominantly a weapon used by southern Plains tribes. Ewers is of the opinion that because of direct contact with Spanish–Mexican soldiers, who were trained and skilled lancers, possible encouragement was given to its greater use. (Ewers, 1954, p. 201). The Omaha called their lances *moṅdehi* (bow tooth) 'which bears out a tradition that in ancient times the Omaha used to attach a blade to one end of the bow to be used like a bayonet for thrusting' (Fletcher and La Flesche, 1904–1905, p. 448).

By 1830 such bow lances – often a long bow with a metal lance head at one end – were ceremonial objects and might serve to signify membership of a warrior society; for example the Cheyenne Bow-String society members carried an eight foot long bow spear which was a copy of one carried by the Great Prophet when he last visited the tribe (Dorsey, 1905, p. 24).

Bodmer painted a portrait of an Assiniboin warrior carrying such a lance in 1834 and two years earlier George Catlin painted a Blackfoot medicine man with a similar – but somewhat shorter – ceremonial weapon. It is this lance, or a virtually identical specimen, which is now preserved in the ethnological collections at Peabody Museum of Harvard University. The metal blade of traditional style – used on both functional and ceremonial weapons of this type – was standard for the pre-1850 period.

Comanche warriors – the lords of the southern Plains – traditionally employed a lance six to seven feet in length. In early days the points were of 'chipped stone, often leaf shaped' (Wallace and Hoebel, 1954, p. 110). Later the heads were of metal perhaps as long as thirty inches. A batch of lances which I examined in the Office of Anthropology at the Smithsonian Institution in 1969 had a number of heads made from the blades of cavalry swords. Swords were prized possessions of Plains warriors. Mako-shon-kush was painted in 1837 by the Government artist, George Cooke, proudly carrying a sword.

Elderly Comanche warriors relating warpath experiences at the Laboratory of Anthropology, Santa Fe in 1933, stated that 'Only a brave man carried a spear, because it meant hand to hand combat.' A spear carrier could never retreat and live to face his fellow warriors. There was no alternative for him but victory or death. The war lance ranked higher as a symbol of a war chief than any headdress and warriors who carried the spear went without a war bonnet. Chikoba's (Breaks Something) own brother, after the battle of Adobe Walls, gave up his spear, and all his family were glad. 'A spear is a big responsibility.' (Wallace and Hoebel, 1954, pp. 110–111).

George Catlin's dramatic sketches of southern Plains warriors clearly show that the lance was never thrown javelin wise but rather carried under the arm and thrust into the quarry – man or buffalo had little chance of survival when wounded by such a formidable shock weapon.

As early as 1833, however, Maximilian observed that Crow warriors carried their lances merely for show and later, during the latter part of the 19th century, it became fashionable in parades for Crow women to carry swords in ceremonial cases shaped in the form of a lance. Slung on the right side of a woman's horse they were generally elegantly ornamented with red cloth, paint and beads and were amongst the finest examples of Crow art. The artist Charles Schreyvogel collected a fine specimen which is now at the Linden Museum, Stuttgart, Germany.

The war club or battle axe was considered a formidable weapon in early days and had wide distribution. It was mentioned by the explorers Lewis and Clark when they visited the Lemhi Shoshone of the Plateau region west of the Great Plains in 1805 and was apparently a commonly used and evidently ancient weapon. Nearly thirty years later, Maximilian was to collect such a weapon from the Mandan one thousand miles east of Shoshone country. In the north, Blackfoot warriors generally carried similar clubs and Berlandier observed them amongst the Comanche in 1829. The heads of such clubs might weigh up to four pounds and were made of flint, quartzite, steatite and at times even catlinite. They were usually of an elliptical section, perhaps four to six inches long and two to three inches wide at the centre, tapering towards the ends. This head was attached to the end of a long handle, which in early days was usually covered with rawhide, an extension of this covering looping over a groove in the head. The rawhide was sewn in place when wet and after drying held the stone end firmly in position. A buckskin thong at the other end could be looped over the wrist, avoiding loss in a running battle.

Probably as early as 1830, in the east, many of these weapons were being displaced by metal axes or tomahawks. Certainly by the mid-19th century Rudolph Kurz was moved to observe that the style was considered 'old fashioned' by his Hidatsa friends who lived in close proximity to the Mandan of the Upper Missouri; farther west, and as late as 1870, Blackfoot warriors continued to employ the war club both on foot and horseback. (Ewers, 1954, p. 202). The fur trader, Denig, observed that any attempt to ward off the blow of a stone war club 'must be attended with a broken arm' and that if the stroke was not fended the strongest man

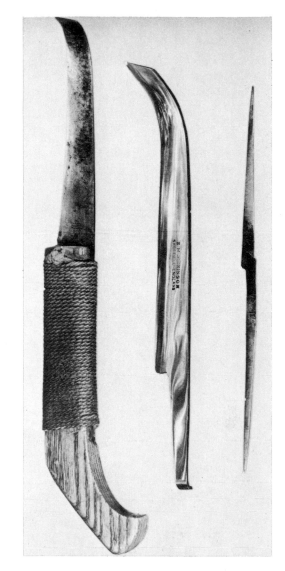

Trade knives. Hudson's Bay Company. These were popular trade items offered to the North American Indians at an early date. The best ones were made in Sheffield and found their outlet through the large fur companies. The large knife at the left with brass mounting was referred to as a chief's knife, the next is a scalping knife with a redwood handle. The others were employed for everyday use and were identified by the trade names 'imitation stag' and 'small roach'.
Hudson's Bay Company, London.

must fall beneath it. (Denig, 1930, p. 555). Weasel Tail, a Blackfoot informant, summarized its manner of use on foot when he advised 'if any enemy tries to stab you with a knife, hit him on the arm or wrist and make him drop it. Then hit him over the head with your club'. (Ewers, 1952, p. 202).

In later years these war clubs were carried only on ceremonial occasions; no longer functional weapons, they were then frequently decorated with wrapped or sewn beadwork and small tin cone jingles, while many of the heads were smaller, and often of a soft stone which would shatter on impact. They appear to have been popular early tourist items, made by old warriors who had undoubtedly used the style in their fighting days. The workmanship was invariably of a high quality and they have now become a scarce collectors' item.

While the stone-headed club was the commonest form of early Plains Indian shock weapon, other types were employed of more limited distribution and in general of a more complex construction. Thus ball-headed clubs, while predominantly an Eastern Woodland weapon, were also to be found amongst the Plains tribes, particularly those in the prairie region where Woodland and true Plains culture were integrated to form a subculture, primarily Plains but with a number of Woodland characteristics. The ball-headed club, called *zhopazhna* by the Omaha, was generally

Crow warrior in war dress carrying a gun-shaped war club, c. 1850. He also carries the highly decorated combined quiver and bow case for which the Crow were particularly famed, and wears a soft tanned buffalo robe slung across his left shoulder and held in place with the strap of the quiver. His leggings are decorated with broad strips of porcupine quillwork fringed with hair which only distinguished warriors were entitled to wear.
The gun-shaped club with the metal blade was a weapon which found particular favour farther east among the Omaha, Oonca, and Chippewa but a number of specimens have also been found among the Sioux.
From a painting by Bill Holm, Seattle.

made from the root of an ash. It was elegantly shaped and traditionally a weasel was carved on the top above the rounded head. (Fletcher and La Flesche, 1904–1905, p. 448). Maximilian collected a fine example of one of these clubs, probably from the Yankton Dakota, in the early 1830s and also a bladed type with one edge notched – very reminiscent of some western Plains quirts – from the Ponca, a small tribe often associated with their linguistically related brethren the Omaha of eastern Nebraska. Ball-headed clubs were virtually non-existent amongst the more westerly tribes but an elegant club with a beautifully carved handle and elk horn head collected by Maximilian from the Assiniboin may be representative of another popular style. Elderly Blackfoot warriors interviewed over a quarter of a century ago stated that they had used both wooden and elk horn clubs in their youth. (Ewers, 1955, p. 201).

Gunstock clubs – so named because they were carved in the form of a gun stock – were popular in the Eastern Woodlands as early as the beginning of the 17th century. They were also occasionally employed by some Plains tribes, although west of the Missouri they tended to be an exception to the rule, being found predominantly amongst those tribes who lived near the banks of that great waterway. Rudolph Kurz collected an elegant gunstock club in his travels up the Missouri in the mid-19th century, and although unidentified the unusual panel of porcupine quillwork suggests eastern Plains origin.

Maximilian, Prince of Wied Neuwied, collected at least one which is now housed in the Linden Museum in Stuttgart while another fine and early example is in the British Museum. By the 1860s such clubs were considered old fashioned and were hardly used. A variant of the style appears to have become popular amongst some western Sioux for in the 1880s Nelson A. Miles collected a slender gunstock club from the Sioux leader, Sitting Bull. A particularly vicious weapon, the traditional single triangular metal blade had been replaced by three knife blades set firmly into the wooden stock. H. L. Peterson, who made a special study of the American tomahawk, was of the opinion that such styles were popular in the period 1860–1880.

So much then for predominantly native-made shock weapons. In fact most of these were overshadowed by axes and tomahawks which were traded to Plains tribes at an early period. Native metal working was entirely unknown to early Plains tribes, and although a little pewter and lead work was done during the reservation period they were entirely dependent on the skill of the white man for practical iron or steel weapons. From the very earliest contact with North American Indians – as early as the 16th century – metal axes both for domestic and military use were high on the list of goods demanded in the Indian trade. For example, the trade goods listed in 1750 by York Factory, one of the Hudson's Bay Company's principal trading posts, included not only a wide range of beads, cloths, brass bells, buttons and thimbles but swords and 'Hatchets "middling and smaller".' (York Factory Trade Goods List, Hudson's Bay Company Archives, London).

When Lewis and Clark visited the Mandan villages of the Upper Missouri, Meriwether Lewis wrote in his journal for 5 February 1805: 'They (the Mandan) are particularly attached to a battle axe formed in a very inconvenient manner in my opinion, it is fabricated of iron only, the blade is extremely thin, from 7 to 9 inches in length and from 4¾ to 6 inches on its edge from whence the sides proceed nearly in a straight line to the eye where its width is generally not more than an inch – the eye is round and about an inch in diameter – the handle seldom more than 14 inches in length, the whole weighing about one pound – the great length of the blade of this axe, added to the small size of the handle renders a stroke uncertain and easily avoided, while the shortness of the handle must render a blow much less forceable even if well directed still more inconvenient as they uniformly use this instrument in action on horseback.' (Lewis and Clark, 1804–1806, p. 36).

Thirty-odd years later, Carl Bodmer was to paint Mato-tope, second chief of the Mandan, carrying such a war axe. Peterson is of the opinion that such axes were in popular use in the regions below the great bend of the Missouri river to the junction with the Mississippi, being employed by such tribes as the Iowa, Sauk, Fox, Kansa, Pawnee, Comanche, Mandan, Dakota, Osage and Oto. They rarely appeared in other areas. (Peterson, 1965, p. 22). Used for more than half a century, the height of their popularity seems to have been in the period 1810–1830 – its predecessor was the spontoon type tomahawk, its successor the pipe tomahawk.

Pipe tomahawks were 'invented before the turn of the eighteenth century probably by an Englishman'. (Peterson, 1965, p. 33). This ingenious weapon, as its name implies, was a combined weapon and pipe, an acorn shaped or later tubular metal bulb serving as a receptacle in which tobacco was placed, a hole running the entire length of the handle. There were many variations of the basic style. Commonest amongst Plains Indians was the half hatchet form 'with an outward flare on the side toward the hand only' – it was especially apparent among the English specimens. While in early days a good number of pipe tomahawks were manufactured in both France and England, local blacksmiths later made them, often employing old rifle barrels to produce the entire head – blade, eye and bowl from one piece of metal. 'Pipe tomahawks made from rifle barrels in this fashion can readily be recognised by the traces of rifling still inside the bowl.' (Peterson, 1965, p. 36).

A good quality tomahawk forged this way should have an elliptical eye and a piece of steel sandwiched in at the bottom to produce an effective cutting edge: the handle should be tapered so that when the head is first fixed in place the mouth-

Sioux warrior on horseback carrying a gun. Upper Missouri, July 1851. Although guns were used as early as 1746 by the northern Plains Indians they were, even as late as 1850, of an inferior kind and although inexpensive (about five dressed buffalo robes would obtain a gun in 1850) they were inaccurate and cumbersome. They were carried as a status symbol – often in buckskin cases as shown here. Only after the introduction of the breech-loading rifle in the mid-sixties did the Plains Indian seriously consider dispensing with the bow and arrow – but most continued to use it until the end of the buffalo days. This warrior is mounted on an Indian pony (note the typical sheep-like head). He displays the defiant scalp-lock and appears to be tattooed. In his left hand he carries a fan made from turkey tail feathers – a coveted trade item. From the original sketch book of Rudolph Kurz. Historische Museum, Berne.

piece goes first down through the eye making it impossible for the head to fly off on impact. While the English style was widely distributed and used on the Plains some tribes – notably the Crow – were particularly fond of the Spontoon-type pipe tomahawk which according to Peterson received this name because the blade 'itself' resembled the military espontoon, 'a pole arm carried during most of the 18th century by commissioned officers who fought on foot'. (Peterson, 1965, p. 24). Evidence suggests that the style was first introduced by the French – indeed one theory has it that the shape was directly derived from the fleur-de-lys – but it was undoubtedly copied by both British and American blacksmiths. Many tomahawks – especially those employed in the last quarter of the 19th century for ceremonial occasions – were elaborately decorated. The blade itself was pierced, heart shapes being particularly popular, and the handle was studded with small brass tacks or, and this was particularly true of the wealthy Crow, wrapped with costly otter fur. The handle was covered with buckskin terminating in a beaded (occasionally quilled) and fringed triangular drop

Blackfoot horse raiders in warm-weather dress.
Sketch by Calvin Boy, Blackfoot Reserve, Montana.
Horse raiders generally set out on foot as shown here.
Except for a little dried meat, no food was taken as this
could be procured on the way. The war leader
selected his party carefully, the two most important
members being the kettle bearer and the scout; the former
might be entrusted with the care of a powerful war
medicine bundle and it was his responsibility to ensure
that no taboos associated with the bundle were violated.
From J. C. Ewers *The Horse in Blackfoot Indian Culture.*
Washington, 1955.

to which were attached small brass trade bells.

Most large museums containing American Indian material have representative examples of pipe tomahawks. Particularly fine collections however are those at the Museum of the American Indian in New York and the outstanding private Pohrt-Chandler collection in Flint, Michigan. The British Museum have amongst others an interesting specimen collected by the Englishman, William Blackmore, probably from the Ute, while one of the most elegant that I have handled was donated to the Historische Museum in Berne, Switzerland by the descendants of Rudolph Kurz who had collected it in Missouri country over a century and a quarter ago.

Knives were common trade items. The commonest, often referred to as a 'scalping knife', was, according to the chief trader at Fort Union in the mid-19th century, of English manufacture with a logwood or brazil-wood handle having a steel blade some eight inches long and one and a half inches wide and it was 'sharp on one edge and with the point turned like a butcher's knife' (Denig, 1930, p. 555). Other knives were the so-called Wilson's butcher, Cartouche, and 'eye dagues'. Trade lists of the Hudson's Bay Company for the years 1750–1820 identify a wide selection of trade knives offered by that company to Canadian Indians, such as the Cree, Assiniboin and Blackfoot. A broad double-edged knife commonly referred to as the beaver-tail knife was a favourite weapon of Blackfoot warriors in hand-to-hand fighting.

'The warrior grasped the handle so that the metal blade protruded from the heel on his fist. He used a powerful downward chopping motion to penetrate the opponent's body above the clavicle or a sidewise sweep to strike him between the ribs or the stomach. It was a deadly weapon for close infighting afoot, of little use in opposition to a mounted enemy armed with war club or lance. It was a favourite weapon for finishing off a wounded or disabled enemy and served as the scalping tool.' (Ewers, 1955, p. 202). The style was probably particularly popular amongst the Blackfoot because of its adoption in the Bear-knife medicine bundle. In early days, perhaps prior to 1850, there were many such Bear-knife medicine bundles. The chief object of the bundle was a large beaver-tail type knife, the handle of which was the jaw of a grizzly bear.

Traditionally both sides of the knife blade were painted in a zigzag of blue and its 'power was thought to be very great, so great that its owner was seldom killed, for its appearance frightened everyone into submission, after the manner of bears. There were many songs in the ritual. All war songs, since the bear is a fighting animal.' (Wissler, 1912, p. 134). Dr Wissler, researching among the Blackfoot in 1906, was of the opinion that such Bear-knife bundles were virtually extinct at that time. One reason given for the decline was the brutality of the transfer ceremony and the associated life-long obligations. Only a few years ago a distraught Blackfoot woman presented Dr Harold McCracken, the curator of the Whitney Art Gallery in Cody, Wyoming, with a Bear-knife bundle stating that she had been plagued with bad dreams ever since she had ceased carrying out the obligations of the most powerful of war medicine bundles.

All knives were carried in sheaths, often highly decorated with quill or beadwork. While generally carried on the left side at the back of the belt, in early days some eastern Sioux apparently carried knives in sheaths which hung round the neck. The Piegan warrior, Saukamappee, told the explorer David Thompson that his father's weapons were knife and axe, stating that 'he carried his knife on his breast and his axe in his belt'. (Thompson, 1916, p. 328). An interesting ethnological theory is that the triangular neck yoke commonly displayed on typical Sioux war shirts was a conventionalized symbol of the early neck sheath. Two particularly distinctive styles of sheath were the large heavy rawhide Blackfoot or northern type frequently decorated with brass tacks and beadwork and having a triangular opening through which a belt could be passed. The smaller central Plains or Sioux type (often with an inner sheath of rawhide to enclose the blade) had an outer sheath of heavy buckskin usually fully beaded and was tied to, rather than threaded on, the belt. In both types the

An Indian War Party. Although after about 1850 the raid
for scalps was far less popular than the raid for horses,
when it did take place warriors, after much ceremonial
preparation and parade in large groups followed the war
trail on horseback – in contrast to horse raiders who
generally left under the cover of darkness in small
parties on foot. From a painting by N. C. Wyeth.
Joslyn Art Museum, Omaha, Nebraska.

knife went deep down in to the sheath, only an inch or so of the handle protruding. An ingenious addition to prevent loss of sheath and contents was a wooden or horn bobbin attached to one end of a long braided thong which was attached to the back of the sheath, the bobbin being pulled over and under the belt. As with the pipe and gun, the knife was integrated within the symbolic lore of the tribes – mention has already been made of the famed Bear-knife of the Blackfeet. Additionally it was employed to seal an oath.

The anthropologist and explorer Lewis Henry Morgan wrote of the Crow in 1862 that when they wished to clear themselves from some charge they took an oath by swearing on the gun, knife or pipe. In the case of the knife it was raised in the right hand and pointed towards the sky with the words 'I have stated the truth.'

'They then draw it between the lips and are required to touch the tongue to the blade. Those who swear falsely in this way attempt to avoid touching the tongue, which appears necessary to complete the oath.' (Morgan, 1959, p. 175).

Before the introduction of powerful and accurate rifles the shield was an important part of military costume. It was effective against arrows and would deflect or deaden the effect of a musket ball. Additionally, there is good evidence to suggest that an attenuated form of body armour was utilized by early equestrian warriors, while the heavy buckskin shirts with short sleeves which were still to be observed among so widely separated groups as the Cree and Ute as late as the mid-19th century probably gave considerable protection to the wearer.

In pre-horse days the shield was usually some three feet in diameter and carried by warriors on foot, affording considerable protection. By the 1830s these were greatly decreased in size – undoubtedly the introduction of the horse which drastically changed warfare tactics and demanded a greater degree of mobility, was the prime mover in the development of a smaller shield, perhaps eighteen inches or so in diameter. Large ones were, however, still in vogue especially on the southern Plains. Lino Sánchez y Tapia painted both sedentary and equestrian Comanche warriors in 1828 carrying large shields which I estimate to be at least three feet in diameter (Berlandier, 1969, Plate 3). A few years later George Catlin sketched Comanche warriors carrying shields at least thirty inches in diameter.

The basic technique of making shields differed only slightly. The rawhide which was used in their construction came from the shoulder hide of a bull buffalo – the thickest part. To increase the thickness it was heated over a fire or steamed over hot water; while still hot it was placed in a shallow hole and weighted at the centre with stones. On drying the shield had a permanent set so that the side presented to the enemy was convex. Many shields, however, which I have examined in museum collections lack the curved surface, consisting simply of a heavy flat disc of rawhide perhaps up to half an inch thick. A variation on the style, apparently favoured by the Comanche, was to use two discs of rawhide, sewing them together around the edge of a wooden hoop. The space between the discs was then packed with hair, feathers, grass or other material to further reduce the momentum of the impinging missile. One observer related that a shield he captured from a Comanche warrior was packed with pages of a book dealing with the complete history of Rome! 'Before discovering that paper was used for padding inside the shields, Anglo–American pioneers were quite puzzled at the Comanche interest in books!' (Wallace and Hoebel, 1952, p. 106).

While shields had considerable practical value in the mechanical protection they afforded, it was primarily the 'medicine power' of the painted designs on them which was believed to offer the desired protection if, as in later days with the

Map drawn by an Assiniboin Indian showing war path to the Rocky Mountains. December 1853. Maps were frequently drawn by Plains Indians which were accurate and could be understood by whites. This is one of the north bank of the Missouri leading from Fort Union to beyond Fort Benton, 200 miles away. The names were written in at the direction of the Assiniboin by Edwin Denig, fur trader, at Fort Union. Nez Percé, who often travelled east into buffalo country, used maps drawn on rawhide. From the original in the National Anthropological Archives, Smithsonian Institution.

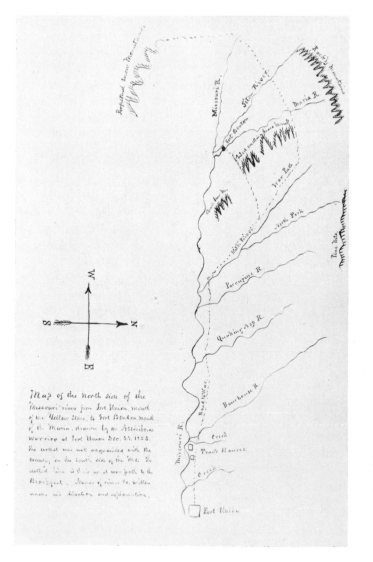

introduction of the high-power rifle, the shield failed to protect its owner its short-coming was accredited to the fact that the 'medicine power' associated with the fire-arm was greater than that of the shield. This concept was widespread. Studies show that the designs on shields had dream or vision origins at least among the Crow, Sioux, Blackfoot, Assiniboin, Hidatsa and Kiowa.

It is on record that at one time the American Fur Company attempted to introduce polished metal shields among the Blackfoot but 'this was opposed by the medicine men, who would thus have been deprived of an important source of revenue, and the superstitious feelings of the Indians induced them to prefer their own which alone could undergo religious dedication and enjoy the favour of the Great Spirit'. (Bradley, in Ewers, 1955, p. 203).

The Crow, one of the most superstitious of all Plains tribes, with a strong belief in 'medicine power', were credited by Maximilian as being suppliers of shields to the Blackfoot. 'We saw the Blackfeet ride to battle half naked, but some, too, in their finest dresses, with the beautifully ornamented shields obtained from the Crows, and their splendid crowns of feathers, and, on these occasions, they all have their medicines, or amulets, open and hung about them.' (Maximilian, 1843, p. 117). Maximilian collected a number of such shields from the Crow; one of them, now at the Linden Museum in Stuttgart, is particularly interesting as it is virtually identical with one in the collection of the Museum of the American Indian, New York – considering the unique and individual nature of shield designs it is highly probable that it was made by the same man.

Shields could be transferred along with strict ritualistic observances and some men who were particularly renowned for shield making abilities obtained high prices for their goods. Indeed, because it cost at least a horse to obtain a shield ceremonially blessed by a medicine man, a poor man 'sometimes carried a buffalo robe folded several times, over his left arm'. (Bradley, in Ewers, 1955, p. 258).

Another shield which I believe is also Crow is in the Hooper Collection in England. It is uniquely interesting in that it has three buckskin covers each painted with a different design. Many Plains shields, especially those from the Crow, often had the protective design painted on a buckskin cover placed *over* the rawhide disc; this was in turn covered with another plain buckskin cover which was removed before battle commenced. In later years only the *painted cover* itself might be carried into battle. A Sioux specimen which is credited as having originally belonged to the famous war chief, Crazy Horse, and now housed in the Smithsonian Institution is decorated with symbols having, in Sioux mythology, strong protective powers, the dragon fly and thunderbird.

One of the most famous of all shields was that which belonged to Rotten Belly, head chief of the River Crow, decorated with a black conventional-

ized human figure having disproportionately large ears. It was said to have remarkable powers of prophecy. 'Once when a revenge expedition against the Cheyenne was contemplated, Rotten Belly was implored to lead the large Crow war party. He rolled his shield from a high pile of buffalo chips, promising that if the painted side fell next to the ground when the shield stopped rolling he would not proceed against the enemy; but if the painted side was up he would lead the expedition. The painted side was turned upward when the rolling shield stopped and Rotten Belly led his people to a great victory over the Cheyenne on the Arkansas River.' (Lowie, in Wildschut, 1960, p. 72). Legend has it that the shield prophesied Rotten Belly's imminent death in a battle against the Blackfoot in 1834. The design was copied on another shield at least once for there is one at the Natural History Museum in Chicago, which is virtually identical.

By 1860 it was uncommon for Crow (and this is probably true for other central Plains tribes such as the Sioux, Cheyenne and Arapaho) warriors to carry shields into battle. The anthropologist, Lewis Henry Morgan, was told in the spring of 1862 after examining a Crow shield that those people now seldom carried them in battle because they no longer offered protection against musket balls. (Morgan, 1959, p. 191).

War exploits, on a Cheyenne tipi lining. In full regalia a Cheyenne warrior rides towards his enemy. A captured cavalry sword is given much prominence – such weapons were highly coveted by their owners. A scalp hangs from the bridle of the eagle-feather bedecked warrior and another has been taken from a vanquished enemy. Field Museum of Natural History, Chicago.

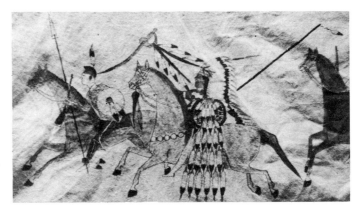

Crow warriors interviewed by Wildschut in the first quarter of this century told him that shields were considered 'too cumbersome and heavy, and they hampered the movements of warriors in close battle. Two Leggings said that on one occasion he did take a shield on the warpath. When he returned the skin on his left arm and shoulder were chafed raw by the continual rubbing of the heavy shield, caused by the jogging of his trotting horse.' (Wildschut, 1960, p. 65). The same *magical* powers were apparently obtained if part of the shield or even a miniature were carried into battle and although no longer functional as a weapon it was not unusual to see, in the 1870s, shields carefully supported on a tripod placed outside the owner's tipi – religious taboos were carefully observed even in this simple operation. For example, Hump's shield carried precepts that while so displayed a child must not walk or crawl under the tripod from which the shield was suspended and at sunset the shield was to be taken inside the tipi and fastened to the rear pole and when in this position 'no one might pass in front of it or between it and the centre of the tipi'. (Wildschut, 1960, p. 68).

There was no great wealth in guns prior to the 1870s although as mentioned earlier even by 1740 some Piegan Indians had them. These early guns were however of an inferior kind – even as late as 1854 one observer described the common gun carried by Blackfoot Indians as 'an inferior type of shotgun'. He was probably referring to the single shot smooth-bore flintlock first introduced by the Hudson's Bay Company and later commonly referred to as the 'North-West gun'. By the early 19th century they were the commonest type of gun employed by the Plains Indians and in 1850 they were traded to the Plains Cree for five buffalo robes or three silver fox skins (see Denig, 1927, p. 122). Such guns were, in the earlier period at least, manufactured in Europe, principally by firms in London and Birmingham, the manufacturer 'Barnett of London' being particularly well known. They were inexpensive and hard wearing but notoriously inaccurate, slow to reload and particularly awkward on horseback with barrels some three feet in length. They were frequently shortened and the iron salvaged commonly being re-used to make a scraping tool employed for tanning buffalo and deer hides – little was wasted by the Plains Indians.

Guns made a deep impression on the Indians. One early traveller observed of the Indians of the Lake Superior region that guns so astonished them that they declared 'there was a spirit within the gun, which caused the loud noise made when it was fired'. (Ewers, 1967, p. 38). Francis Parkman stated that his Sioux friends called a gun *Manzawakan* meaning 'metal (or iron) possessed with a spirit'. (Parkman, 1883, p. 231) and Maximilian mentioned a Mandan ceremonial for consecrating firearms.

Probably, like the Comanche who stated that when the gun was first introduced 'everyone wanted them', after the novelty wore off and the limitations of such weapons became apparent most Plains tribes still relied primarily on the bow.

After the annihilation of Brevet Lieutenant Colonel Fetterman and eighty men near Fort Phil Kearny on 21 December 1866, it was the opinion of Dr S. M. Horton, the post surgeon, who examined the bodies after that bloody encounter, that not more than 'six were killed by balls' – thus the Oglala Sioux who were the victors were at that time still largely armed with the bow and arrow.

The American troops who fought against Plains Indians were largely armed with antiquated muzzle loaders, relics of the Civil War, and it was not until 1865 that breech-loading 50-calibre Springfield rifles were issued. Such rifles gradually found their way into Indian hands; they were supremely better than the muzzle loaders (where a ramrod had to be used, making it virtually impossible to load on horseback) since all that was necessary for reloading was to simply throw open the breech block, eject the empty shell and slip in a fresh one, an operation which could be done in a few seconds. Although repeating rifles were available to Plains Indians by the mid-1860s few could afford them. Indeed, few Indians apparently used such weapons in the Custer Battle of 1876, and most still used muzzle loaders or percussion guns, or at best single-shot breech loaders.

Guns were precious items and coveted when owned. Like the bow they were put in buckskin cases often highly ornamented with beadwork. Thus, armed with his own favourite weapon, the Plains warrior set out on the war-trail. An efficient leader generally selected his war party carefully and the role of supporting personnel was not overlooked. Thus a well organized group of perhaps between ten to fifty often included youngsters who were not yet of warrior age and possessed no 'medicine'. They joined the expedition as apprentices, their work mainly concerned with preparing the food, looking after captured horses and generally making themselves useful. Occasionally, women would also go along, especially those who had no children. They rendered valuable service in mending worn clothing, particularly moccasins. Except for a little dried meat, no food was taken as this could be procured on the way; each man carried his own wooden bowl or large horn spoon from which he could eat or drink. The war leader, as he was called if *he personally* possessed the necessary supernatural power to give some guarantee of success, and had not sought the help of another, appointed assistants who acted on his behalf.

The two most important posts were those of kettle-bearer and scout. The kettle-bearer not only organized the cooking arrangements but also took care of 'certain eating and drinking customs which were common features of war party practice'. (Smith, 1938, p. 440). For example, the great Cheyenne war leader, Roman Nose, possessed medicine power which forbade the eating of food which had been cooked in an iron vessel, and only after elaborate purification ceremonials could a violation of that rule be rectified. The kettle-bearer might also be entrusted with the care of the war medicine bundle. The scout took on the practical role of locating the enemy and protecting the war party from surprise attack. Leading a war party was a heavy responsibility and occasionally even the best men cracked under the strain. Old Kiowa informants related the case of a leader who after a few days 'lapsed into some type of schizophrenic condition, obsessed with the delusion that all of his men were horses'. One day 'he stopped the party, lined up the warriors and examined the teeth of each man. Another day he forced all of them to bray in chorus, threatening to shoot any man who did not bray or obey him or who deserted!' This situation would have been particularly amusing had the outcome been less dismaying for most of the party were ambushed and almost exterminated. (In Miskin, 1940, p. 33).

A typical war adventure for the capture of horses from their traditional Flathead enemies who lived near the 'Backbone-of-the-world' (the Rocky Mountains) was related by the Blackfoot warrior, Many White Horses.

'We followed the south bank of the Missouri, the berries were ripe, game was plenty and fat and the journey was pleasant. We followed up the Bear Tooth, or South Fork, where the railroad runs now. When one day's march from the Flathead country, a storm came up and beat the grass flat. In jest, I said to Calf Necklace "Let us go alone. I believe that when we get out the wind will go down." Soon we came to an open country and to a cliff. Looking over we saw a river and a Flathead camp. We returned to tell our party but lost them. We could not trail them as the grass was down. Then we gave the call for having seen an enemy. The party answered and soon joined us. Then we made a medicine smoke and gave prayers for success. I have a warbonnet with four songs. When transferred to me, my face was painted and the songs taught. When near the enemy I go through this in the same way. I painted my powder horn and bullet pouch. I carried two awls, mending materials and extra moccasins.'

While Many White Horses does not mention the use of any maps he indicates that the geography of the country was well known to his expedition. The fur trader, Edwin Denig, found that his Assiniboin informants were both capable and accurate in rendering the topography of their country. In December 1853 he obtained from an Assiniboin warrior a detailed and well scaled map of the area, north and west of Fort Union as far as Fort Benton and was further moved to write, 'In conversation with most elderly Indians regarding locations, travels or to explain battles and other events, resort is had by them to drawing maps on the ground, on bark with charcoal, or on paper if they can get it to illustrate more clearly the affair in question. In this way the Chief of the Crow Nation three years since made and left with us a map of his intended travels during the entire fall

A back view of a fully developed flaring warbonnet, to the crown of which are attached two small ermine skins which were probably war fetishes and formed part of the warbonnet's protective power. In later years such animal skins were replaced by a conventionalized 'major' plume which was a large bird quill attached to the centre of the crown and was said to represent the owner of the warbonnet. Crow, 1832. From George Catlin's *Albums Unique*. Museum of Mankind, London.

and winter succeeding, embracing a circumference of 1500 miles, with the different encampments to be made by that nation in that time, and so correct was the drawing that we had no difficulty in finding their camp the following winter in deep snow, one months travel from this place.' (Denig, 1927, p. 605).

My own Nez Percé informants also indicated that maps on rawhide of 'the buffalo country' were familiar to them in early days. Travel at night was helped by observation of the stars, the north star in particular was familiar to most Plains tribes and in times of heavy cloud the direction of the wind helped in indicating the correct course towards the enemy. Enemy signs could tell much. Thus, camp fires would tell the number of persons there; the condition of the ashes and horse droppings, remains of meals, the terrain – broken or bent grass – and tracks by water's edge would

Capturing the best horse. Sioux pictograph, 1874.
The favourite horse was often picketed at night outside
the owner's lodge. The stealing of such a horse in the
very heart of an enemy's camp required great skill and
courage, it ranked as a high war honour and sustained
a 'game' element which found its way through most
Plains Indian intertribal warfare. This pictograph,
together with a number of others, was collected in 1874
by the Englishman William Blackmore from a party of
Oglala Sioux near Sidney Barracks, Nebraska.
Museum of Mankind, London.

indicate how recently occupied. Tribal identity
might be confirmed by observation of discarded
and worn out moccasins, arrowheads, even a bead
or two. A skilled Indian scout could, by consideration of all these factors, assess with remarkable
accuracy most of what he wished to know.

Old time Plains Indians had acute sight. 'At a
distance of 12 or 15 miles they will distinguish
animals from timber, even supposing they are not
in motion. If moving they will discern between
horses and buffalo, elk and horses, antelope and
men, a bear and a bull, or a wolf and a deer etc.
But the greatest mystery is how they make out
anything living to be there at such a distance on
the instant, when they themselves are in motion
and the animal at rest. This they do when it is
surrounded by a hundred other objects as like to
living creatures as it is. Once pointed out, the

movements are watched and its character thus
determined. Their powers in this respect are truly
astonishing and must be acquired. They also judge
very correctly of the relative distances of objects,
either by the eye or to each other. Smoke can be
seen rising on the plains at a distance of 60 miles
and they will tell from that or any lesser distance
within a few miles of the place where it rises.'
(Denig, 1927, p. 528).

Rivers were crossed by use of bull boats if time
permitted otherwise a small makeshift coracle of
hide and sticks to carry clothing and powder only
was employed by the swimming warriors. This is
shown in a sketch made by Rudolph Kurz in 1852.

It was not unusual for war parties to leave messages for their members who scouted ahead or
were following. Many comments of early observers
of Plains Indians indicate that picture writing and
a system of signs was well developed and understood. On leaving camp, Blackfoot war parties
frequently left a willow stick bent V-like and stuck
in the ground, the apex pointing in the direction
taken. Stragglers or other parties would know
that if the angle was acute, the distance to the
next camp was small. More precise instructions
were frequently left by a kind of map marked on
the ground. The V symbol was again employed to

indicate direction, rivers and streams were mapped out, while pebbles coloured black or pieces of charcoal marked the proposed camping places, the number in each case was to indicate the resting time. Stops by day (indicating travel by night) were conveyed by the use of yellow pebbles, and the fact that two parties had joined was indicated by V shaped symbols converging. (From Wissler, 1911, p. 43).

The messages were of course doubly useful; not only did they convey information to warriors actively engaged in the same war expedition, but if the war party was overdue it would be possible for searchers to follow the sequence of events. In the mid-19th century the system was so well developed that by the use of ingenious signs and sketches an Assiniboin war party was able to convey the following detailed information: 'We are a party of twenty men and have stolen 39 horses from the Blackfeet. The camp turned out and killed one of us and recaptured 14 horses. We forted, and fought with them. In the battle three of us were wounded and six horses were killed, we got off with 19 horses. The first night away from the enemy camp we encamped on the plains near a spring and in this encampment we left a wounded man, we made two more encampments after that, when we now leave this painting and intend pursuing our course home to the right. A band of buffalo was seen on the opposite side of the river on a creek while the battle was going on, which are all we have yet seen.' This remarkable message is reproduced, page 60. The end of the dotted line conveys as far as the war party have then gone, while the other marks show the road that they intend to pursue. (Denig, pp. 78 and 606).

A highly developed system of signalling was employed both to convey information to distant members of the war party and on return to those in camp. A forward scouting party, on sighting the enemy, commonly conveyed this intelligence to the main group by rapidly riding backwards or forwards or in a circle; blanket signals were also commonly employed and mirror signals were particularly popular. Often the system to be used was first discussed and agreed; thus there was no universal code although the discovery of a large band of enemy was commonly conveyed by vibrating the mirror, giving a continuously moving beam. Smoke signals were employed in a similar way but according to one reliable authority they were used in a very limited manner by Plains Indians. (Clark, 1885, p. 415).

The first camp made after leaving the confines of the village was considered particularly important for it 'reflected the substitution of the road of war, for that of peace'. (Smith, 1938, p. 442). Such a camp might be quite close to the village; as well as having religious significance it also served as a base for both pre-battle and post-battle ceremonials; here the outward party performed some of the necessary medicine power obligations to ensure success, and on return prepared for a ceremonial victory entrance to the village.

Nearer to enemy territory, war lodges were commonly used by war parties. These were permanent structures of wooden poles set somewhat like those of a tipi but closer together. On average the poles were some twelve feet long and tied at the top. Lighter poles were leaned against the foundation poles and the whole framework was usually covered with slabs of cottonwood bark. The lodge was entered through a passage-way barely four feet high and ten feet or more long. 'Informants said that in the time of their youth there were a great many war lodges in the country of the Blackfeet and their enemies. The lodges were located in heavily timbered areas near rivers or streams, or on thickly wooded heights, conveniently near well-known war trails. There were many along the Missouri River, and it was the business of leaders of Blackfoot war parties to know where they were located.' (Ewers, 1968, p. 118).

The anthropologist, Lewis Henry Morgan, remarked on the large number of such lodges which he observed in his journey up the Missouri in the early 1860s. Not only did the war lodge provide both protection from enemy attack and unpredictable weather, it also served important functions as a supply and information base and was an important part of the Plains Indian war complex. 'While the main body was active in other duties in preparing for the raid in comparative seclusion near the lodge, the leader sent out scouts to locate the enemy camp and report its size and wealth in horses. No time was lost in aimless wandering in enemy country on the part of the main body, nor did it expose itself needlessly to discovery by the enemy.' (Ewers, 1968, p. 127).

As they neared the enemy, and anxiety and tension increased, Sioux warriors commonly pledged the Sun Dance vow. Such times would surely be a moving experience to any observer for these hardy warriors of the Plains were also sensitive, family loving people. Many had children, relatives and friends who they dearly wished to see again. 'They felt that no extreme of heroic endurance would be too great an expression of thankfulness if they were reunited with their friends.' (Densmore, 1918, p. 101). Mato kuwa-pi (Chased by Bears) spoke such a vow for his party: 'Just before sunrise I told the warriors to stand side by side facing the East. I stood behind them and told them to raise their right hands. I raised my right hand with them and said: "Wakan-tanka, these men have requested me to make this vow for them. I pray you take pity on us and on our families at home. We are now between life and death. For the sake of our families and relatives we desire that you will help us conquer the enemy and capture his horses to take home with us. Because they are thankful for your goodness and will be thankful if you grant this request these men promise that they will take part in the next Sun Dance. Each man has some offering to give at the proper time.' (Densmore, 1918, p. 97).

Some warriors performed personal ceremonies before a battle, such as the famous Rotten Belly with his shield which was said to have powers of prophecy. While the Crow warrior, Blows Down, the owner of a sacred hoop which was also believed to possess prophesying powers, describes holding the hoop in the rising smoke of sweet grass and upon looking into the hoop, he and his companions saw a vision of many horses. (Wildschut, 1960, p. 46).

Ideally, before going into battle, warriors painted their bodies and faces and at times their horses as well, the designs being in accordance with dreams or bestowed by some successful warrior, thus the painted design on the body could often be a form of protective power. Neither was painting confined solely to the battlefield. Further, there is abundant evidence which clearly indicates that painting was seldom done purely for ornament. The Omaha, for example, 'When going to battle, on the surround at the tribal buffalo hunt, when taking part in the Héde-wachi ceremony, at the races, at the Hethúshka society and the Pebble society, the painting on their faces and bodies had a serious significance, partaking of the nature of an appeal or prayer.' (Fletcher and La Flesche, 1905–1906, p. 350).

The Wet. A Crow warrior and successful horse raider of about 1890. Interesting costume details are the two scalps attached to each shoulder of the Wet's highly decorated buckskin war shirt. The fact that he has been able to garnish his shirt with beaded strips and ermine mark him as a man who has gained high distinction on the war trail. The Wet's shirt is now in the collection of the Field Museum of Natural History, Chicago. From a painting by De Cort Smith.

Some warriors sought the services of a medicine man who specialized in making war medicine. Thus Tasún-ka-wakań (Holy Horse) painted four warriors' faces brown with a white line across the forehead which extended down the cheek and forked at the end. He also painted their horses with white clay 'drawing zig-zag lines from the mouth down the front legs, branching at the hoofs, and the same on the hind legs; there was also a band across the forehead and spots on the chest'. (Densmore, 1918, p. 353). As he painted the men and their horses, Holy Horse sung the following song concerning the paint:

le	this
maká	earth
wéćićon kin	I had used as paint
on	causes
oyá te	the tribe (of the enemy)
iní han wayé lo	much excitement.

Song Concerning War Paint,
sung by Śiyáka, (Densmore, 1918, p. 353).

After the painting was finished one of the songs to be sung by the warriors explains the intended function of the painting:

lé na	these [the painted horse and the herbs]
wanlá ka nunwé	may you behold
mitá śunke	my horse
wakiń yan iyé ćeća	like the thunderbird
wanlá ka nunwé	may you behold

Behold my horse
sung by Śiyáka, (Densmore, 1918, p. 355).

The painting on both horse and man was undoubtedly representative of *Wa-kí-yan* the lightning or thunder spirit so respected and feared by the Sioux and other Plains tribes (the channel cut on arrows, the reader will recall, was symbolic of this deity). On the great treeless plains the death-dealing qualities of lightning were terrifyingly apparent – animals and men were often struck. The thunder spirit was usually imagined as a huge bird, the lightning was the flashing of his eyes and the thunder his voice, and according to Sioux mythology the horse was the gift of the thunder. 'The horse always appealed to them as a creature of mysterious origin, and in many cases was assumed to have been given by the thunder. In any event there is an association in their minds between the power of the war horse and the thunder.' (Wissler, 1907, p. 193).

The Omaha maintained that the thunder bird lived in a 'forest of cedars' (Fletcher and La Flesche, 1905–1906, p. 457). It is interesting in this context to note that many Siouan tribes believed that cedar – a post, bough or even a twig – gave protective power against malign spirits. For example the shrine which stood in the centre of the Mandan villages was a red cedar post which represented the body of Lone Man who figured prominently in Mandan mythology – a benevolent and protective deity – while the Omaha's Tent of War contained an ancient cedar post believed to be related to thunder and war. Many other tribal in-

Return of the Warriors, from a painting by Charles M. Russell, 1906. Most successful war parties would make camp before entering the village. There the warriors rehearsed their victory songs and went carefully over their war exploits; then, dressed and painted, they rode into camp singing their common war song and all rejoiced. The leading warrior is carrying a crooked pole wrapped with otter skin that together with the horned headdress is probably the insignia of the war society to which he belonged. Whitney Gallery of Western Art, Cody, Wyoming.

stances could be cited. On a more individual basis the symbolic war-exploit talismans of the Mandan chief, Mato-tope are probably carved from cedar wood. Half a century later a visitor who met the famed Sioux warrior Rain-in-the-Face was led to observe 'I entered his cabin one day and found a small cedar tree, four or five feet high, standing in the centre of it. When asked the reason for this strange encumbrance he answered *"Wa-kí-yan lí-la ko-kí-pa"* (The Lightning is very much afraid of it!) which I took to be another way of saying that for some reason he was very much afraid of the lightning. It showed that even this terrifying power can be controlled through its fears.'

Rain-in-the-Face is one of the few Indians I know of who gained his name through his warpaint. As a young man he joined a war party which successfully captured horses from the Gros Ventres; the party found themselves pursued and it was necessary to make a stand. Rain-in-the-Face had painted his face to represent the sun 'when half covered with darkness – half black and half red'. Fighting for a whole day in the rain his face became streaked with the red and black warpaint which confirmed his boyhood name of Rain-in-the-Face. (Hodge, 1907, p. 353).

As was noted earlier the Plains tribes seldom guarded or coralled their horses unless there was evidence that the enemy were in the vicinity. By hobbling the lead mare and selecting good pasture it was generally possible to contain the herds overnight within a comparatively small area. Youths were often given the task of daily caring for horses and it was they – at the instructions of the owner – who drove them to pasture at night and retrieved and watered them the next day. There was no central responsibility from the band leaders or council, it being recognized that each family was responsible for his own herd. Although the majority of horses were largely unguarded at night a significant exception was that the favourite and best horse was commonly picketed outside the owner's tipi. The stealing of such a horse in the very heart of the enemy's camp required skill and courage. It was an objective which most ambitious warriors sought for, not only did it guarantee a quality animal but such a deed ranked highly in the scale of recognized war honours. Further, it sustained a 'game' element which so characteristically threaded its way through Plains Indians inter-tribal warfare.

A successful horse raiding party might capture at least one hundred or more horses; more were seldom taken unless the party was unusually large since there were practical difficulties in containing them especially if the warriors of the ransacked camp were in close pursuit. Although on such horse-raiding expeditions, close contact with the enemy was generally avoided, face to face encounters inevitably occurred and scalps were taken on both sides. The artist, De Cost Smith, vividly described an abortive attempt by a young Sioux warrior to capture the favourite horse of a prominent Crow warrior known as The Wet.

'Fully awake now, fully alive to the situation with his eye at the peephole, he felt for his rifle and raised it noiselessly to be ready. Outside a tall form had just cut the lariat, made a half hitch around the horse's jaw and was starting to lead it away. Quickly, with soft, swift tread The Wet stepped over the threshold, and with the muzzle of his gun almost touching his enemy's back, fired. The horse started at the flash; the man fell. Instantly The Wet shouted his coup cry "I, The Wet, have just killed an enemy. I am first to strike." Bird Head then struck the dead man, and, finding his gun at the same time, announced in a loud voice his claim of second to strike an enemy, and the first to capture an enemy's gun.' (De Cost Smith, 1949, pp. 145–146).

The development of such a situation could subsequently give rise to a revenge party but as has been demonstrated earlier, post mid-19th century inter-tribal warfare became synonymous with the horse raid. The ethnologist, George Grinnell, summarized a wide-spread attitude when he wrote 'there were many brave and successful warriors of the Cheyenne . . . who on their war journeys tried to avoid coming into close contact with enemies, and had no wish to kill enemies. Such men went to war for the sole purpose of increasing their possessions by capturing horses; that is, they carried on war as a business – for profit.' (Grinnell, Vol. 2, 1923, p. 2).

As soon as safety was reached the loot was distributed among the members of the party – generally the older, more experienced warriors receiving the most. It took a number of such expeditions for young men to accumulate sufficient wealth to even consider marrying.

With the possible exception of the Arikara (Smith, 1938, p. 443), all successful war parties made camp before entering their home village. Here they prepared for a grand entrance and the subsequent rejoicings in the form of victory and perhaps scalp dances. Here warriors could go carefully over their war exploits, rehearse their victory songs and dances, don their war dress – all

for the maximum dramatic effect. Then, approaching the village they rode in singing their war songs.

The return of a successful war party was an occasion for rejoicing and celebration, the victory dances and recounting of war honours which were acted out in a dramatic and realistic fashion putting emphasis on the superiority of the group over the enemy. Generous warriors gave away captured horses, thereby elevating their prestige further. Such actions 'served as a stepping stone to leadership'. (Ewers, 1955, p. 189).

If scalps had been taken then, and this was undoubtedly embedded in the early lore of the tribes, returning warriors rode into camp with faces painted black, shooting their guns into the air and carrying the scalps on long poles. 'The people were excited and welcomed them with shouts and yells. All was joy. The women sang songs of victory. . . . In the front rank were those who had . . . counted coups. . . . Some threw their arms around the successful warriors. Old men and women sang songs in which their names were mentioned. The relatives of those who rode in the first rank . . . testified to their joy by making gifts to friends or to poor people. The whole crowd might go to where some brave man lived or to where his father lived, and there dance in his honour. They were likely to prepare to dance all night, and perhaps to keep up this dancing for two days and two nights.' (Grinnell, Vol. 2, 1923, pp. 6 & 22).

Such a returning Assiniboin war party was observed and sketched by the Swiss artist, Rudolph Kurz, in 1851 and even after the time that the scalp raid took on a minor role Sioux warriors still continued to sing war songs containing the phrase 'the black face paint I seek' (Densmore, 1918, p. 359), and definite rituals were observed in its use. Thus Sioux war parties which had defeated the enemy without loss to themselves allowed not only the first four who had killed enemies to use the black face paint but it could also be used by their women relatives who participated in the scalp dance.

Although there were few restrictions placed on active participation in post-warpath dances those who had been honoured by the gift of a scalp – perhaps to put an end to their period of mourning – frequently joined the scalp dance as did the female relatives of the victorious warriors. The predominance of females in the scalp dance has led at least one anthropologist to observe that 'the role of the woman was so marked as to make its description practically synonymous with descriptions of the scalp dance'. (Smith, 1938, pp. 450–451).

The emphasis on a display of uninhibited triumph, the recognition that prayers had been answered, the complete lack of concern with any dread or danger associated with the dead enemy not only exemplified the Dionysian character of the Plains Indians but contrasted markedly with and set them well apart from other cultural groups in North America where scalping also found a place in warfare. Elsewhere there was emphasis on

rituals directed at removing from the slayer the curse and 'dangerous supernatural potency of the scalp'. (Benedict, 1932, p. 16). The Papago, for example, engaged in an almost three weeks' purification ritual after the taking of a scalp: then its medicine became subservient to the owner and was used as an aid in rain-making and the promotion of crops.

By contrast the successful Plains warrior utilized the loot of war to attain rank; he gave away his horses to the needy, his scalps to the grieved. However, in a society which put so much emphasis on freedom – and evaluation – of the individual it was necessary to ensure that all were aware of his standing and thus his honours were well displayed for all to see.

Return of a successful Assiniboin war party, Fort Berthold, Upper Missouri, July 1851. If scalps had been taken – and two are shown here attached to a stave carried by the right-hand warrior – returning warriors generally painted their faces black. Many war songs contained the phrase 'the black face paint I seek' referring to the painting custom of successful scalp raiders. The reason for the nose tips being left unpainted is not recorded but it is interesting to observe that amongst the Osage, a linguistically related group who lived to the south of the Hidatsa, the tip of the nose of a captive was, in the war ceremony, scratched with the sharp point of a sacred knife. From a sketch by Rudolph Kurz, 1851. Historische Museum, Berne.

Exploits of the War Chiefs

*Mato-tope had fastened transversely in his hair a wooden knife
. . . because he had killed a Cheyenne chief with his knife; then
six wooden sticks . . . indicating so many musket wounds
received . . . for an arrow wound he fastened in his hair the
wing feather of a wild turkey . . . on his arms from the shoulder
downwards he had seventeen yellow stripes which indicated
warlike deeds . . . on his breast the figure of a hand, of a
yellow colour, as a sign that he had captured prisoners. A
warrior so adorned takes more time for his toilette than the
most elegant Parisian belle.*

Maximilian, Prince of Wied-Neuwied, 1834

THE VERY BASIS OF RANK differentiation was success in war, and all able Plains males above the age of fifteen or sixteen strove towards the achievement of military distinction. Warriors of any Plains tribe could broadly be divided into two classes 'the warriors who had arrived and those who had not' (Mishkin, 1940, p. 2). Touching an enemy with the hand or with a harmless 'coup stick', the taking of a horse, gun or scalp, were all counted as deeds of honour but a hierarchy of distinction was also made within the ranking group: some deeds were much more highly regarded than others and the methods of recording them differed. Thus the credit-bearing deeds of the Kiowa, for example, may be classified roughly into three groups, each deed having more or less equal value within the group:

Group I
1 Counting first coup.
2 Charging the enemy while party is in retreat, thereby covering retreat.
3 Rescuing a comrade while party is retreating before a charging enemy.
4 Charging the leading man of the enemy alone before the parties have met (which was tantamount to suicide).

Group II
5 Killing enemy.
6 Counting second coup.
7 Receiving wound in an honourable action (hand-to-hand combat).

Group III
8 Dismounting, turning pony loose and fighting on foot.
9 Counting third and fourth coup.
10 Frequent service as a *toyopki* (a war party leader).
11 Success in stealing horses.
12 Efficiency in war camp life (obeying orders, good scouting, etc.).
(Adapted from Mishkin, 1940, p. 39).

The three groups have been listed in order of the degree of honour they confer. A similar listing may be cited for the Omaha where six grades of honour could be counted on the body of an enemy:

1 The highest honour was to strike an unwounded enemy with the hand or bow.
2 Striking a wounded enemy.
3 Striking with the hand or bow the body of a dead enemy.
4 To kill an enemy.
5 To take a scalp. (This honour ranked with number 3, since the dead man could not resist, although the friends of the slain might rally around the body and strive to prevent the act by carrying it away).
6 To sever the head from the body of an enemy.
(Adapted from Fletcher, 1905–1906, p. 437).

In cases 1, 2, 3 and 5 two persons only could take the same honour from the same enemy.

The sixth grade is of particular interest, for the custom of scalping probably goes back to the days when the entire head of the enemy was commonly taken as a war trophy. The Sioux, a people who of all tribes put much emphasis on the hair fringed war-shirt, cultivated the defiant scalp lock – a kind of 'come and get it if you can' gesture. In haste on the battlefield there was no particular ceremony in taking a scalp; a knife was run around the cranium, a foot placed on the dead warrior's neck and ideally a sudden jerk would take it off. It was not, however, always so easy. Referring to the adventures of a Frenchman one white observer recorded the following tale.

'During one of the earlier skirmishes with

Assiniboin scalp dance, Fort Union, 1853. Military achievements were advertised in the widespread scalp dance. The scalps were displayed on poles and it was a dance in which women could participate. Their rôle was important and usually the wife of the successful warrior carried the scalp as shown here while victory songs were sung. The woman on the right carries a spontoon-type war axe whilst the men are beating small hand drums. The breechclouts worn by the warriors are not actually around the waist, but passed under the legs and hung down front and back over a belt. Since the material was continuous the Indian has drawn it as he knew it to be rather than as it appeared to the observer. After a sketch by an Assiniboin warrior. Smithsonian Institution, Washington.

Scalp Dance.

Apaches he had sighted an Indian hidden in a tree, who, with a rifle which was modern for those days, was doing considerable damage among the dismounted soldiers beating through a bushy ravine. With a lucky shot in the head he killed the Indian. An old trooper stepped up and said "Now, scalp him." The Frenchman, believing this to be routine procedure, with some difficulty loosened the edges of the scalp with his knife, grasped the hair and pulled. To his surprise it clung tenaciously. "Give it a good yank" said his instructor. Heaving with boyish strength, the scalp tore loose, pieces of shattered skull adhering, spattering blood, brains, and matted hair into his wide eyes and gaping mouth. "I never scalped another Indian," he said!' (Smith, 1949, p. 250).

Early accounts of Blackfoot warfare even before the introduction of the gun or horse clearly indicate that the scalp 'was regarded as a very valuable war trophy' (Ewers, 1955, p. 213). To most tribes the hair of a person was believed to have vital connection with the life of the body. Upon the scalp lock the war honours of a warrior were worn and its taking was considered a great triumph. Thus returning war parties who had taken scalps would prepare them at their final camp before entering the village. 'They selected a man who had dreamed of a carnivorous animal which attacks human beings, if such a man were in the party. This man scraped the flesh from the inside of the scalp, and having mixed the fat from it with gun-powder, rubbed it on his face and hands. He did this because of his dream of an animal that devours human beings. Then, making a little hoop, he sewed the scalp inside it and fastened it at the end of a pole.' (Information from Eagle Shield in Densmore, 1918, p. 360).

In 1833 Maximilian observed the return of a successful Blackfoot war party who had taken scalps. 'When the warriors come near their camp, after a battle, they sing, and one rides or runs before, often in serpentine lines, backwards and forwards about the tents, holding up and shaking the scalp, and displaying it at a distance. If any one has taken a weapon, he displays it in the same manner, loudly proclaiming his name as having taken it. After a successful engagement, the men sing a song which they call *aninay*, that is "they are painted black".' (Maximilian, Vol. 23, 1906, p. 119).

Military achievements were widely advertised by the successful warrior. At the victory dance, at society meetings, or during the annual Sun Dance each garnished his deed to give it a personal flavour – modesty had little place in war honours; the final outcome of which was to give each warrior a definite and undisputed rating in the hierarchy of rank. The victory or scalp dance was widely popular and the prepared scalps were put on prominent display. The men and women danced and sang their victory songs, frequently taunting and boasting in character. 'Each pole (with a scalp attached) is borne by a squaw, usually a relative

Sioux scalp taken by an Omaha, 1840. The scalp is stretched on a hoop, decorated with webbing, and probably has religious significance. Although the hoop is more associated with the western Sioux, where it was a symbol of the Great Mystery, the concept of the circle as symbolic of continuity was widespread. Unlike customs found in other areas in North America, there were none associated with the removal of any curse connected with the scalp on the Great Plains. The main emphasis was on a display of triumph.
Paul Dyck Foundation.

of the warrior who took it, who leads in the dance, the warriors and squaws all arrayed in their best attire following her in a circle of a size proportioned to the number of dancers. The step of the dance is little more than a march in quick time, to the music of a song peculiar to the dance. Where the number of dancers is considerable several rings are formed in different parts of the tent and the dance is frequently kept up with intervals of rest for twelve or fourteen days.' (Bradley, 1923, pp. 269–270).

The Omaha had a special ceremony, the *Wate' gictu*, ('the gathering together of facts accomplished') where war deeds were solemnized (Fletcher & La Flesche, 1905–1906, p. 434). Here the keepers of the four Packs Sacred to War reminded the men to state the truth, for the bird messengers contained within the packs would report their deeds to Thunder, the god of war. For each of the honours he was to claim a warrior painted a small stick red which, when called upon to recite his deed, he held above the Pack of War. At a given signal he dropped the stick onto the pack; if the deed had been disputed or the stick fell to the ground it was believed that the man had not spoken honestly 'and the man lost the honour he had sought to gain'.

Sun Dance Ceremony; torture at the pole and dragging buffalo skulls. Sioux pictograph by Jaw about 1910. Two warriors at the left dance with right hands raised in prayer towards the Sun Dance pole; another is overcome by the ordeal of dragging buffalo skulls attached by thongs through the flesh of the back (on the right). Another warrior is attached to the pole by means of cords fastened to wooden skewers thrust through the skin of the chest invoking the higher powers to observe that he is fulfilling his vow. 'I will give my flesh that I may conquer my enemies!' The wearing of warbonnets is unusual and these have probably been added by Jaw to give effect. Note the buffalo and human figures attached to the pole.

At the large summer camps when the bands came together after the winter sojourn, warriors who on recent war expeditions had 'made the vow' were expected to actively participate in the Sun Dance ceremony. This involvement could take a number of forms. When *Tatan'ka-iyo'take* – Sitting Bull – fulfilled his Sun Dance vow in the early summer of 1876 he gave one hundred pieces of flesh to *Wakan Tanka*. Jumping Bull, who had agreed to do the cutting, used an awl which he stuck into the skin to lift it clear of the flesh and then with a very sharp knife 'ground down to a thin narrow blade' (Vestal, 1957, p. 149) he proceeded to cut fifty small pieces of skin from Sitting Bull's right arm working upwards from near the wrist. He did the same with the left arm and within a short time of commencing the operation – which took half an hour – Sitting Bull's arms were covered with blood. 'Sitting Bull remained perfectly still, he was wailing all the time – not because of pain – but for mercy to *Wakan Tanka*, the Great Mysterious.... Sitting Bull sat there, wailing never wincing, while the endless piercing, endless cutting went on, cruel and sharp over and over' (Vestal, 1957, p. 150).

It was while acting out his Sun Dance vow that Sitting Bull had his famous vision – predicting the complete annihilation of Custer and his two hundred odd officers and men on the 'Greasy Grass' of the Sioux, better known to the white man as the Little Big Horn (but that is a tale for another time – see Chapter 7, 'The Dispossessed'). When Sitting Bull carried out that Sun Dance vow he was about forty-two years old. It was a most severe ordeal for a man of his age and the Sioux recognized that Sitting Bull was offering to *Wakan Tanka* the only thing, his body, that really belonged to him. Lesser men might offer material gifts – a horse, tobacco or a pipe – but comparatively few gave part of their bodies as was demanded in the more exacting rituals of the Sun Dance.

The Sun Dance ordeal could take other forms. George Dorsey, who made a detailed study of the ceremonial amongst the Cheyenne recorded a warrior dragging a buffalo skull fastened to the flesh of the back and arms. Others would be attached to the Sun Dance pole by means of cords fastened to wooden skewers thrust through the skin of the chest and in extreme cases piercing the pectoral muscles; the length of the cords might be such that only the participants' toes could touch the ground. Each man attempted to free himself as quickly as possible and those tied to the centre pole each held an eagle bone whistle on which they blew as they danced with a rhythmic raising and lowering of the body on the ball of the foot staying on the same spot but slowly rotating so as to continually face the sun. Still others might be entirely suspended just as in the Mandan O-kee-pa ceremony.

There was considerable room for individual variation although not strictly concerned with the Sun Dance ceremony itself. Thus some successful warriors might carry their bridles and whips which they had taken on the warpath, these now attached to the flesh of the arm as they danced. The extension of the flesh under the above conditions was astonishing. Lieutenant Henry E. Maynadier, who described similar torture ceremonies amongst the Mandan in the 1860s remarked, 'I was amazed to see how far the skin would stretch, pulling out a distance of 12 or 15 inches' (Reynold, 1868, p. 150). Personal observations at the Oglala Sun Dance at Pine Ridge, South Dakota in the summer of 1966 in part confirmed Maynadier's description although the piercing was slight in comparison to the earlier severe ordeals. When the cord was under tension the skin of the dancer's chest stretched at least some five or six inches.

All Sun Dance participants were painted. After the customary 'sweat bath' which warriors took prior to their ordeal, selected men painted the warriors; amongst the Cheyenne the painting was uniform for most of the dancers, there being a prescribed form of painting on each of the four days of the ceremony. The designs were highly symbolic of the earth and growth, or represented the roads of prayer 'Go to my heart and make me strong'. (Dorsey, 1905, p. 171).

The Plains warrior devoted his best efforts to displaying his heroic deeds by a complex system of heraldry. It is difficult to generalize for the whole Plains area but the use of feather insignia was widespread. Although many types of feather were used as decoration, eagle feathers were the most coveted. Bald or spotted eagle tail-feathers were seldom used. Tradition had it that only those from the tail of the young golden eagle (*Aquila heliaca*) must be used for war honours. Such feathers, perhaps fourteen or fifteen inches long and three inches or so in width, were white with dark brown or black tips. Little wonder that they were chosen – not only was the 'war' eagle a magnificent and brave bird but combined with ermine, red horsehair tips, brightly coloured porcupine quills or beads they made a striking effect. Such feathers were costly and difficult to come by. The bird was too fierce to domesticate by a nomadic people so it was generally trapped, certain men specializing in the procuring of the feathers for others – at a price. In the mid-19th century, fifteen feathers would cost a horse and 'two tails of the war eagle of 12 feathers each would be worth two horses if wrought into a cap, or something more than a horse without'. (Denig, 1930, p. 589).

The Omaha called war honour decorations *u'kion* (from *kion* 'to decorate oneself by painting

Rawhide cut-outs attached to Sun Dance pole. Sioux 1881. The Sun Dance was rich in symbolism and lasted four days. Recognition was given not only to the powers of the Sun but also to the earth, sky, thunder, stars and mother earth. The four cardinal directions and the symbolism of war and the buffalo were recognized in the rituals involving painting, song and dance. These effigies were collected by the ethnologist Alice Fletcher at the last great Sun Dance held by the Sioux at Pine Ridge, South Dakota, in 1881. (Note that the penis has been rejoined to the body. It was cut off by an embarrassed Indian who passed these effigies on to Alice Fletcher at her request after the dance. She demanded and got the penis back, and Agent McGillycuddy effected the repair). Peabody Museum, Harvard University.

or by wearing regalia or garments'). A feather worn erect at the back of the head indicated a war honour of the first grade while among the Sioux it was worn horizontally to represent the same deed. Worn erect by these people it signified that the warrior had killed an enemy without injury to himself. Hanging from the scalp-lock it signified amongst the Omaha the striking of a dead enemy (an honour of the third grade). The Hidatsa, observed in 1881, designated some war achievements by painting the feather; thus an eagle feather bearing two red bars signified that the wearer was the second person to count coup on a fallen enemy, while a red feather denoted a wound received in battle (Mallery, 1888–1889, p. 437).

Rites in the Cheyenne Sun Dance. The Sun Dance – a powerful and important ritual which gave unity to The People – was inevitably resented and feared by ninteenth-century missionaries, Bureau of Indian Affairs Officials and the Army. Finally in 1884, the Interior Department produced a criminal code forbidding Indian religious practices and established severe penalties. The rituals were still carried out, however, and in some instances witnessed by understanding white men. This photograph was taken early one morning in a Cheyenne camp at the turn of the century. Field Museum of Natural History, Chicago.

Coup feather symbolism was most highly developed by the Siouan speaking tribes such as the Sioux, Hidatsa, Mandan, Crow and Omaha. It was predominantly a north-eastern and central Plains trait but as the examples quoted above indicate, interpretation of meaning was by no means uniform. However, in general these were the people who traditionally used one of the best known of

Heroic exploits were displayed by use of a complex system of feather heraldry of which warbonnets were the most sophisticated style of headgear. It is difficult to generalize but such regalia shown here could only be worn by distinguished warriors. In general amongst Siouan-speaking groups each feather did represent a deed of honour–but not necessarily that of the wearer; rather it was a recognition of the best warrior and an acknowledgment of the interdependence of men. The straight-up style headdress was more common amongst the Blackfoot and came to be associated with Horn Society regalia; however, it was not worn exclusively by men of that Society. The two trailer bonnets are Sioux. The one shown on the left is a simple early style. It dates from about 1850 and is at the Pitt Rivers Museum, Oxford. The one shown right belonged to the Oglala Sioux Cinte Mazza or Iron Tail who was a companion of Buffalo Bill for many years. It is now in the author's collection. Drawn by Edward H. Blackmore.

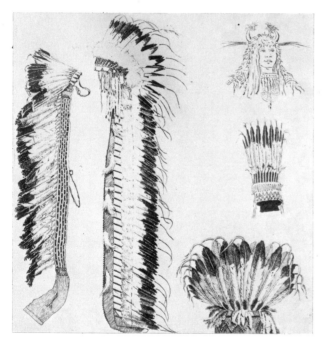

all headdresses – the eagle-feather warbonnet. It is not surprising, therefore, to learn that the flaring warbonnet had very limited use prior to 1850. More popular and with wider distribution in early days was the horned bonnet (Taylor, 1962, p. 7). The German traveller Maximilian described the appearance and the *function* of such a bonnet. 'They likewise wear the large horned feather-cap, this is a cap consisting of strips of white ermine, with pieces of red cloth hanging down behind as far as the calves of the legs, to which is attached an upright row of black and white eagle's feathers beginning at the head and reaching the whole length. *Only distinguished warriors who have performed many exploits may wear this headdress.*' (Maximilian, Vol. 23, 1906, p. 25a). While Maximilian specifically refers to the horned bonnet his statement of the significance of the headdress could equally apply to the Sioux style warbonnet.

The large number of brave exploits which each feather in a warbonnet represented were not necessarily those performed by the wearer. Rather the feathers represented the sum total of the feats of arms performed by the followers of a proven war leader. It was a recognition of the best warrior and an acknowledgment of the interdependence of men.

Traditionally, a man who desired to wear a warbonnet and had obtained the consent of the leading men prepared a feast to which he invited members of the warrior fraternity. As the feathers were prepared and handed to the maker of the warbonnet for lacing into place a warrior recited the honour which the feather was to represent. Warbonnets might contain up to sixty or more eagle feathers – the warbonnet which once belonged to the Oglala warrior Cinte Muzza (Iron Tail), in my collection, contains 64 feathers, 28 in the crown and 36 in the long tail – thus the ceremony of making it could have taken many days.

The Blackfoot traditionally wore another style of bonnet in which the feathers were set rigidly into a simple headband. Such headdresses were simpler in construction than the Sioux-style bonnet where the feathers were free to move, and without doubt they were older – the simple headband having wide distribution in North America.

Tradition states that this style of headdress amongst the Blackfoot originated as regalia of the Bull society and several versions of the origin myth for this society mentioned the acquisition of the straight-up bonnet from the buffalo. They were not however exclusively worn by members of the society – some privileged men made and wore them according to instructions obtained in dreams or visions. In battle it was considered a very brave thing to wear the straight-up headdress 'as it made the wearer exceptionally conspicuous and a likely target for enemy fire'. However, some Plateau tribes did prefer them to the Sioux style 'because they were best for windy weather and for riding' (Taylor, 1962, p. 5).

The decorated buckskin shirt was likewise a sign of rank. It could, in early days, only be worn by men of distinction. Amongst the Sioux there was a tradition of the 'shirt wearer' probably relating to the time when heavy buckskin armour was worn by warriors. Traditionally these were fringed with hair and contrary to popular belief the hair was usually donated by relatives rather than cut from scalps. In addition, the true war-shirt was decorated with quilled or beaded bands across the shoulders and down the arms, often highly diagnostic of tribal origin, and on northern costume – that of the Blackfoot and Assiniboin especially – there would be additional decoration in the form of rectangular or circular quilled units.

The Crow were particularly strict in the usage of the decorative bands. William Wildschut, who did a great deal of research work amongst these people in the early years of this century, was told that a man who struck the enemy first was entitled

Sioux warshirt, about 1850. The shirt is painted with the deeds of valour of the original owner. The warriors on horseback are not riding side-saddle, rather it is a depiction of what the artist knew was there rather than what the eye actually perceived. At least one of the enemy is Crow or Hidatsa – note the distinctive hair ornament worn by the central pedestrian warrior who is being speared by the feathered lance. The tracks painted on the left-hand arm probably represent horses captured from the enemy. Musée de l'Homme, Paris.

to wear a war shirt; this could only be decorated with the quilled or beaded arm and shoulder strips when the owner had earned the right by virtue of striking an enemy, thus it was a mark of distinction to which only a few were entitled. Since the end of intertribal wars another way was found whereby young people could gain the privilege of wearing such a garment.

'A number of young Crow, led by an older man, offer a visiting Indian of a different tribe many presents to induce him to act as an enemy. This "enemy" is given a good horse and starts out from camp in the evening. Next morning before dawn the Crow start out on the trail of this "enemy". The Crow who manages to overtake him and strike the first coup is entitled to wear the honors formerly earned by this act in actual combat. Four times, and on different occasions, this young man must strike the first coup, which is usually done by hitting the "enemy" lightly with a stick or with the hand, before he is entitled to wear the decorated war-shirt. This is the reason why they are valued very highly by the Crow and are scarcer among them than among other Plains Indians.' (Wildschut, 1960, p. 38).

Warriors frequently decorated their costume with painted figures, symbolic of success in warfare. Thus triangular-shaped figures terminating in a knob are often to be seen on early Blackfoot shirts which according to Maximilian represented whips indicating the number of horses given as gifts – the sign of a successful horse raider. A shirt decorated with figures of guns might represent the number taken in battle, with pipes the number of

war expeditions led and with the red hand – a widely-used symbol painted on the horse, the body or shirt – that the enemy had been slain. Scalps might be neatly decorated with beadwork and attached to costume, as on the shirt of the Crow warrior The Wet. The author Clare Sheridan collected two such scalps in 1937 from the Blackfoot warrior Crazy Crow, he had taken them from Crow and Kootenay enemies in the days of his youth.

A favourite place which Blackfoot warriors used for graphic recording of their war deeds was on the lining inside their tipis, the 'dew Cloth' already referred to in Chapter I.

A painted lining of a lodge which formerly belonged to the Blackfoot warrior, Red Crane, was described by the eminent anthropologist Dr George Bird Grinnell in 1895. It is a fine example of Blackfoot picture writing, although lacking the aesthetic quality of the realistic figures painted by Sioux, Kiowa, Cheyenne and Mandan contemporaries. However, it does adequately serve to tell others who were familiar with pictographic art just what Red Crane's claims to distinction were. According to Red Crane the dotted lines which run irregularly through the cut represent his tracks as he travelled about over the country. On one occasion he started out with a gun and soon shot an elk; then he went on farther and met an enemy, armed only with a bow and arrow, whom he killed.

Motifs on a Sioux pipe bag, c. 1875. This close-up of the panel on a Sioux pipe bag shows a realistic figure worked in beadwork of the owner of the bag riding into battle. Traditionally the shield and bow were carried on the left and this side is presented to the enemy. The tail of the warbonnet thus generally hung on the left as shown here. A scalp hangs from the bridle and the warrior carries a sword which is worked in tiny metal beads. The crosses on the bag may signify the deed of rescuing a friend under enemy fire or may represent the dragon fly a symbol of protective power.

A little farther along three scalps, with a hand painted at the corner of each one, show his success on his war journey, while later he took a gun, three more scalps and a mule. Almost at the centre of the lining stands a horse tied by the fore-leg to a peg in front of a lodge; he cut this animal loose and rode it away. In another place a picture tells of the day when Red Crane, with six companions, was surrounded by his enemies in a patch of brush. The two charging grizzly bears call up dangers to which he was exposed while hunting, and the figure of the eagle recalls some peculiar experience that he had while catching these birds. Other strange adventures, in which a beaver, a squirrel, a fisher and an otter had some part are also shown. Grinnell commented 'this is, in fact, a primitive manuscript, a diary or note book which served to keep fresh in its writer's mind the events of his whole life. The size of the skin was five by seven feet.' (Adapted from Grinnell, 1895, p. 244). It is interesting to note the curious 'button-hook' drawn for a hoof on all the horses shown on this pictographic record. A moment's reflection tells that this in fact is not a hoof but a hoof-print. Plains Indians employed this method of identification for animals – the track of a bird or animal. In the case of the single-toed horse – an oddity in itself – it is the hoof *print* not the hoof which is sketched so as to identify beyond question the animal drawn and the Blackfoot continued to employ this notation long after most of the other tribes had abandoned it.

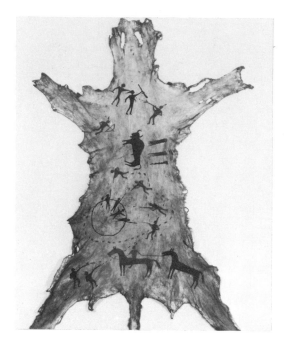

Hide decorated with war and hunting exploits. Sarsi Indian. The Sarsi were a small tribe associated with the Blackfoot. Judging from this specimen their artwork was similar to that of the Blackfoot, lacking the realistic forms which the more southern tribes – such as the Sioux, Mandan, Hidatsa, Kiowa and Cheyenne developed possibly after contact with white artists. The figures probably represent a successful war expedition where horses were captured, and some enemy killed and scalped. Although guns are obviously carried, one scene shows the hunting of a buffalo with a bow and arrow which probably occurred on an expedition where stealth would be of prime importance. Rymill Collection. University Museum of Archaeology and Ethnology, Cambridge.

Blackfoot warrior. Brulé Flats, Fort McKenzie, about 1833. Here the war exploits painted on a buffalo robe are clearly shown. The painted guns and bows are probably significant weapons captured in battle while the triangular waisted figures represent enemy warriors slain; the hoofs, tracks to the enemy, and the triangular figures within the circle horses proffered as gifts. The warrior carries a long pipe with the typical Blackfoot acorn shape. From a lithograph by Carl Bodmer in Maximilian's *Atlas*. British Museum.

Buffalo robes were the chief article for everyday dress for most Plains warriors. Nearly thirty years after Lewis and Clark's memorable trip, Maximilian observed of the Blackfoot '[Their] large buffalo robe, is, for the most part, painted on the tanned side, but less skillfully than among other nations. In general, there are black parallel lines mixed with a few figures, often with arrow heads, or other bad arabesques; others, again, are painted with representations of their warlike exploits, in black, red, green, and yellow. The figures represent the taking of prisoners, dead or wounded enemies, captured arms and horses, blood, balls flying about in the air, and such subjects. Such robes are embroidered with transverse bands of porcupine quills of the most brilliant colours, divided into two equal parts by a round rosette of the same. The ground of the skin is often reddish-brown, and the figures on it black. All the Missouri Indians wear these robes, and it is well known that those of the Minitaries and the Crow are most beautifully worked and painted.' (Maximilian, Vol. 23, 1906, p. 102).

At the same time however some Mandan art work had become considerably more sophisticated probably due to the influence of white artists – particularly Catlin and Bodmer.

Combining his new-found skill with established tradition the Mandan chief, Mato-tope, emblazoned his personal buffalo robe with highly symbolic hieroglyphics relating his outstanding war

The Silk Robe. From a painting by Charles M. Russell, 1890. The scene shows two women hard at work on a fine buffalo hide which they will dress to a velvet-soft texture. The work of defleshing the hide is obviously over – the tools which they are using being those for removing fur or reducing the hide to an even thickness are made from elk horn. Two warriors look on, no doubt discussing the war exploits with which the robe will be finally decorated. This is a good study of an Indian camp scene. The tipi cover on the left has been raised to facilitate air circulation, revealing a willow stick back-rest and a saddle – probably a woman's to judge from the high pommel and cantle. Resting on a tripod, produced by using a travois, is the warrior's shield together with his medicine bundle. Amon Carter Museum, Fort Worth, Texas.

exploits. Although Four Bears was second chief of the Mandan, his superior Wolf Chief was, according to George Catlin who stayed with the Mandan during the summer of 1832, 'a haughty austere, and overbearing man, respected and feared by his people rather than loved'. By comparison Mato-tope was 'free, generous, elegant and gentlemanly' and undoubtedly the first and most popular man in the nation. In a society where successful military prowess was so coveted, it was Mato-tope's outstanding success in battle against hostile bands of Assiniboin, Cheyenne and Arikara which put him high in the social rank of his tribe and it appears that he was unsurpassed in this field. 'Four Bears himself, though of slight build and medium stature, claimed to have killed five enemy chiefs and to have taken 14 scalps.' Upon his return from a coup counting session in the other Mandan village of Ruhptare in January 1834, Four Bears told his white friends 'with great satisfaction and self complacency that he had enumerated all his exploits, and that no one had been able to surpass him' (Ewers, 1957, pp. 5 & 6).

Mato-tope personally presented to both Catlin and Maximilian his handsomely painted robes and at least one other to an unknown collector shortly afterwards. Even in those early days a chief who coveted fame was well aware of the great advantage of the publicity which could be gained by presenting his painted robes to distinguished white travellers 'especially those intending to write books' (Smith, 1949, p. 174).

Fortunately for ethnology George Catlin spent a considerable amount of time with Mato-tope documenting each outstanding exploit, recording 'such are the battles traced upon the robe of Mato-tope or Four Bears, interpreted by J. Kipp from the words of the hero while sitting upon the robe, explaining each battle as represented' (Catlin, Vol. 1, 1841, p. 154).

These explanations are published at length in Catlin's volume and may be followed by reference to the robe which is now in Berne, Switzerland. One particular exploit which was recorded by both Catlin and Maximilian concerned a battle between Mato-tope and a Cheyenne chief. Maximilian explains, 'He had killed many enemies, among whom were five chiefs. He gives a facsimile of a representation of one of his exploits, painted by himself, of which he frequently gave me an account. He was, on that occasion, on foot, on a military expedition, with a few Mandan, when they encountered four Cheyenne, their most virulent foes, on horseback. The chief of the latter, seeing that their enemies were on foot, and that the combat would thereby be unequal, dismounted, and the two parties attacked each other. The two chiefs fired, missed, threw away their guns, and seized their naked weapons; the Cheyenne, a tall, powerful man, drew his while Mato-tope, who was lighter and more agile, took his battle axe. The former attempted to stab Mato-tope, who laid hold of the blade of the knife, by which he, indeed, wounded his hand, but wrested the weapon from his enemy, and stabbed him with it, on which the Cheyenne took to flight.'

Catlin related the same exploit and although it differs in details the two accounts are substantially the same. Mato-tope's rendering of that particular battle appears on all three of the war-exploit robes known to have been painted by this famous chieftain. The guns are shown which had been discharged and then thrown aside, the footsteps of the two warriors with wolf-tails at their heels – a distinguished mark of success in battle – while the Cheyenne is clearly identified by the otter skin headdress and blood is shown flowing from the wounded Mandan chief's hand. So proud was Mato-tope of this particular exploit that he henceforth wore a carved wooden knife on both his magnificent horned headdress and also within his exploit feathers. This knife is clearly shown both in Carl Bodmer's detailed paintings of this chief which he did at Mi-ti-was-kos – the principal Mandan village – in 1834 and Catlin's portrait of the chief executed in the same village two years previously. Maximilian briefly referred to this symbolic wooden knife when he wrote 'the wooden knife painted red and fastened transversely in his hair indicates that he had killed a Cheyenne chief with this knife' (Maximilian, 1843, p. 399). This knife was collected by Maximilian together with six other highly symbolic hair ornaments. The knife itself, as Maximilian accurately described, is painted red, evidently with flat water paint. It is just over 195mm long; just below the handle is a perforation through which a buckskin thong has been passed to facilitate attachment to the head. The hair ornaments are also referred to by Maximilian: 'the six wooden sticks, painted red, blue and yellow with a brass stud at one end indicates the number of musket wounds which he had received' (Maximilian, 1843, p. 339). Since these were of considerable importance to Mato-tope they probably refer to the battle with the Assiniboin where Mato-tope first received his name 'Several hundred Minatarees (evidently Hidatsas) and Mandan attacked by a party of Assiniboin – all fled but Mah-to-toh-pa, who stood his ground, fired, and killed one of the enemy, putting the rest of them to flight and driving off sixty horses . . . here he got the name of "the four bears", as the Assiniboin said he rushed on like four bears.' (Catlin, Vol. 1, 1841, p. 154). The robe shown on page 48 shows at least two exploits where musket bullets are depicted by a line terminated by a dot, whilst Catlin in his detailed facsimiles shows still more. These exploit sticks are approximately 230mm in length and carefully whittled to a slim point, the thickest end being about 8mm in diameter. About halfway down is an interesting effect produced by shaving the body of the stick and allowing the free ends to curve and bunch around the main stem. The significance of this is open to conjecture but could it possibly be meant to represent the puff of smoke so characteristic of old time muskets? Driven in the butt end are small brass tacks just as Maximilian described them.

The wood from which the exploit knife is carved is both soft and light and possibly cedar; could this have an even deeper significance, considering that the symbol of the Ark of the First Man (see Chapter I) was also both made of cedar and painted red? This we shall probably never know for certain.

We can however be more positive about the subsequent fate of Mato-tope. Sadly, it was through the very people whose friendship Mato-tope so encouraged that this stout-hearted warrior died – from the white man's smallpox at the age of fifty-three on 30 July 1837, cursing the day the white man first set foot in the Mandan villages just under a century before (from Taylor, 1973, p. 43).

Badges of honour as worn by Mato-tope were by no means a unique custom, although the object and its interpretation was frequently highly individualistic. Mow-way, a great Comanche war-chief, commonly wore a large grizzly bear claw tied to his scalplock to commemorate a personal encounter with a huge grizzly which he subsequently killed with his knife (Nye, 1968, p. 298). Sitting Bull, that great spiritual leader of the Teton Sioux, generally wore a bunch of shed buffalo hair painted red, fastened on the side of his head. To the Sioux in general shed buffalo hair was said to 'signify the times when buffalo were plenty and also a remembrance of the coming of the White Buffalo Maiden' (Densmore, 1918, p. 458). While no exact interpretation of his hair ornament was ever obtained from Sitting Bull, it must be remembered that in earlier days he had been a great warrior, had opposed the encroachment of the white man and was deeply distressed at confinement on a reservation – the hair ornament was probably his way of showing grief for the passing of the old ways.

Kicking Bear, one of the leading men in the

Mato-tope in war regalia. January, 1834. The painted buffalo robe of this outstanding warrior is shown in the colour plate. The decorated feathers which he wears in his hair symbolize warlike deeds. An arrow wound is signified by the wing feathers of a wild turkey, and at the back of his head is a large bunch of owl feathers dyed yellow with red tips, indicating membership of the Dog Society. The knife, which is carved from wood and tied to his hair, symbolises a particularly bloody encounter with a Cheyenne chief, and the painted sticks musket wounds received in battle. His left hand is painted yellow, to show that he has captured prisoners. From the original water colour by Carl Bodmer. Joslyn Art Museum, Omaha, Nebraska.

Sioux exploit robe, 1830. This robe formerly belonged to the Yankton Sioux Monka-ush-ka who took it to Washington in 1837. On the robe are over forty pedestrian and a dozen or so equestrian warriors shown in various phases and modes of Plains Indian warfare. We can positively identify some of the enemies as Crow by the manner of their hairstyles; others are more difficult but they are probably Mandan and Hidatsa. Many are armed with guns and carry their powder and ball in a horn flask and buckskin pouch of a style popular with the Crow and their brethren the Hidatsa. The leader (possibly Monka-ush-ka himself) is identified by a pipe—note the equestrian warrior near the top at the left and also the figure wearing the headdress lower right. A number of the enemy have obviously been slain with a sword. Musée de l'Homme, Paris.

Ghost Dance religion of 1890, commonly wore a cross within a circle painted in kaolin on the left hand side of his hair. According to Kicking Bear it was a heraldic device signifying that he had rescued a friend under enemy fire.

Almost contemporary with Mato-tope's robes is a fine example from the Yankton Sioux. This was once the property of Monka-ush-ka, who travelled to Washington in 1837 as a representative of his nation, dying under tragic circumstances at Baltimore before he could return to the Plains country. Monka-ush-ka's portrait was painted by the artist, George Cooke. It shows a fine warrior complete with exploit feathers and wearing a handsome quilled shirt.

A detailed analysis of the figures on robes painted by Plains warriors enables us to deduce a great deal about early Plains Indian ethnology particularly in the area of warfare. A robe in the British Museum undoubtedly painted before 1850 is a good example of this. The warrior wearing the feathered headdress – the owner of the robe – wears a breechcloth of trade cloth exhibiting a selvedge edge, he counts coup on his adversary by means of his society rattle decorated with portions of deer-hooves and wears a feather-decorated sash – perhaps a 'no-retreat' pendant worn only by the bravest warriors (see Chapter III). His opponent is probably a Crow, note the distinctive hairstyle. This man is also breechclothed, carries a quiver of arrows and owns a short bow. The successful warrior's track towards his enemy is also indicated and around his neck he carries a personal talisman in the form of what appears to be a claw or horn.

Not only can painted robes be sources of ethnographical details but it has been suggested that a variant of the warriors' exploit robe – the *Wani yetu iyáwa* (Sioux) or 'winter count' could be a source of Plains Indian history. Several of the Plains tribes developed the custom but it was probably first used by a creative Yanktonai warrior in 1871 and subsequently copied by fellow tribesmen.

The war record of Running Antelope (Ta-to-ki-un-ki) one of the four chiefs recognized by the Hunkpapa at the Fort Laramie treaty of 1851, was studied in detail by Garrick Mallery in the late 19th century. Running Antelope was an outstanding chief of the Hunkpapa Sioux, and it was he who helped escort Father Pierre Jean De Smet, the Jesuit missionary, to the 'hostile' Sioux camps on the Powder River in May 1868 and who presided over the subsequent council. Being an older man than Sitting Bull, he settled early on the Standing Rock Reservation, and rather like Red Cloud in the 1880s sought peace in his twilight years. It was he who pleaded with Sitting Bull to make amends with a United States Government Commission who travelled to the western reservations in 1883 to investigate the condition of the Indian tribes of

Mato-tope in ceremonial regalia, Fort Clark, 1834. From the original engraving by Carl Bodmer in Maximilian's *Travels*, 1843. Smithsonian Institution, Bureau of American Ethnology.

Montana and Dakota. At that time Sitting Bull had just been released from Fort Randall after his surrender at Fort Buford on 19 July 1881. It was the aged Running Antelope who was concerned with the everyday problems at Standing Rock, and his camp down near the Grand River, now the township of Little Eagle, was a favourite meeting-place for tribal gatherings.

To judge from his exploits, starting as early as 1853, the war record of Ta-to-ki-un-ki is impressive and eclipses that of Mato-tope the Mandan chief of a generation before. It must however be borne in mind that either customs were different from one tribe to the next or had changed in the half-century or so which separated the completion of the counts. It is certain that the exploits enumerated by Running Antelope were, as has been discussed earlier, not only those which he himself had personally performed but those of his followers as well – a well established and perfectly legitimate custom, not unlike that of Generals in our modern armies who gain the major credit for victorious combat.

In 1856 he led a war-party against the Crow and he and his followers annihilated ten men and three squaws; in the same year he killed two – probably also Crow – chiefs. A distinguishing feature of the Crow was the pompadour hair cut and this is used to identify them tribally in Running Antelope's pictographs.

Although Sitting Bull's hieroglyphic autobiography suggests to the uninitiated that he had performed sixty-three warlike exploits before 1870 when he was interviewed under guard at Fort Yates on 1 August 1881 (pending his transfer down river to Fort Randall for two years confinement), he described raids upon enemy tribes and said that he had 'stolen horses 22 times' and that he had personally killed 16 enemies but had 'never killed a white man'. One of his pictographs now preserved at the Smithsonian Institution shows him chasing a mounted white man in a fringed buckskin coat and shooting him between the shoulders. His biographer, Stanley Vestal, comments 'this was Sitting Bull's first white victim' (Vestal, 1957, p. 318). That in fact is probably an erroneous statement and critics of the day all used such incorrect evidence against him.

Although Sitting Bull's military record against enemy tribes was better than most – it had to be for the very fabric of the culture to which he belonged pivoted on the war game – to a discerning far-sighted man such as Sitting Bull the personal killing of a white man was another matter. In fact the deed portrayed was performed by Shonka Ku'-tei-ye-ha – better known to whites as Low Dog. Low Dog was a member of Sitting Bull's band and it was both the leader's privilege and duty to publicize the war exploits of his followers in this way. The name of the white man was Mac-Donald, who acted as mail carrier between Forts Totten and Stevenson (Dakota Territory) and he was killed on 15 May 1868. The artist De Cost

Smith relates an interesting story referring to this particular incident. The fringed buckskin coat shown in the pictograph came into his possession via Low Dog but it was not until years later that he deduced that it had originally belonged to MacDonald. On close examination he discovered unmistakable bloodstains under the otter fur border and patches on the left front and back beneath the fringes where the bullet fired by Low Dog had found its mark.

One of the most outstanding deeds Sitting Bull ever performed and one which the old-timers frequently related was the celebrated battle between him and a Crow chief. That battle made its life mark on Sitting Bull in more ways than one, for not only did it establish his reputation as an outstanding warrior – he was afterwards invited by the Midnight Strong Hearts, the cream of the Strong Heart military society, to become their leader – but he was severely wounded in the left foot which for the rest of his thirty-four years of life caused him to walk with a perceptible limp. The event is also well worth relating for it tells us much of the lone-hand warfare so typical of the warriors of the Plains and is reminiscent of the deed of valour performed by that other incompatible warrior of another generation, Four Bears of the Nuitadi Mandan.

It was the winter of 1856 when *Wapáha Wan Yuksápi* ('the warbonnet was torn'). The Hunkpapa were short of horses so they decided to steal some from their wealthy enemies the Crow. Thus, according to the Sioux version, over one hundred warriors went on this quest for *shonka wakan*. Most were on foot, they carried lariats and empty saddle pads 'which could be stuffed with grass when they had captured ponies'. Locating a Crow village on Porcupine Creek north of the Yellowstone River, they drove off a great herd of horses under cover of darkness. At dawn the loss was discovered by the Crow who soon caught the slow moving body of horses and men. 'All at once the skyline sprouted lances, tossing like long grass blades against the sky, then black and white warbonnets, the heads of horses, naked, painted warriors. They rushed over the brow of the hill like water through a spillway. The charge was on. Here they came, slapping their open mouths to make the pulsating terrible war cry. "Yip, yip, yi-ip!" they yelled. And puffed through loosely closed lips, like an angry buffalo: "Ploo! Ploo!"' (Vestal, 1957, p. 28).

Three Crow leaders came on ahead of the main body, who had halted when they saw the Sioux make their stand. One charged in amongst the Sioux, counted two coups and turned to get away. It was then that Loud Bear 'snatched the man's warbonnet by its long tail, which came away in his hand' (Vestal, 1957, p. 28). Hence the year designation in the Sioux winter count.

Sitting Bull rode forward to confront one of these daring warriors, he dismounted and called 'Come on, I'll fight you. I am Sitting Bull!' He was

Assiniboin Warrior Naopah. Painted by Carl Bodmer in 1833. He wears a horned headdress which marks him as a warrior of distinction. His shirt is painted with brown stripes representing coups counted in battle. Maximilian's *Atlas*. Museum of Mankind, London.

chief of all those bands – some call them tribes – that made the Teton, the Hunkpapa, Oglala, Minneconjou, Sans Arc, Blackfoot, Brule and Two Kettles, he was one of the ablest leaders they ever produced. That they recognized this is reflected in his name. The buffalo was honoured by all the Plains Indians, he was the most wise, the most powerful and closest to the Great Spirit. A man named for a buffalo bull was rated of high status. The chief's name is rendered Tatánka-iyòtake, strictly the translation is Buffalo-bull-sitting-down but to get a thorough understanding of what the Sioux really meant when they named Sitting Bull it should be rendered 'A Buffalo Bull Resides Permanently Among Us' (Marquis, 1934, p. 8). Such was the warrior leader who faced the on-coming white men, who were to subsequently brand him a coward, a liar, a fraud, even a half-breed Frenchman who wrote poetry; but he was none of these things. Sitting Bull was a pure-blood North American Plains Indian, the epitome of a warrior of the Plains.

Red Feather, Chief of the Sans Arcs, c. 1870 or earlier. It is difficult to be objective about photographs taken in a studio such as this one since the costume may be part of the photographer's props which some subjects were not strictly entitled to wear. This man wears a fine quilled buckskin shirt fringed with human hair. At the throat is a rectangular neck yoke which seems characteristic of some eastern Sioux groups. His leggings are decorated with painted stripes which signify heroic deeds in warfare and he wears a necklace of grizzly bear claws. In his hand he carries the wing of an eagle as a fan.

wearing the no-retreat sash so characteristic of a number of the 'No flight' warrior societies – in this case the Strong Hearts – and as he ran forward he noticed that the Crow wore a red shirt trimmed with ermine, 'the insignia of a chief' (Vestal, 1957, p. 29). 'When the Crow saw his enemy so near, he threw up his gun to shoot. Sitting Bull instantly dropped upon one knee, threw his shield before him and took aim at the Crow. The Crow fired first. Sitting Bull felt his shield jump as the ball pierced it, felt the jolt and the pang of the wound it made in the sole of his left foot. The Crow was blotted from sight by the white smoke, but not before Sitting Bull had taken aim and pulled the trigger. He saw his enemy leap into the air and fall mortally wounded, shot through the body. Sitting Bull jerked his long knife from its scabbard, and, limping forward, plunged it into the heart of the Crow chief.' (Vestal, 1957, p. 29). The bullet had struck Sitting Bull just under the toes and ploughed back to the sole of the heel; when it healed the foot contracted and from that day Sitting Bull walked with a limp.

'The importance of this single combat was very great in Sitting Bull's life. When the Sioux wish to say a thing is excellent of its kind, they say it is sha, red. The killing of the Crow chief, that was Sha-sha, very red! A hundred Hunkpapa were witnesses to Sitting Bull's single handed courage, to his success, and among Indians, nothing succeeds like success.' (Vestal, 1957, p. 31).

In subsequent years Sitting Bull rose to hold a unique position amongst the Sioux nation and although there was and never could be a head

The Only Good Indian...

'You steal the country before the red man says yes or no.'

Red Cloud. Sunday 16 June 1866

*One Plains Indian tribe has a tradition of their first contacts
with the white man – it refers to 'prints of a foot shaped
differently to theirs. There was a deep mark at the heel; the tracks
were not flat like those made by people'.*

Grinnell, 1895, p.226

'ONE PLAINS INDIAN TRIBE has a tradition of their first contacts with the white man – it refers to "prints of a foot shaped differently to theirs. There was a deep mark at the heel; the tracks were not flat like those made by people".' (Grinnell, 1895, p. 226).

The history of the Canadian fur trade enables us to reconstruct more positively these early encounters, for some of the earliest white contacts with Plains Indians were with the fur traders in Canada, initially indirect – the Piegan for example acquired their first trade goods, including several guns, from the Cree in about 1728. Later, when the French started to develop extensive fur trading enterprises in the Canadian Northwest, the Hudson's Bay Company sought trade with the more remote tribes and by 1754 Anthony Henday, their emissary, had made contact with the *Architinues* (Blood or Gros Ventres) with a view to inducing them to bring their beaver and wolf skins to York Factory on the Hudson Bay to trade for guns, ammunition and cloth. But they refused the offer, saying that the journey was too far and too hazardous and ultimately both the Hudson's Bay Company and the Northwest Company (formed in 1784) were forced to build trading posts within easy reach of Blackfoot territory.

By 1821 more than a dozen had been established. The main demand was for beaver skins, but only a few Blackfoot bands responded since most had never previously trapped that animal, on the other hand the Cree were adept at the art and boldly ventured into Blackfoot territory. Because of their comparative greater use to the traders they were better armed and this tended to upset the balance of power in the area. Further, as the beaver east of the Rockies became progressively scarce, the fur traders made contact with the Kutenai, Kalispel, Flathead and other Plateau tribes who thus armed with guns pressed the Blackfoot from the west.

The situation was in part reconciled however by utilizing the immense food and horse resources which the Blackfoot could offer; they became the main source of dried and pounded meat, pemmican, dried berries and backfat and horses to transport supplies to the outlying posts, principally to the vast forest regions above the North Saskatchewan river. The Blackfoot were thus *forced* into a position of dependence for they needed trade goods – particularly guns – in order to maintain their

dominance. Unlike the weaker tribes, such as the Cree to their east and the Kutenai and Flathead to their west who particularly needed the resources of modern technology in order to survive, they had refused to become subservient to the whites.

In 1794 Duncan M'Gillivray of the Northwest Company made the reason clear when he observed, 'The inhabitants of the Plains are so advantageously situated that they could live very happily independent of our assistance. They are surrounded with innumerable herds of various kinds of animals, whose flesh affords them excellent nourishment and whose skins defend them from the inclemency of the weather, and they have invented so many means for the destruction of animals that they stand in no need of ammunition to provide a sufficiency for their purposes. It is then our luxuries that attract them to the fort and make us so necessary to their happiness.' (M'Gillivray, 1929, p. 47).

The trade in beaver and other fur-bearing creatures during this period was enormous. The returns by the Northwest Fur Company for a typical year (1805) were:

77,500	beaver skins
51,250	muskrat
40,400	martin
1,135	buffalo robes

Little wonder that by 1830 the hey-day of the fur trade in Canada was over. The white man had taken what he wanted, caused the virtual extermination of the beaver east of the Rockies merely for the sake of fashion, and reduced the trade to a mere trickle.

In general, however, that half century period of frenzied trade in Canada was both peaceful and beneficial to both sides and the Hudson's Bay Company treated the Indians well. 'Inspired though they may have been by prudence and self interest, rather than by enlightened motives of native welfare, their dealings with the Indians were marked by a sense of trusteeship and strict integrity.' (Stanley, 1936, p. 197). Additionally, many of these early fur traders were educated and perceptive men and wrote extensively about the Indians they met and the country they explored. Today's ethnologists owe much to the journals of David Thompson, Matthew Cocking, Anthony Hendry and others.

The situation was to be somewhat different in the United States. Relations with the Blackfoot started off on a bad footing when two Piegan were killed by Meriwether Lewis in 1806. The situation was further aggravated by the American Fur Company's policy 'of sending white trappers into Blackfoot country rather than depending upon the Indian supply. The Blackfoot resented this competition of the white trappers and attacked them as trespassers. . . . In large measure, the greater harmony in the relations of the Blackfoot and the Canadians as compared with the Americans, was due also to the differences in organization, personnel, and administration of the respective trading companies. The American fur trade reflected the rugged individualism and lack of organization of the newly developing capitalist economy of which it was part. In contrast, the Hudson's Bay Company with its highly centralized and efficient organization was part of the long-established and smoothly functioning British Empire. The Hudson's Bay Company had years of experience in dealing with Indians and exercised the strictest control over its employees'. (Lewis, 1942, pp. 27–28).

Eventually capitulating to Blackfoot demands, the American Fur Company built Fort Piegan in 1833 in the heart of Piegan territory, but this was burned by a party of Blood Indians due to a misunderstanding, so a year later Fort McKenzie was established about two miles farther up the Missouri, not far from the present township of Loma, Montana. It was here that the German scientist, Maximilian, together with his talented Swiss artist companion, Carl Bodmer, stayed from 9 August to 14 September 1833, making outstanding ethno-logical records of the Blackfoot who were encamped on adjacent Brulé Flats and observing an incredibly bloody hand-to-hand battle between a combined force of Assiniboin and Cree and a small Piegan camp which took place outside the fort on 28 August 1833. (See Chapter VIII).

The same year an extensive trade in buffalo hides was set up – a commodity which the Blackfoot could easily supply – and trade became friendly. Good relationships were established still more firmly when Alexander Culbertson, one of the most able agents of the American Fur Company, married the daughter of a Blood Indian chief. Then in February 1844, Francis Chardon, as an act of revenge for the killing of an employee by Blackfoot the previous year, murdered thirty Blackfoot Indians (including women and children) by firing a cannon loaded with bullets into the midst of them as they came to trade. Fort McKenzie was burnt to the ground by the furious

Fort Pierre, Dakota Territory, c. 1855. This bird's eye view – which lacks perspective but gives excellent detail – shows one of the fur trading posts built along the Missouri River between 1820 and 1850. They were found from St Louis to Blackfoot country 2,000 miles to the northwest. The lucrative fur trade was to soon bring disaster to the Missouri tribes. On June 19th the company steamboat *St Peter* unloaded its smallpox-infested cargo at Fort Clark and by the end of the summer seven-eighths of the Mandans and more than half the Aridara and Hidatsa were dead of the disease. Note the scenes painted over the gates, which in a recent study of Folk Art on the Upper Missouri, the ethnologist J. C. Ewers interpreted as 'See here, this is the place. You can see that we are your friends. Come in and trade with us.' These fur trading posts came to be of particular significance in the conquest of the Plains Indians for as game became scarce and profits dwindled they were sold to the United States Government and became military posts of which, in 1855, Fort Pierre was the first in Dakota Territory. From a watercolour by F. Behran. National Archives, Washington.

Fort Berthold, 1868. This important trading post was built in 1845 some years after the smallpox epidemic struck Fort Clark. In 1844 groups of the decimated Hidatsa and Mandans had established a small earth lodge village called 'Like-a-fish-hook' on a peculiar bend of the Missouri and the following year the American Fur Company established Fort Berthold a short distance away. Here can be seen a commanding position across the Missouri – a typical location for the river tribes. Near the water's edge, goods unloaded from a steamboat (which had probably travelled a thousand miles upstream from St Louis) are being checked and transported to the Fort while seated Indians look on. By 1864 Fort Berthold was a military post. From a sketch by General Regis De Trobriand. State Historical Society, North Dakota.

Blackfoot and trade ceased. Two years later, Alexander Culbertson returned to the Upper Missouri and established Fort Benton near the junction of the Marias and Missouri Rivers in 1846 (an area which had long been a rendezvous for Indians and traders). It helped patch up the old enmities.

Very favourable terms in trade could now be offered to the Blackfoot, for the introduction of the steamboat to the Upper Missouri in 1833 provided comparatively easy transport down to the fur trading capital of St Louis, and this trade continued well into the 1870s until suddenly the buffalo, like the beaver a generation before, became scarce. The northern Plains Indians would soon be facing starvation.

The pattern which developed south of the Blackfoot was in part an extension of existing Indian trade. The Upper Missouri villages of such tribes as the Mandan, Hidatsa and Arikara had long been centres of trade where the nomadic tribes traded the products of the chase for the products of agriculture. In 1805 explorer Mackenzie described a typical trading session between the Hidatsa and their nomadic cousins, the Crow.

'Les Gros Ventres made the (Crow) . . . smoke the pipe of friendship, and, at the same time, laid before them a present consisting of two hundred guns, with one hundred rounds of ammunition for each, a hundred bushels of Indian corn, a certain quantity of mercantile articles, such as kettles, axes, clothes, etc. The (Crow) in return brought two hundred and fifty horses, large parcels of (buffalo) robes, leather leggings, shirts, etc., etc. This exchange of trading civilities took place dancing, when the dancing was over, the presents were distributed among the individuals in propor-

tion to the value of the articles respectively furnished; this dance therefore is a rule of traffic. The Mandan villages exchanged similar civilities with the same tribe.' (Mackenzie, in Masson, 1889, p. 346).

Recognizing this well-organized and balanced trade pattern, the earlier white traders were initially content to journey to them and acquire what furs were available. Most of these came from the nomadic Crow and Flathead to the west or the Cheyenne, Kiowa and Arapaho to the southwest but the source was not a dependable one, the nature pattern of trade goods placing emphasis on other commodities. Recognizing the immense trade potential this balanced situation was drastically changed as the white man sought to create a demand for luxury goods made principally in Europe.

In 1804 trader Tabeau observed, 'It is evident that with the bow and arrow the Savages of the Upper Missouri can easily do without our trade, which becomes necessary to them only after it has created the needs . . . it is not to be doubted that custom, intercourse, the spirit of imitation, rivalry, the idea of luxury will give birth among the Savages to new needs and the necessity of enjoying will produce the activity required to procure the means for them.' (Tabeau, in Abel, 1939, pp. 72 & 166).

Although most of the tribes who lived along the banks of the Missouri had for obvious reasons attempted to prevent white traders from progressing beyond their own villages, James Kipp, a seasoned and experienced Canadian of German descent succeeded in establishing Kipp's Trading Post in 1826. Situated on the north bank of the Missouri some two miles above the White Earth River (in present-day Mountrail County, northwestern Dakota) it was a decisive step in forging direct trade with the powerful Siouan speaking Assiniboin. Two years later a much larger trading post – Fort Union – was established near the confluence of the Missouri and Yellowstone Rivers and Kipp's Post was abandoned. Union was to become one of the principal trading posts of the American Fur Company in the Upper Missouri region and Edwin Thompson Denig – one of its most able superintendents – an outstanding authority and author on the surrounding Plains tribes.

The position of the Upper Missouri village tribes, whose whole economy pivoted on their 'middlemen' role, was considerably weakened and 1831 onwards saw their progressive decline. The Mandan, however, have won a particular place in the chapters of history for the establishment of Fort Clark within a stone's throw of their principal village of Mi-ti-was-kos gave a unique opportunity for explorers and scientists of the day to minutely observe their customs and manners. For example, George Catlin visited them in the summer of 1832, attended their incredible O-kee-pa ceremony and wrote about them extensively. As far afield as London and Brussels, the name of Four Bears, Chief of the Mandan, was known to a vast mid-19th century public.

Trade with the southern Cheyenne and Arapaho and to a lesser extent with the Kiowa, Comanche, Ute and Plains Apache (until the 'Great Peace' of 1840 when most of these tribes struck up friendly relations in order to fight an encroachment of their territory by whites and displaced eastern Indians), was through the famous Bent's Fort which was located on the Arkansas River along the Santa Fe Trail in present-day southeastern Colorado. Completed in 1832 by William Bent it was the principal trading post amongst these southern plains tribes. 'Colonel' Bent was a 'man of intelligence, good sense and strong character' (Vestal, 1948, p. 64). In 1835 he married Owl Woman, a daughter of one of the principal men of the Cheyenne and keeper of the sacred medicine arrows. It was a diplomatic and oft-taken step in Plains Indian trade relations. (Culbertson, it will be remembered, married the daughter of a principal Blood chief.) In later years when the crisis of war with the white man reached the southern plains it was to William Bent that the chiefs turned for advice.

The important trading post for the southern divisions of the Teton Sioux – particularly the Oglala and Brulé – was Fort Laramie, which stood on the level land near the junction of the Laramie and North Platte Rivers. It was named after an unfortunate Frenchman one Jacques La Ramée who was killed by Indians in 1821. Fur trading had early been established in the area.

In the winter of 1812–1813 Robert Stuart had passed that way on his path-finding expedition from Astoria on the Columbia River to St Louis (he is also credited with the discovery of the Oregon Trail). Stuart made mention of the wooded stream flowing from the southwest into the North Platte River, the home of many prized beaver. By 1825 there were annual trappers' rendezvous held in the Green and Wind River valleys; 1834 saw the establishment of Fort William, the first Fort Laramie and in 1841, a more permanent adobe walled post. This coincided with the abandonment of the rendezvous system as the beaver trade declined. It was here in the spring of 1846 that young Francis Parkman stayed, vividly describing the Fort in his now famous book *The Oregon Trail*. He noted that the American Fur Company virtually monopolized the Indian trade of the region and that prices were extortionate. 'Sugar, two dollars a cup; five-cent tobacco at a dollar and a half; bullets at seventy-five cents a pound. The company is exceedingly disliked in this country; it suppresses all opposition and, keeping up these enormous prices, pays its men in necessities in these terms.' Parkman made some interesting ethnological observations

Fort Laramie, c. 1837. This stood near the junction of the Laramie and North Platte Rivers in present day south-eastern Wyoming. It was built in 1834 and then known as Fort William. The later, more permanent, adobe-walled post which replaced it became a military garrison in 1849. Fort Laramie was the scene of a number of important historical events in the history of the American West and was visited by the young Francis Parkman in 1846. He observed that the American Fur Company virtually monopolized the Indian trade in the region and that prices of furs were extortionate. It was here – on Christmas night 1866 – that John 'Portugee' Phillips, after a four-day ride from Fort Phil Kearny through appalling weather conditions, brought the news of the Fetterman disaster. From a painting by Alfred J. Miller. Walters Art Gallery, Baltimore, Maryland.

(1) Rushing Bear, Head Chief of the Rees (Arikara) c. 1865. (r) Chak-uk-t-kee, a Pawnee chief. The sedentary Missouri tribes reduced in numbers by the ravages of smallpox had little choice but to throw in their lot with the white man as he pushed his way west. Intertribal warfare which had been largely limited by recognized war customs was turned to advantage and the army tended to exploit tribal rivalries by employing the smaller tribes as scouts. This photograph was probably taken some years before 1870; one taken of Rushing Bear in 1872 by the frontier photographer S. J. Morrow shows almost identical costume but a definitely older man. Birmingham Reference Library.

on the Sioux of the area and amongst other Indian accoutrements collected a fine Oglala Sioux war-shirt which is now in the collection of the Peabody Museum at Harvard University.

The great fur trading post was soon to take on another, more sinister role; a pattern which was to be repeated many times over from Fort Benton to Fort Pierre, along the whole length of the mighty Missouri. The white man coveted another commodity, which by right of heritage belonged to the Warriors of the Plains – their land.

Up to 1840 it was largely traders, explorers, missionaries and Indians who dominated the scene at Fort Laramie but 1843 saw the first of the great migrations to Oregon and covered wagons became a familiar sight along the Oregon trail in early summer of each year. Initially, the migration of whites was a trickle, 1000 in 1843, 3000 in 1845 but by the summer of 1850 it became a raging torrent reaching nearly 40,000. By then the Sioux were becoming increasingly alarmed. The emigrants not only brought diseases to which the tribes had no resistance (Asiatic cholera amongst them) but destroyed or frightened away the game. The danger from Indians was well summed up in the popular emigrant campfire refrain:

> The Injuns will catch you while crossing the plains
> They'll kill you, and scalp you, and beat out your brains

Uncle Sam ought to throw them all over the fence
So there'll be no Red Injuns a hundred years hence

In an attempt to keep misunderstandings between emigrants and Indians to a minimum, steps were taken by the government to establish military stations along the Oregon Trail. Thus, early in 1849, a battalion of 'Missouri Mounted Volunteers' established Fort Kearney. Situated on the south bank of the Platte River near the head of Grand Island, it was the first of the military posts on the Oregon Trail. Then, on 26 June 1849, Lieutenant Daniel P. Woodbury purchased Fort Laramie from one Bruce Husband, agent of the American Fur Company. The price was $4000. By 12 August 1849, when two officers and fifty-three men of Company G, Sixth Infantry arrived the garrison was complete; the economic game of the fur trade was over. Fort Laramie had become a strategic military post. In subsequent years it was to be one of the most important military posts in the history of the wars against the central Plains Indian.

'It offered protection and refreshment to the throngs who made the great western migration over the Oregon Trail. It was a station for the Pony Express and the Overland Stage. It served as an *important base in the conquest of the Plains Indians*, and it witnessed the development of the open range cattle industry, the coming of the homesteaders, and the final settlement which marked the closing of the frontier.' (Hieb, 1954, p. 1).

The great council held at Horse Creek near Fort Laramie in 1851 attempted to bring permanent peace to the area. In return for safe emigrant travel up the Platte west to the mountains the United States government agreed to 'make an annual payment to the Sioux in goods valued at $50,000 per year for fifty years, to be delivered in the Fort Laramie area'. Additionally, amid bitter protests from the Sioux, for it completely ignored the basic structure of a Plains nation (see Chapter II), a headman of the Brulé, Conquering Bear, was 'appointed chief of all the Sioux'. Conquering Bear, who emerges as a man of intelligence and unquestioned ability and courage, had an impossible task. Consider 'The aforesaid Indian nations do hereby agree and bind themselves to make restitution or satisfaction for any wrongs committed after the ratification of this treaty by any band or individual of their people on the people of the United States while lawfully residing in or passing through their respective territories.' (Article 4).

Further 'It is agreed and understood that should any of the Indian nations, party to this treaty, violate any of the provisions thereof, the United States may withhold the whole or a portion of the annuities mentioned in the preceding Article from the nation so offending until, in the opinion of the President of the United States, proper satisfaction shall have been made.' (Article 8)

(McCann, 1956, pp. 3 & 4).

When the bands scattered, to pursue their usual nomadic hunting life, they would be wandering over an area comprising the southern part of present North and South Dakota and at least the northern portions of Nebraska and Wyoming; clearly Conquering Bear could have no jurisdiction over such a widely-scattered and loosely-held group of individuals. His first task was to reconcile the virtual rejection of the Treaty by the United States Senate who reduced the terms from fifty to ten years. Additionally he had no power whatever over the completely independent Oglala division, who although not exactly adverse to sharing the goods had flatly refused to sign the Treaty in the first place anyway. Said Conquering Bear: 'Father' (addressing Colonel D. D. Mitchell, one of the Commissioners who presided at the Treaty) 'I am not afraid to die but to be chief of *all* the nation, I must be a big chief, or in a few moons I shall be dead on the prairie. I have a wife and children I do not wish to leave. If I am not a powerful chief, my enemies will be on my trail all the time.' Even Conquering Bear could not have foreseen how soon his prophesy would be a reality.

The slow war of suppression of the Plains Indian all began with a cow, so thin and emaciated that it had been abandoned by its Mormon emigrant owner. Desiring a piece of rawhide and perhaps a questionable meal into the bargain High Forehead, a visiting Miniconjou Sioux, shot the cow dead on the afternoon of 18 August 1854 'to make restitution or satisfaction for any wrongs committed . . . by any band or individual . . . on the people of the United States . . .'. How clearly those words must have echoed in Conquering Bear's thoughts as he hurried to Fort Laramie. The emigrants demanded compensation and although Conquering Bear immediately offered a horse in payment, Lieutenant Hugh B. Fleming considered the matter so trivial that no decision was reached that night. Probably the matter would have rested there but next day Lieutenant John Grattan strongly supported the emigrants and claimed the right to command a detachment of infantry to arrest the offending Indian. Reluctantly, Fleming agreed to the proposal, instructing Grattan 'to receive the offender, and in case of refusal to give him up, after ascertaining the disposition of the Indians, to act upon his own discretion, and to be careful not to hazard an engagement without certain success'. (McCann, 1956, p. 8).

Grattan was an unfortunate choice for such a diplomatic mission. A somewhat boisterous, swash-buckling youth of twenty-four who had only graduated from West Point the previous year, he was evidently itching for honour and a break from the monotonous, routine army life. He believed in severe dealing with any Indian misdemeanour. Grattan, along with Sergeant W. Faver, twenty-six infantrymen, two musicians, and a terrified (by this time half-drunk) interpreter – one Lucian Auguste – rode toward the Sioux encampment. Twice Grattan was forcibly warned of

Indians Attacking Emigrants. The Marauders. By the mid-1840s the great migration was underway and in 1850 nearly 40,000 white people in search of new horizons followed the Oregon Trail. With them they brought diseases to which the Indians had no natural resistance; additionally, they frightened away the deer and buffalo on which the nomadic tribes were so dependent. Fort Laramie became a haven in a wilderness for the footsore and weary pioneer and the necessity of using the fort as a military base was early recognized. The picture shows an attack by the vengeful warriors. It is unlikely however that either warrior would be armed in this way. Indians seldom used a gun on horseback and when they did the barrel was cut down; the bow and arrow would be much more effective. The long lance and shield carried by the warrior wearing the horned headdress would probably be reserved more for parades and certainly not used in close combat against gun-armed pedestrians as shown here. From a pencil and wash drawing by Felix Octavius Carr Darley. Joslyn Art Museum, Omaha, Nebraska.

the potentially dangerous situation. Obridge Allen, a professional emigrant guide, rode up and pointed out to Grattan 'that the Oglalas had begun driving in their pony herds – typical Indian preparation for battle'. (McCann, 1956, p. 12). Shortly after James Bordeaux, an experienced and shrewd trader at that time trading directly with the Sioux, observed to Grattan 'Why don't you let the old cow go. It was laying there without food or water and would soon die; it was too lame to walk; its feets (*sic*) was worn through to the flesh. It was shot by some boys who wanted a piece of skin'. (McCann, 1956, p. 6).

Bordeaux could see the foolish Auguste abusing the waiting Indians; he told the Sioux 'they were all women', 'he would have them all killed', 'by sundown he would eat their hearts' and running his horse in the manner Indians did before a fight, to give them their second wind, he was waving his pistol and giving war whoops. Turning to Grattan he said that Auguste would make trouble 'and that if he would put him in my house I will settle the difficulty in thirty minutes'.

Many chiefs were born diplomats, and especially so when their women and children were around. Their weapons were fair words, an appeal to reason and if necessary even friendly coaxing. Conquering Bear was no exception to this rule. Plains Indian psychology is well illustrated in the subsequent tragic events.

Grattan told Conquering Bear that he had come to take High Forehead back to the Fort. Reported Man-Afraid-of-His-Horses 'The Bear said to me, "You are brave, what do you think of it?" I said to him, "You are chief, what do you think?" Then Conquering Bear told Grattan that High Forehead was "a guest in his village and not subject to his authority"'. Although Grattan was made further offers of ponies to pay for the cow and was urged to delay any action until Major John W. Whitfield, the Indian Agent, arrived, he ordered his troops into the Brulé village announcing that he would 'go himself to High Forehead's lodge'. He halted some sixty yards from High Forehead's lodge which stood near that of Conquering Bear's, and then he ordered the howitzers primed and aimed 'in the general direction of Conquering Bear's lodge, and disposed his men on either side of the cannon'. (McCann, 1956, p. 16).

A further conference lasting three quarters of an hour was held. Conquering Bear offered liberal compensation for the cow. Man-Afraid-of-his-Horses pleaded with James Bordeaux to replace the foolish Auguste as interpreter. 'My friend, come on. (That) interpreter is going to get us into a fight and they are going to fight if you don't come.' The parley had become increasingly bitter and even the diplomatic Conquering Bear was beginning to lose patience with the arrogant Grattan. Reported Man-Afraid, 'The Bear said it was hard as it was a poor cow and that today the soldiers had made him ashamed that he was made chief by the whites and today you come to my village and plant your big guns. . . . For all I tell you you will not hear me. I would strike you were I not a chief. But as I am a chief and am made so by the whites will not do it.' As Man-Afraid and the reluctant Bordeaux rode back towards the conference it suddenly broke up.

'At about this time the frustrated Grattan broke off the parley and moved towards the troops, giving a command that the Indians did not understand. Conquering Bear strode toward his own lodge. Two or three shots were fired, and an Indian was hit. Bordeaux was then near enough to hear the chief's shout to the warriors not to fire – that perhaps this was just a shot to protect the honour of the troops and they would leave since they had wounded a good man. Bordeaux fled to his trading post.' (McCann, 1956, p. 18).

The situation was explosive; while the second parley was in progress, warriors – amongst them the young Red Cloud – rode down from the Oglala encampment just north of the Brulé camp circle, while behind the wild roses and brush on the left flank of Grattan's line of troops, hundreds of mounted Brulé were donning their warpaint and bonnets. The twenty-four year old Lieutenant had just two alternatives; he could withdraw and perhaps lose face or by a further trial of strength attempt to win the day. Too fat with pride, predictably he chose the latter course. Thus John L. Grattan, a '53 graduate from West Point, ended his days at the hands of Sioux warriors . . . and gained immortality. 'But Grattan was now convinced of the need for a demonstration, and ordered the infantry to fire a volley. This time Conquering Bear went down mortally wounded. Arrows began to fly from the bowmen on the flank. Grattan then fired the mountain howitzer and afterwards the twelve pounder, but the canister charges whistled harmlessly through the conical peaks of the Brulé lodges.' (McCann, 1956, p. 19).

Grattan's command, few if any of which had any experience of Plains Indian warfare, scattered in panic. Grattan himself crashed to the ground struck by arrows. When his body was found afterwards it had twenty-four arrows in it 'one going completely through his head. He could be identified only by his pocket watch.' (McCann, 1956, p. 20). Within a short time the entire command, except one, was wiped out. The sole survivor was Private John Cuddy who although badly wounded had crawled into the wild rose bushes. He died two days later without giving any account of the battle.

The above account is based on the research of Dr Lloyd E. McCann of Butler University, Indianapolis, Indiana. Pieced together from data in House and Senate Executive Documents, a narrative of Man-Afraid-of-his-Horses now in the National Archives, and an interview with Red Cloud by Judge E. S. Ricker at Pine Ridge, South Dakota, 24 November 1906, it records the first substantial defeat of the United States Army by Plains Indian warriors. The clash underlined the vast differences between the two cultures, and served as a warning to other would-be 'paper chiefs'. The 'war game' was over; the Grattan Massacre, as it became known, heralded the beginning of a slow war of suppression which was to last for nearly forty years.

Even as early as 1825 the Comanche of the southern plains – who broadly claimed the area of present-day Texas but also ranged as far north as present-day Colorado and Kansas – noted with some concern the movement of eastern Indians to the very borders of Comanche territory. The passing of the Indian Removal Act of 1830 had given President Andrew Jackson the power to order the transfer of any Indians who had managed to survive east of the Mississippi to lands west of that great waterway. This is not the place to discuss the terrible consequences of that sinister power. Sufficient to say that at least one modern student has pointed out that in the light of the Nürnberg Laws such action would now be classed as genocide (Farb, 1969, p. 250). By 1832 white settlers were also moving westward from Arkansas territory and the Comanche were becoming increasingly hostile.

'About 1832 war and confusion seemed to be increasing in the country west of Indian territory between the Arkansas and Red rivers. The Plains tribes were fighting the one with the other, intruding Indians from the east were going into the prairies and antagonizing the native Indians by killing their game, and the Great Plains country was anything but safe for the few white persons who dared enter it.' (Richardson, 1933, p. 79). Thus, in June 1834, a Dragoon Expedition under Colonel

Village of Brulé. A number of the southern bands of Sioux tended to stay near to the trading posts and ultimately became particularly dependent on the products of the white man; here, for example, most tipis are made of canvas and many have wagons. A scene probably very similar to this – but with less evidence of white contact – met Lieut. John Grattan, as he rode with his small detachment on the afternoon of 19 August 1854 to Chief Conquering Bear's village, in search of a visiting Miniconjou Sioux who had shot an emigrant Mormon's cow. Library of Congress, Washington.

Henry Dodge travelled into Comanche/Wichita territory with a view to laying the foundation for a peace treaty with these hostile tribes; the expedition was successful and led to a treaty at Camp Holmes in 1835. The artist, George Catlin, was on the 1834 expedition, having been granted permission by the Secretary of War. Two years previously, Catlin had visited the Upper Missouri tribes, made the best of the opportunities which came his way during that expedition and not only produced some of the earliest views of the Arkan-

sas River valley but also left us priceless pictorial documents of a number of the southern Plains tribes – including Comanche, Kiowa and Wichita – and he was much impressed by the Comanche's horsemanship recording 'I am ready without hesitation to pronounce the Comanches the most extraordinary horsemen that I have seen yet in all my travels, and I doubt very much whether any people in the world can surpass them.' (Catlin, Vol. II, 1841, p. 66).

About the same time as eastern Indians and

Cheyenne and Arapaho Chiefs, 1859. An historically important photograph; the central figure is Black Kettle, a chief of the Cheyennes. The earliest known photograph of this chief was taken in 1857. The group were photographed at Leavenworth on their way to Washington with interpreter John Smith who figured prominently in the history of the southern Cheyenne. Black Kettle tried to avoid war between his band and the U.S. Army but on two occasions – at Sand Creek in 1864 and at Washita in 1867 – his village was attacked and destroyed. Black Kettle was killed in the latter conflict. From an old photograph collected by the Englishman William Blackmore, about 1865. British Museum.

whites started moving west into Comanche territory another threat loomed from the north. The Cheyenne – an Algonquian tribe who came to the Great Plains from the northeast, becoming completely equestrian by the end of the 18th century – split into two divisions. One remained in their old possessions between the Cheyenne and White Rivers and along the Black Hills, while the other division for reasons of trading (principally at Bent's Fort) moved south to the valleys of the Platte and Arkansas Rivers, and made an alliance with the southern Arapaho. Together they defeated the Comanche alliance (Comanche, Kiowa and Plains Apache) at the battle of Wolf Creek in 1838 and forced the Comanche to accept the Arkansas River as their northern boundary. Southern Cheyenne–Arapaho territory thus encompassed the Santa Fe Trail and the mail routes to Denver, Colorado. Recognizing the danger of the approaching white man and well-armed eastern Indians, the tribes made an alliance two years later, thereby ensuring supplies of horses to the Cheyenne and Arapaho and guns and ammunition to the Kiowa, Comanche and Plains Apache. It was called *The Great Peace* and it produced a formidable barrier to the development of the southern Plains for it substantially reduced inter-tribal warfare, enabling the warriors' best energies to be directed against the white intruder.

The Cheyenne had a legend which told how 'after a disastrous encounter with some other tribe, they all decided they would become terrible fighters and so become great men' (Vestal, 1948, p. 63). The formation of the *Hotaṁ itaṅ iu* 'Dog Men' was a living reminder of that legend. The 'Dog Soldiers', as they became known to the whites, considered that they were the watchdogs of the Cheyenne people and to them, especially, territory once gained was not easily relinquished.

In the fall of 1864, Black Kettle, Left Hand, White Antelope, and other chiefs were camped on the south bend of Sand Creek. This was some thirty miles northeast of Fort Lyon and about 100 miles southeast of Denver where Black Kettle and other chiefs had met Governor Evans and Colonel J. M. Chivington earlier that summer. This particular group of Cheyenne and Arapaho were generally considered 'friendlies' – the more hostile bands, including the Cheyenne Dog Soldiers, were camped near the headwaters of the Republican River more than 150 miles farther north. On the morning of 29 November 1864, Chivington, a former Methodist minister and once described as a 'fiery abolitionist convinced of the righteousness of his decisions', heading a regiment of 'Colorado Volunteers' – a state militia who had been recalled by the territorial governor – attacked Black Kettle's and White Antelope's camp of some 100 tipis. Vain attempts by the chiefs to convey their peaceful intentions were to no avail. White Antelope fell under a hail of bullets but miraculously Black Kettle survived the onslaught and ultimately made his escape together with the other members of the village who survived the attack. Completely destitute, the Cheyenne retreated to Big Timbers, a cottonwood grove about fifty miles northeast of Sand Creek and eventually joined other Cheyenne bands. At least sixty-nine Cheyenne and Arapaho had been slaughtered, many of them women and children; to say that they were scalped and mutilated in a brutal manner would be to understate the horror for 'it rivaled, if it did not surpass, in barbarity and savagery any outrage committed by Indians'. (Nye, 1968, p. 20).

After Sand Creek, Black Kettle slowly moved south into Comanche territory and attempted to avoid trouble. The Cheyenne Dog Soldiers, however, under Tall Bull and White Horse, continued to reside in their old domain, extending an invitation to northern tribes to help keep the white man from their territory. They were joined by Roman Nose of the Northern Cheyenne and Pawnee Killer of the Sioux. Between them they developed a policy of continuous harassment. 'The hostiles raided nearly every stage station, ranch and settlement between the forks of the Platte and Denver, killing and burning and tearing down the telegraph line. . . . It was the beginning of a long and bitter war.' (Vestal, 1948, p. 75).

By June 1867, Denver was virtually isolated, provisions were becoming desperately short, and trade ground to a virtual standstill. Such was the situation which the Englishman, Dr William A. Bell, found when he stayed at Fort Wallace in western Kansas in June 1867. Bell had sailed to America in early spring, 1867, being a charter member of the Ethnological Society of Great Britain, he had more than a passing interest in the American Indian and seized the opportunity to join a government expedition to survey routes for a southern trans-continental railway. The terrain to be covered was to stretch from Fort Wallace, Kansas, to Albuquerque on the Rio Grande and possibly also to extend well down into New Mexico and California. The only vacancy on the expedition which could be offered to Dr Bell was

The Sand Creek Massacre, November 1864, from a painting by Robert Lindneux, 1936. The attack on a Cheyenne village was by a regiment of Colorado Volunteers led by a former Methodist minister, Colonel J. M. Chivington. Although the Cheyenne were flying both a U.S. and a white flag above their village as a sign of their peaceful intentions nearly seventy Indians – many of them women and children – were slaughtered. State Historical Society, Colorado.

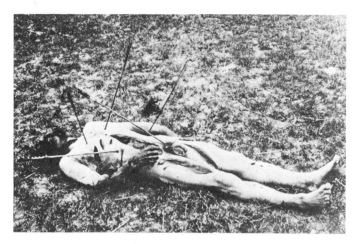

Sergeant Frederick Wylyams. Fort Wallace, Kansas, 26 June 1867. Massacres such as Sand Creek caused further retaliation and the Red and White confrontation took on a brutal turn. This U.S. cavalryman—an Englishman who according to the photographer was a graduate of Eton – was unfortunate enough to be ambushed by a party of Cheyenne led by Roman Nose. Photograph taken by Dr W. A. Bell 1867. Smithsonian Institute, National Anthropological Archives.

that of photographer, so he 'apprenticed himself to the best teacher in Philadelphia – Mr John Browne. In the shortest possible time he learned the art of wet-plate photography and the uses of the necessary developing equipment'. (Watson, 1966, p. 4). Bell was evidently impressed by the Indians he observed, particularly their horsemanship, and of this he wrote, 'The Buffalo Indians are probably the finest horsemen in the world. Accustomed from their childhood to chase the buffalo, they live half their time in the saddle.' (Bell, Vol. I, 1869, p. 58).

During their surveying activities the expedition met up with Lieutenant George A. Custer's 7th Cavalry and Bell befriended a fellow Englishman, one Sergeant Frederick Wylyams, in Captain Albert Barnitz's G Troop of the Seventh. Sergeant Wylyams was, according to Bell, a graduate of Eton who 'while sowing his wild oats had made a fatal alliance in London and gone to grief'. (Bell, Vol. I, 1869, p. 46).

On Saturday, 22 June 1867, a mixed band of Cheyenne, Arapaho and Sioux attacked Fort Wallace which was at that time considerably under strength, most troops having accompanied General W. S. Hancock on a treaty-making expedition to Fort Larned on the Santa Fe Trail. The attack was repulsed but it gave Bell his first opportunity to see 'how the "noble red men" fought'. (Bell, Vol. I, 1869, p. 53). Following the short engagement on the 22nd, fifty soldiers under Captain Barnitz, including Sergeant Wylyams and Dr Bell, scouted in the vicinity of Fort Wallace. They were observed by a large war party – four hundred or so in number. The leader was a tall warrior with a lance on a white horse 'who was so conspicuous in the fight on Saturday'. (Bell, Vol. I, 1869, p. 59). The Indians signalled to one another by walking their horses in a circle, whilst the chief signalled to more distant warriors by means of a mirror 'which flashed brilliantly in the sun'. (Bell, 1869,

p. 59). The following is an account of the engagement; it illustrates the typical ambuscade tactics which the mounted warriors of the Plains were to employ so successfully time and again in the increasing clashes with the cavalry. It also tells much of the horrors of Indian–white warfare – the 'no quarter' attitude which was so apparent at Sand Creek only three years before.

'No sooner had the cavalry followed the retiring band beyond the ridge, exchanging shots and skirmishing all the way, than on either flank, two fresh bodies of warriors suddenly appeared. They halted a few minutes; a powerful-looking warrior fancifully dressed, galloped along their front shouting suggestions; and then, like a whirlwind, with lances poised and arrows on the string, they rushed on the little band of fifty soldiers. The skirmishers fired and fell back on the line, and in an instant the Indians were amongst them. Now the tide was turned. Saddles were emptied, and the soldiers forced back over the ground towards the fort. The bugler fell, pierced by five arrows, and was instantly siezed by a powerful warrior, who, stooping down from his horse, coolly stripped the body, and then, smashing the head of his naked victim with his tomahawk, threw him on the ground under his horse's feet. On the left of our line the Indians pressed heavily cutting off five men, among them Sergeant Fredcrick Wylyams. With his little force, this poor fellow held out nobly until his horse was

Chest skin scalp showing tattoo, 1867. This was taken from the chest of Sergeant Frederick Wylyams by the Cheyennes and recaptured from them some time later. It was given to Captain Isaac P. Baker, MD, by one of the cavalry officers. It measures $5\frac{3}{4}$ inches by $5\frac{1}{4}$. Paul Dyck Collection, Paul Dyck Foundation.

killed, and one by one the soldiers fell, selling their lives dearly. The warrior who appeared to lead the band was up to this time very conspicuous in the fight, dashing back and forth on his grey horse, and by his actions setting an example to his warriors. In the mêlée however one of our cavalry men was thrown to the ground by the fierceness of the Indian onslaught, when this leader, who I have since learned was the famous Cheyenne war-chief Roman-nose, attacked the prostrate man with his spear. Corporal Harris, of "G" company was near him, and struck Roman-nose with the sabre which he held in his left hand. Quick as thought, the chief turned on him, but as he did so, the faithful "Spencer" of the corporal met his breast, and with the blood pouring from his mouth, Roman-nose fell forward on his horse, never again to lead his "dog soldiers" on the warpath. By this time it was more than evident that on horseback the soldiers were no match for the redskins. Most of them had never been opposed to Indians before; many were raw recruits; and their horses became so dreadfully frightened at the yells and the smell of the savages as to be quite unmanageable so Captain Barnitz gave the order to dismount.

'When the dismounted cavalry commenced to pour a well-directed volley from their Spencers, the Indians for the first time wavered, and began to retire. For two hours Capt. Barnitz waited with his thinned ranks for another advance of the Indians, but they prudently held back; and, after a prolonged consultation, retired slowly with their dead and wounded beyond the hills, to paint their faces black and lament the death of one of the bravest leaders of their inhuman race.

'I have seen in days gone by sights horrible and gory – death in all its forms of agony and distortion – but never did I feel the sickening sensation, the giddy, fainting feeling that came over me when I saw our dead, dying and wounded after this Indian fight. A handful of men, to be sure, but with enough wounds upon them to have slain a company, if evenly distributed. The bugler was stripped naked, and five arrows driven through him while his skull was literally smashed to atoms. Another soldier was shot with four bullets and three arrows, his scalp was torn off and his brains knocked out. A third was riddled with balls and arrows but they did not succeed in getting his scalp, although, like the other two he was stripped naked. James Douglas, a Scotchman, was shot through the body with arrows, and his left arm was hacked to pieces. He was a brave fellow, and breathed out his life in the arms of his comrades. Sergeant Wylyams lay dead beside his horse and as the fearful picture first met my gaze, I was horror stricken. Horse and rider were stripped bare of trapping and clothes, while around them the trampled, blood-stained ground showed the desperation of the struggle.

'I shall minutely describe this horrid sight, not for the sake of creating a sensation, but because it is characteristic of a mode of warfare soon thank God – to be abolished; and because the mu-

tilations have, as we shall presently see, most of them some meaning, apart from brutality and a desire to inspire fear.

'A portion of the sergeant's scalp lay near him, but the greater part was gone; through his head a rifle-ball had passed, and a blow from the tomahawk had laid his brain open above his left eye; the nose was slit up, and his throat was cut from ear to ear; seven arrows were standing in different parts of his naked body; the breast was laid open, so as to expose the heart, and the arm, that had doubtless done its work against the redskins was hacked to the bone; his legs, from the hip to the knee, lay open with horrible gashes, and from the knee to the foot they had cut the flesh with knives. Thus mutilated Wylyams lay beside the mangled horse. In all there were seven killed and five wounded.

'As I have said almost all the different tribes on the plains had united their forces against us, and each of these tribes has a different sign by which it is known.

'The sign of the Cheyenne or "Cut arm", is made in peace by drawing the hand across the arm, to imitate cutting it with a knife; that of the Arapaho, or "Smaller tribe" by seizing the nose with the thumb and forefinger; of the Sioux or "Cut throat" by drawing the hand across the throat. The Comanche or "Snake Indian" waves his hand and arm, in imitation of the crawling of a snake, the Crow imitates with his hands the slapping of wings. The Pawnee or "Wolf Indian" places two fingers erect on each side of his head to represent pointed ears; the Blackfoot touches the heel, and then the toe, of the right foot; and the Kiowas' most unusual sign is to imitate the act of drinking.

'If we now turn to the body of poor Sergeant Wylyams, we shall have no difficulty in recognizing some meaning in the wounds. The muscles of the right arm, hacked to the bone, speak of the Cheyenne, or "Cut Arms", the nose slit denotes the "Smaller tribe" or Arapaho; and the throat cut bears witness that the Sioux were also present. There were therefore amongst the warriors Cheyenne, Arapaho and Sioux. It was not till some time afterwards that I knew positively what these signs meant, and I have not yet discovered what tribe was indicated by the incisions down the thighs, and the laceration of the calves of the legs, in oblique parallel gashes. The arrows also varied in make and colour according to the tribe; and it was evident, from the number of different devices, that warriors from several tribes had each purposely left one in the dead mans body.' (Bell, Vol. I, 1869, pp. 61–64).

Other than the fact that Bell was erroneously informed that the slain chief was Roman Nose (who was actually killed at Beecher Island in September of the following year) the above account which was written in his book *New Tracks in North America* after his return to London in February 1868 is perhaps one of the most accurate and vivid first-hand accounts of a small scale Indian-

white engagement ever recorded by an unbiased, scientifically trained observer.

Bell went on to explain that Wylyams had promised earlier on that fateful day to help him print some photographs which he had taken en route 'so I had to print off my negatives alone, and to take a photograph of him, poor fellow, as he lay; a copy of which I sent to Washington that the authorities should see how their soldiers were treated on the Plains'. (Bell, Vol. I, 1869, p. 64).

Such was the pattern of warfare on the southern Plains – particularly in Kansas, where the warring tribesmen bitterly opposed the building of the Union Pacific Railroad through their very hunting grounds. The horrors of Indian-white warfare were not however always reported with such stark reality as the Wylyams affair. The time William Thompson shammed dead as a young Sioux slowly scalped him with a very blunt knife, and his efforts to preserve his scalp in a bucket of water until surgeons could sew it back on again in Omaha, was the bones of many a frontier tale. Colonel Dodge tells us the operation was not successful, remarking wryly 'I saw the man some months afterwards, perfectly recovered but with a horrible looking head.' (Dodge, 1876, p. 400).

The Treaty held with the southern tribes on Medicine Lodge Creek near Fort Dodge, Kansas, 19–20 October 1867 attempted to reconcile both Indian and white grievances. The Treaty followed

Attack at Dawn. This might be the way it happened when Custer attacked Black Kettle's village of Cheyenne at Washita in November 1867. More than 100 Indians – including women and children – were killed. Employing a brutal scorched-earth policy Custer and his men rounded up nearly 900 Indian ponies and killed them and then burnt the village to the ground. The Indians look a little over-dressed for a surprise dawn attack since most Indian males habitually slept naked. From a painting by Charles Schreyvogel, 1904. Thomas Gilcrease Institute, Tulsa, Oklahoma.

from the findings of a Special Joint Committee who published *Condition of the Indian Tribes* in 1867. A general Peace Policy was advocated, for it pointed out that most of the trouble on the Plains was due to white encroachment. Medicine Lodge Treaty met with little substantial success for a variety of reasons. First, the government of the day was slow in carrying out the terms with those bands that did sign the Treaty. Also, the Treaty failed to get the Comanche to 'touch the pen' and further the Kiowa and Comanche still found it difficult to get used to the idea that the annexation of Texas in 1845 made its people citizens of the United States – raids in Texas to them had traditionally been the 'warriors' path to glory and wealth'.

The tribes were particularly incensed by the continued building of the Kansas and Pacific railroad to Denver, and the guerilla-type warfare continued. Roman Nose had bluntly stated the Indian viewpoint at a council held at Fort Ellsworth early

93

in 1866. 'This is the first time that I have ever shaken the white man's hand in friendship. If the railway is continued I shall be his enemy forever.' (Brady, 1904, p. 73). But Roman Nose was soon to die when his medicine power failed him during a charge at the famed Battle of Beecher's Island on the Arikaree Fork of the Republican River (in present-day eastern Colorado), in September 1868. He was 'buried' in the true Plains tradition reserved for their most exalted warriors – in a buffalo hide tipi complete with his accoutrements of war.

Two months later came another devastating blow to the Cheyenne. Generally known as 'The Battle of the Washita' the more informed often call it 'Custer's Massacre'. The hostile attitude of the southern Plains tribes led to demands by Nebraska, Colorado, Kansas and Texas settlers for effective military protection. By November 1868 a campaign was under way – the plan was to strike the hostiles in their winter camps and by destroying their food supplies force them into a state of subjugation. The problem was deciding who were the hostiles. On 20 November, Black Kettle, in company with a number of Cheyenne and Arapaho chiefs and headmen visited Col. William B. Hazen at Fort Cobb. He requested permission to move his people to the vicinity of the Fort during the winter as a demonstration of his peaceful intentions. 'I have always done my best to keep my young men quiet, but some will not listen and since the fighting began I have not been able to keep them all at home. But we all want peace, and I would be glad to move all of my people down this way.' Black Kettle made it quite clear that he spoke only for his band and as a further indication of his peaceful attitude he told Hazen that his camp of 180 lodges was on the Washita, forty miles east of Antelope Hills. The request was refused, Hazen explaining that General Sheridan 'the great war chief' was already in the field and intent on punishing the hostiles 'therefore you must go back to your country and if the soldiers come to fight you you must remember they are not from me but from that great war chief, and it is with him you must make your peace'. (Watson/Russell, 1972, p. 3).

On 23 November Lieutenant-Colonel George A. Custer moved out from Camp Supply. His orders from General Sheridan were 'to proceed south in the direction of the Antelope Hills, thence toward the Washita River, the supposed winter seat of the hostile tribes, to destroy their villages and ponies, to kill or hang all warriors and to bring back all women and children'. On the morning of 26 November, they discovered a fresh Indian trail in the snow and by evening had located a Cheyenne village; the Seventh moved to within a half mile of the village and waited for dawn. One of Custer's biographers – Van De Water – was later to write that neither Custer nor Sheridan believed in the existence of 'innocent Indians' Custer's orders were clear – *kill Indians*. 'Now he has found his Indians' wrote Van De Water. 'He has no know-ledge of what band, what tribe sleeps in the tree-shielded lodges beside the Washita, on land secured by treaty. Kiowa – Cheyenne – Arapaho? Hostile? Friendly? Custer does not know but he sends a scout back to halt the column and summon all officers to prepare retribution for "the number and atrocity" of the slumberers' crimes'. (Watson/Russell, 1972, p. 3).

Custer divided his regiment into three detachments. Major J. H. Elliott was assigned three troops to attack from the left, Captain Thompson with three troops to attack from the right, while Custer at the head of a column consisting of six troops and a company of sharpshooters was to attack from the centre. The plan was for them all to strike the village simultaneously. Strung for many miles along the banks of the Washita were – as is typical of Plains Indians during the winter season – a series of small encampments a mile or so apart, each probably consisting of at most one hundred or so tipis. Custer struck the western-most village and it happened to be Black Kettle's. This time Black Kettle was less fortunate than at Sand Creek; when the fighting was over he, together with 102 other Cheyenne – men, women and children – were dead. Although completely surprised, the Cheyenne put up a considerable fight. One group of troops led by Major Elliott chased a party of Indians who were fleeing to the villages farther down river. Elliott's rallying call was 'Here goes for a brevet or a coffin!' He, together with the nineteen troopers who followed him, were never seen alive again – for which Custer was to be subsequently severely criticized. Two weeks later their bodies were to be found in a small circle some two miles from the Washita site. They had obviously been overwhelmed by reinforcements from the other villages scattered down the Washita. The full fury of the distraught Cheyenne was borne by these men 'their heads had been battered in, and some of them had been entirely chopped off; some of them had had the Adam's apple cut out of their throats; some had their hands and feet cut off, and nearly all had been horribly mangled in a way delicacy forbids me to mention'. (Graham, 1953, p. 212).

It is however of significance to record that only *one* soldier was killed within the village – Captain Louis M. Hamilton – three other officers and eleven enlisted men were wounded. One gains a strong impression of an utter rout and massacre, for as Custer subsequently wrote 'except for women and children under eight, they did not try to take captives'. (Nye, 1968, p. 136). Custer early employed what we would now call a scorched earth policy: 875 Indian ponies were captured – and shot. Fifty-three women and children were taken prisoner and the village burned. That evening Custer, probably now much concerned over the reports of large numbers of Indians in the vicinity, left the Washita valley. He apparently made no attempt to ascertain the fate of Elliott and his men.

Captain F. W. Benteen, who would finally

emerge as one of the most respected and brave officers the Seventh Cavalry ever commissioned, was obviously disgusted by the carnage, and devastation of the village and wrote to a friend. 'A great deal remains to be done. That which cannot be taken away must be destroyed. Eight hundred ponies are to be put to death. Our Chief (George A. Custer) exhibits his close sharp-shooting and terrifies the crowd of frightened, captured squaws and papooses by dropping the straggling ponies in death near them. Ah! He is a clever marksman. Not even do the poor dogs of the Indians escape his eye and aim as they drop dead or limp howling away. . . . Now commences the slaughter of the ponies. Volley on volley is poured into them by too hasty men, and they, limping, get away only to meet death from a surer hand. The work progresses! The plunder having been culled over, is hastily piled; the wigwams are pulled down and thrown on it, and soon the whole is one blazing mass. Occasionally a startling report is heard and a steamlike volume of smoke ascends as the fire reaches a powder bag, and thus the glorious deeds of valor done in the morning are celebrated by the flaring bonfire of the afternoon. The last pony is killed. The huge fire dies out; our wounded and dead comrades – heroes of a bloody day – are carefully laid on ready ambulances, and as the brave band of the Seventh Cavalry strikes up the air "Aint I glad to get out of the wilderness" we slowly pick our way across the creek over which we charged so gallantly in the early morn. Take care! do not trample on the dead bodies of that woman and child lying there! In a short time we shall be far from the scene of our daring dash, and night will have thrown her dark mantle over the scene. . . .' (Graham, 1953, p. 212).

Washita was to become, and still is, a controversial episode in the annals of warfare against the Plains Indian; '(it) will undoubtedly remain as contentious as recent events at My Lai and on a "Bloody Sunday" in Londonderry'. (Taunton, 1972, p. 1). In defence of Custer it is said that there was evidence in the village to indicate that at least some of its inhabitants had recently made raids on settlers' cabins – unopened mail, daguerreotype albums, for example. Further, the Indians were camped off the reservations (but on what was frequently referred to as unceded land) as defined by the 1867 Treaty. The question remains, however, of just how much can the wrongs of a comparatively few aggressive individuals be blamed

Map of the Fetterman Massacre, based on one drawn by Colonel Carrington, commander of Fort Phil Kearny. The fort occupied one of the best strategic positions in the American West. It was in the very heart of the Sioux country and the audacity of its position infuriated Red Cloud, whose warriors constantly harassed the occupants. Just before Christmas 1866 Brevet Lieutenant Colonel Fetterman with 80 officers and men rode into a Sioux trap northwest of Lodge Trail Ridge. There were no survivors. The route Fetterman took when he left the Fort (shown between the two branches of the Big Piney) is clearly shown. The places where various groups took their stand are indicated by the letters A B C. Although the map gives a wealth of detail of the rugged terrain the Lodge Trail Ridge has been somewhat foreshortened, possibly deliberately by Carrington, who had ordered Fetterman not to proceed beyond this point. This strengthened Carrington's claim that Fetterman disobeyed orders.

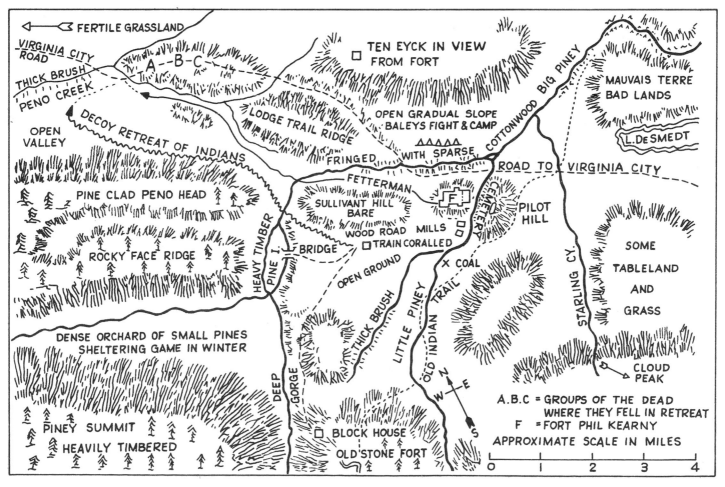

on an innocent majority? In a society where a warrior's path to glory lay in the theatre of warfare, acceptance of Treaty terms by the chiefs meant a blocking of a vital activity of Plains Indian culture; alternative values need time to develop. The People, resentful of the curtailment of their right to live as they pleased, were probably in spirit at least with their young men; nevertheless, viewed as a whole the Cheyenne were in the right and history concedes that Washita was 'Custer's Massacre' for which the *Glory Hunter* was to die for his sins less than a decade hence.

Washita was the beginning of the end for the southern Plains Indians. The ability of the cavalry to take the field in winter – something seldom done in Indian warfare – the superior weapons and resources of the white man, the progressive lack of game and the added burden of protecting their families, wore them down. By 1870 some of their best leaders were dead – Black Kettle, Roman Nose, Tall Bull – and even the more remote Kiowa and Comanche were being beaten to their knees.

Councils followed raids, and raids followed councils. The army took on more of a role of policing and arrested the trouble-makers (or patriots depending on which way you look at it). Satank of the Kiowa chose death to jail, Satanta committed suicide. To add to their troubles the professional 'buffalo skinners' moved in slaughtering the buffalo – the Indians' life-blood – in incredible numbers. When the Englishman, William Blackmore, travelled through Kansas in the autumn of 1873 he observed 'there was a continuous line of putrescent carcasses, so that the air was rendered pestilential and offensive to the last degree'. (Blackmore, 1876, p. 2).

Many – Cheyenne especially – were sent to Florida to be confined in the forbidding St Augustine prison until their spirit was broken. There, like crushed and dying war eagles, they whiled their time away drawing pictographs for tourists depicting their earlier days of glory on the Great Plains – and left for history a priceless record.

In 1867, J. R. Hanson, the Indian Agent for the Upper Missouri Superintendency, had reported, 'We have had but little trouble in this section because immigration has been in another direction and it is along these routes they have mustered their forces to keep back the invaders. Had the course of immigration turned in this direction, here would have been the field of war. Could it be done to bring every hostile Sioux to council today and ask, *what consideration would induce you to give up the war and remain in peace?* They would say "Stop the white man from travelling across these lands, give us the country which is ours by right of conquest and inheritance, to live in and enjoy unmolested by his encroachment and we will be at peace with all the world".' (Blackmore, 1869, p. 307). Hanson was obviously referring to the problems facing the western Sioux and their neighbours.

The Government desired to push to the limit the promise the Sioux had made at the 1865 Harney–Sanborn Treaty to allow the Bozeman Trail, the most northern of the four great transcontinental routes across the United States, to be used by emigrants. The Trail ran through the heart of Powder River country, the best and the last hunting grounds of the northern bands of the Sioux, Cheyenne and Arapaho. It also came to be the most direct overland western route to the goldfields discovered in western Montana. As with the Oregon Trail a decade before, the volume of migration threatened to precipitate the rape of the choicest hunting grounds the Plains tribes ever held. All along the Yellowstone and its tributaries (of which the Powder River was one) the valleys were luxuriant, threaded with clear streams and abundant with game. To the southeast were the Pa Sapa, the sacred Black Hills of the Lakota; to the southwest the imposing Big Horn Mountains dominated by the 9000 feet high Cloud Peak; and north the Bear Paw Mountains (where little over a decade hence the non-treaty Nez Percé were to make their last heroic stand). In this vast area there were few white men and it was the intention of the Sioux to keep it that way.

The 1865 Harney–Sanborn Treaty *did not* get the Sioux to agree to the building of military posts along the route. Nevertheless, demands were made that the highway should be made safe for travel. So on 19 May 1866 Colonel Henry B. Carrington of the Eighteenth Regular Infantry left Fort Kearney in Nebraska with an army of 700 men 'accompanied by four pieces of artillery, two hundred and twenty-six wagons, and a few ambulances containing the wives and children of several of the officers' (Brady, 1904, p. 10). Among the soldiers were skilled carpenters, blacksmiths, and mechanics whilst Carrington himself was a trained engineer. Additionally, the 'government had provided appliances needed for building forts, including tools, doors, sash, glass, nails, stoves, steel, iron, mowers, reapers, scythes, and two steam mills'. (Brady, 1904, p. 10).

Carrington's orders were to take command of the 'Mountain District' (as the Powder River country was then called) and to establish four military posts at strategic points along the Bozeman; one was to be an extension of Fort Connor which had been established by General Connor the previous year and was garrisoned by a few 'galvanized Yankees' – captured Confederates. Fort Connor was to be moved forty miles farther west.

As the Carrington Powder River Expedition rode north on its 500 mile journey along the old Oregon Trail, the apostles of the Indian Peace Policy were attempting to further negotiate with the Sioux to *agree* to the building of the Forts. The Plains Indians were being beaten by the complexities of 'civilized' bureaucracy, for the politicians 'tried to please people in the West by promising a better road to the goldfields and to pacify the pacifists in the East by letting them pursue their treaty-making way. If any of these

Above. The Pink Parasol. Intertribal warfare changed markedly with the coming of the white man. The major emphasis now was to capture horses from the red enemy rather than his scalp: the war for revenge and scalps was now waged against the frontiersman who the Indian saw was his worst enemy. Here a returning war party, society banners waving, parades before an admiring audience. From a painting by Ernst Berke, 1954. Sam Cahoon, New Jersey.

Left. A Reconnoitre, by Alfred Jacob Miller, 1838. Scouting ahead was an important duty for war parties. This picture, though somewhat romanticized (the warrior is overdressed in ceremonial costume) shows accurate details of weapons, since both a bow and a single-shot Northwest gun were frequently carried by warriors even as late as the last quarter of the 19th century. Public Archives of Canada.

Lieutenant Grammond sacrificing himself to cover the retreat. December 1866. To retreat was tantamount to suicide in warfare against Plains tribes and such action generally resulted in a complete rout. That this particular episode actually took place is conjectural but it is known that Lieutenant Grammond made a stand with the more experienced soldiers whose bodies were found farthest from the Fort (near point A on the map).

Again the Sioux warrior in the foreground looks somewhat over-dressed for this action. Most Indians fought wearing only a breechclout. From a painting by Charles Schreyvogel. Thomas Gilcrease Institute, Tulsa, Oklahoma.

gentlemen in Washington had been bold, intelligent, and honest enough to see and tell the truth, he might have lost his job – to say nothing of what might have happened to his party!' (Vestal, 1948, p. 93).

On Sunday, 16 June, in the very midst of the negotiations with the already angry tribesmen, Colonel Henry Carrington rode into Fort Laramie. The situation was explosive; Carrington, an honest and fair-minded man, telegraphed his superiors advising suspension of the expedition until the council reached agreement – only to be told to continue as ordered. As he was introduced to Red Cloud, the chief, who had already grasped the scale of the deception, denounced Carrington as a white [War] Eagle and said 'You steal the country before the red man has a chance to say yes or no.' (Brininstool, 1953, p. 55). Then 'in full view of the mass of Indians who occupied the parade ground he sprang from the platform under the shelter of pine boughs, struck his tepees and went on the warpath' (Brady, 1904, p. 8).

On Friday, 28 June 1866, Carrington's force reached Fort Connor, 160 miles northwest of Fort Laramie bordering Powder River Country. Already severely harassed by Indians, Carrington decided not to attempt to change the site of the Fort. Instead, he garrisoned it and then with the balance of his command (something over 500 men) he advanced north, deeper into hostile territory. In mid-July he camped on the banks of the Big Piney Creek – a tributary of the Powder River – and within a few days began to build Fort Phil Kearny. Carrington designed, drew up the plans, and supervised what was subsequently described as one of the finest forts ever built in the American

West. The site was admirably chosen. Built on a small plateau just large enough to contain the main stockade and situated between the two main branches of the Piney, it commanded virtually uninterrupted views for at least one mile north across the Big Piney to Lodge Trail Ridge, south to the left branch of the Little Piney, approximately west to the bare Sullivant Hills and east across Starling Creek to Lake de Smedt. The surrounding plain was grass, studded with wild flowers and clear fresh water was to hand through cleverly designed water gates built in the stockade which led directly to the Little Piney Creek. The fort itself was rectangular, measuring 800 by 600 feet and it was enclosed by an eight-foot high heavy pine log stockade with firing loop holes at every fourth log and with block houses at the east and west corners. The fort was planned for 1000 men but in its short history it probably never garrisoned more than 500. It was virtually impregnable and the audacity of its position infuriated Red Cloud. As Carrington himself subsequently wrote 'In the establishment of this post I designed to put it where it fell heaviest upon the Indians.' (Brininstool, 1953, p. 46).

Further to his telegram from Fort Laramie on 16 June, Carrington had pointed out in a letter to his superiors the absolute failure of the Treaty regarding the Bozeman Trail; he anticipated the intense hostility that he would face against Red Cloud's warriors and he repeatedly requested reinforcements and better equipment. But even the farsighted Carrington could never have foreseen that before the year was out Fort Phil Kearny, Dakota Territory, would be the witness of a most bloody and desperate encounter from which there would be no survivors.

Within a space of six months more than fifty skirmishes with the Sioux and their allies occurred – some of them severe – and during this period over seventy whites were killed, twenty wounded and 'nearly seven hundred animals – cattle, mules, and horses' were captured. (Brady, 1904, p. 19). One of the casualties was a representative from Frank Leslie's *Illustrated Weekly* who 'appeared to be a perfect gentleman. His thought was, that if the Indians found him they would not hurt him, as he intended to show them his drawings, and also to explain to them that he was not armed.' (Brady, 1904, p. 63). The unfortunate artist completely underestimated the intense hostility and ruthlessness of Red Cloud's younger warriors. He was found dead and completely scalped; on his chest they had cut a cross 'which indicated that they thought him a coward who would not fight'. (Brady, 1904, p. 62).

On 21 December at about 11 a.m. lookouts on Pilot Hill – a vantage point about three-quarters of a mile southeast of the Fort – reported that the wood-collecting train (which left daily under heavy guard to cut pine logs for interior construction of the Fort) was being threatened by Indians who were massing in force on and near Sullivant Hills about one and a half miles to the west of the

Fort (see map). As protection, the train had coralled, and observers at the Fort could hear sporadic firing. Carrington immediately requested Brevet Major Powell to command Company C, 2nd U.S. Cavalry and reinforce the wood train, whereupon Brevet Lieutenant-Colonel Fetterman claimed as senior officer to take out his company, and Lieutenant G. W. Grummond requested to take out the cavalry. To this, Carrington somewhat reluctantly agreed. Fetterman had little experience of Indian warfare, whose fighting ability he held in contempt 'with eighty men we could ride through the whole Sioux nation', whilst Grummond had come close to losing his life in a bloody skirmish less than three weeks before: 'I knew the ambition of each to win honour, but being unprepared for large aggressive action through want of force (now fully demonstrated), I looked to continuance of timber supplies to prepare for more troops as the one practicable duty. Hence, two days before, Major Powell, sent out to cover the train under similar circumstances, simply did that duty when he could have had a fight to any extent.' (Brininstool, 1953, p. 41).

Carrington warned Fetterman that they were fighting 'brave and desperate enemies' (Ibid, p. 41); to Lieutenant Grummond he gave orders to report to Brevet Lieutenant-Colonel Fetterman, to obey his orders, and not to leave him. His instructions to Fetterman were explicit. 'Support the wood train; relieve it, and report to me. Do not engage or pursue Indians at its expense. Under no circumstances pursue over the ridge, viz. Lodge Trail Ridge, as per map in your possession.' (Ibid, p. 42). The regimental quartermaster and acting adjutant, Lieutenant A. H. Wands repeated Carrington's orders to Fetterman and just as the little army of 81 men rode out through the west gates

Sioux Indians at Fort Laramie, about May 1868. The harassing tactics employed by Red Cloud and his Sioux succeeded: the government agreed to abandon the forts along the Bozeman Trail. Another treaty was drawn up which was finally signed by Red Cloud in November 1868. These are some of the principal headmen and chiefs who came to Laramie to sign the treaty. Left to right Spotted Tail (Brulé), Roman Nose (Miniconjou), Old Man Afraid of His Horses (Oglala), Lone Horn (Miniconjou), Whistling Elk, Pipe, an unidentified Indian. Photograph attributed to Alexander Gardner, 1868. Smithsonian Institution, National Anthropological Archives, Washington.

'Fearing that the spirit of ambition might override prudence (as my refusal to permit 60 mounted men and 40 citizens to go for several days down Tongue River valley after villages, had been unfavourably regarded by Brevet Lieutenant-Colonel Fetterman and Captain Brown), I crossed the parade, and from a sentry platform halted the cavalry and again repeated my precise orders.' (Ibid, p. 42).

Carrington had estimated a total of 1500 lodges of Indians camped on the Tongue River north toward the Wolf Mountains and warriors from these large encampments daily reinforced those already harassing Fort Phil Kearny.

When Fetterman left the Fort he did not follow the road directly to the wood train; instead he rode north of Sullivant Hill, skirting the southern slope of Lodge Trail Ridge possibly with a view to cutting off the Indians (or as Carrington subsequently surmised perhaps he took this route intending to disobey orders). Carrington then learnt that no surgeon was with Fetterman and thus instructed Dr C. H. Hines, accompanied by two orderlies, to ride to the wood train and if not required to return with Fetterman. At 11.30 a.m. the picket on Pilot Hill reported that the wood train had successfully repulsed the attack, broken corral and had 'moved forward on its daily duty' (Ibid, p. 46). Within a very short time Hines returned, confirming that the wood train had proceeded safely towards Piney Island but that Fetterman had gone beyond Lodge Trail Ridge towards Peno Creek, and that Indians were on the western slope between him and Fetterman making it impossible for Hines to join them.

Fetterman was moving into an ambush – a technique of warfare in which Plains warriors excelled. The Indians who had attacked the wood train moved parallel and slightly ahead of Fetterman. They skirted the pine clad Peno head perhaps a mile or so from Fetterman's command whilst those on the western slope of Lodge Trail Ridge followed behind, cutting off Fetterman's retreat. At 12 o'clock Carrington was informed of rapid firing in the direction of Peno Creek; he immediately despatched Captain Ten Eyck together with infantry and the remaining cavalry with orders to join Colonel Fetterman 'at all hazards'. Within half an hour, Ten Eyck reached a hill about three miles north of the Fort: about that time 'there had been a short lull in the firing (namely, only scattered shots here and there), succeeded by a very brisk firing, apparently by file at first, and quite regular, and an occasional volley, followed by indiscriminate firing, gradually dying out in a few scattering shots'. (Brininstool, 1953, p. 49).

When Ten Eyck reached the summit of the hill where he was in view from the Fort, all firing in Fetterman's direction had ceased. He could not see Fetterman but on the road below him and less than a mile away were a body of Indians who challenged him to come down and fight. 'Moving cautiously forward with the wagons – evidently supposed by the enemy to be guns, as mounted men were in advance – he rescued from the spot where

the enemy had been nearest, 49 bodies, including those of Brevet Lieutenant-Colonel Fetterman and Captain F. H. Brown. The latter went without my consent or knowledge, fearless to fight Indians with any adverse odds, and determined to kill one at least before joining his company.' (Brininstool, 1953, p. 43).

Ten Eyck then prudently returned to Phil Kearny without loss, having been unable to account for the other 32 officers and men who were with Fetterman. The Fort was now in a virtual state of siege; Indians flashed mirror signals across the valley and at night lit fires to show their presence instilling the occupants (which included women and children) with greater fear and apprehension. The guards were doubled, and in each barrack room three men kept watch throughout the night.

The next morning, anticipating that failure to recover the rest of Fetterman's command would lower the morale of the Fort and encourage the Indians further, Carrington took personal command of a heavily armed force of eighty men and rode to the scene of the action. Having now further reduced the fighting capacity of the Fort by almost fifty per cent, and the situation having become so critically desperate, orders were issued that the women and children were to be placed in the magazine with orders that none should be taken alive in the event of the Indians breaching the stockade.

When Carrington reached the scene of the action all evidence indicated that the command had been suddenly surrounded and overwhelmed by a large force of Indians. At the northwest point on the small ridge farthest from the Fort (Point A on Map), Carrington found the bodies of the two civilians, James S. Wheatley and Isaac Fisher of Blue Springs, Nebraska, who had accompanied Fetterman. They had recently acquired Henry repeating rifles and 'felt invincible'; the ground near the two rocks where the men were found was strewn with cartridge shells which 'told how well they fought'. Wheatley had one hundred and five arrows in him and had been scalped. Near Fisher and Wheatley were the bodies of the more experienced soldiers who probably attempted to make a stand, knowing that retreat was suicide in Plains warfare. Lieutenant Grummond's body was near this group and evidence indicated that he had made a most heroic stand. In his Official Report on the Fetterman Disaster penned on 3 January 1867, Carrington said 'The officers who fell believed that no Indian force could overwhelm that number of troops well held in hand. Their terrible massacre bore marks of great valour, and has demonstrated the force and character of the foe; but no valour could have saved them. Pools of blood on the road and sloping sides of the narrow divide showed where Indians bled fatally; but their bodies were carried off. I counted 65 such pools in the space of an acre, and three within 10 feet of Lieutenant Grummond's body.' (Brininstool, 1953, p. 44).

That the Indians had few guns was evidenced by

the fact that only six soldiers had bullet wounds and of these, two – Fetterman and Brown – had died at each other's hand. The mutilation was brutal and designed to instil fear. Carrington reported:

'I give some of the facts as to my men, whose bodies I found just at dark, resolved to bring all in, viz: mutilations: eyes torn out and laid on the rocks; noses cut off; ears cut off; chins cut off; teeth chopped out; joints of fingers; brains taken out and placed on rocks with other members of the body; entrails taken out and exposed; hands cut off; feet cut off; arms taken out from sockets; private parts severed and indecently placed on the person; eyes, ears, mouth and arms penetrated with spear-heads, sticks and arrows; ribs slashed to penetration with knives; skulls severed in every form from chin to crown; muscles of calves, thighs, stomach, back, breast, arms and cheek taken out. Punctures upon every sensitive part of the body even to the soles of the feet and palms of the hand.

'All this only approximates the whole truth.' (Brininstool, 1953, p. 45).

By Wednesday after the battle all had been buried in the post cemetery just east of the Little Piney. Fetterman, Brown and Grummond were placed in one grave, the rest together in another. Each coffin was carefully numbered for identification. 'In the grave', wrote Carrington, 'I bury disobedience.'

This was not to be their last resting place.

Just under a fortnight before on 8 December 1866 President Andrew Johnson had congratulated Congress on the success of the Laramie Treaty and said that the Indian problem along the Bozeman Trail and in the Powder River country in general had been satisfactorily resolved. The enormity of Johnson's understatement was driven home when news of the Fetterman disaster reached Fort Laramie three days later.

Even before receipt of his Official Report on the Fetterman Fight, General Philip St George Cooke ordered that Carrington be relieved of command at Fort Phil Kearny and transferred as soon as possible to the little frontier post of Fort Casper. It took Carrington twenty years to clear his name.

Despite the fact that warring during the winter months was unusual for Indians, so intent were they on ridding the Powder River country of

Camp of Sitting Bull in the Big Horn Mountain by H. H. Cross, 1873. The northern bands of Sioux whom Sitting Bull represented did not sign the Laramie Treaty and refused to recognize its validity, continuing their hunting and roaming ways and seldom going to the agencies. They came to be dubbed as 'hostiles' or the 'buffalo Indians'; above all they valued their freedom. This rather idyllic scene shows Sitting Bull's retreat in the Big Horn Mountains. Although H. H. Cross painted a large number of Indian scenes and subjects, in this picture the tipis in the foreground are much too large and such villages would probably be sited near a wooded stream. Thomas Gilcrease Institute, Tulsa, Oklahoma.

whites that they continued harassment throughout the rest of the winter and spring of 1867. Although the Fort had been completed, large amounts of wood were required for the long winter months and it was arranged for the contract to be given to the firm of Gilmore and Porter, a stipulation being made that these civilians would be constantly guarded by the soldiers.

On 2 August 1867 there came a second major clash with the Sioux near Piney Island. Referred to as the Wagon Box Fight because the wagon boxes were drawn up for protection, the troopers, who had recently been issued with new Springfield breech-loading rifles, took a terrible revenge on the charging Sioux. During a battle which lasted more than four hours, twenty-six well-armed soldiers under the command of Captain James Powell and Lieutenant John C. Jeness, and four civilians, held off a massive force of Sioux and Cheyenne. So sure was Red Cloud of victory that he allowed the women and children to witness the battle from the surrounding hills. The rapidity with which the soldiers could reload, however, confounded the Sioux tactics previously so effective against the old muzzle-loader, when they rode the enemy down before there was time to reload. But towards noon the command was in a critical condition. Lieutenant John Jeness was dead – he died instantly when a bullet struck him in the forehead at the first assault by the Sioux forces; privates Doyle and Haggerty had also been killed and a third seriously wounded. Only the arrival of heavily-armed reinforcements under Major Smith together with mountain howitzers frightened the Sioux, whose mode of fighting – indeed whose very existence – depended so much on small losses. Like a wounded grizzly Red Cloud prudently withdrew to ponder new tactics. It was estimated he had lost sixty-seven of his bravest warriors (including his nephew) and 120 were wounded, some so severely that they were crippled for life. On the credit side, although he probably didn't know it then, the Sioux had won the Powder River War.

When Powell's party returned to Fort Phil Kearny they were suffering from complete nervous exhaustion from which some, including Captain Powell, never fully recovered. The Wagon Box Fight added an additional burden to Fort Phil Kearny's problem; there had been a sudden badly-planned addition of soldiers after the Fetterman Fight and Carrington, who knew Fort Phil Kearny so well, had been replaced. The poorly balanced diet available, together with the constant harassment by Indians ultimately broke the men's health.

The Government needed to re-think their violation of the 1866 Laramie Treaty.

In April 1868, the Peace Commissioners again came to Fort Laramie and this time they were prepared to grant Red Cloud's demands. He had won a victory for the position that he had taken in 1866 – the complete abandonment of the Forts along the Bozeman Trail and a clear defining of the limits of the lands claimed by the Sioux – but he was so astute that although Brulé and other Oglala headmen had 'touched the pen' by the end of May, he personally refused to sign until 6 November 1868, after the Forts had been burned to the ground.

Article II of the Treaty clearly and precisely defined their reservation, 'commencing on the east bank of the Missouri River where the forty-sixth parallel of north latitude crosses the same, thence along low water mark down said east bank to a point opposite where the northern line of the State of Nebraska strikes the river, thence west across said river, and along the northern line of Nebraska to the one hundred and fourth degree of longitude west from Greenwich, thence north on said meridian to a point where the forty-sixth parallel of north latitude intercepts the same, thence due east along parallel to the place of beginning'. Broadly this was what is now the state of South Dakota, west of the Missouri River.

Recognizing that Red Cloud could not speak for those Northern Sioux tribes, the Hunkpapa and Sans Arcs particularly, Article XI of the Treaty specifically refers to 'tribes *who are parties to* this agreement', whilst Article XVI stipulated that 'the country north of the North Platte River and east of the summits of the Big Horn Mountains, shall be held and considered to be *unceded Indian territory*, and also stipulates and agrees that no white person or persons shall be permitted to settle upon or occupy any portion of the same; or without the consent of the Indians, first had and obtained, to pass through same'.

The clauses in the Treaty were complex and it must have been confusing to most of the Sioux; 'forty-sixth parallel' and 'one hundred and fourth degree of longitude west from Greenwich' took some defining in terms of local streams, mountains and known landmarks. Subsequent events were to prove, however, that another mind as keen as, perhaps even more than, Red Cloud's understood the Laramie Treaty very well indeed. *Tatan'ka-iyotake* – Sitting Bull – Champion of the Sioux, would drive a still harder bargain before the power and spirit of the free Plains Indian was finally destroyed.

The Dispossessed

'The country there is poisoned with blood . . .'

Sitting Bull in Canada, October 1877

SMOULDERING APATHY replaced open hostility and the Treaty obligations now forced Red Cloud into a battle of words; words produced by the white man's philosophy which the Warriors of the Plains failed to fully understand. On the face of it Red Cloud and his followers should have been satisfied; their demands had apparently been met, the Bozeman Trail was closed and the Powder River area, with certain vague provisos, was still Indian country. But what was apparently agreed on paper had a different reality when put into practice.

As the Treaty Sioux attempted to readjust, complaints were rife, and usually directed at their agents whom they regarded, generally with some justification, as authoritarian, thieving scoundrels. Later Red Cloud was to request a *wealthy* agent 'who would not need to steal and would give the Oglala whatever they asked for'. (Hyde, 1937, p. 232).

The dissatisfaction was symptomatic of a disturbed and bitterly disappointed people. Modern day social anthropologists would recognize that the suppressed tribes were in an anomic state where the old values no longer held any meaning and the conditions necessary for self-fulfilment and the attainment of happiness were no longer present.

The conflict was aggravated by the complexity of American democracy, of opposing departmental interests, of shifting political power and the limited authority of individuals. Later, Joseph of the Nez Percé was to summarize it rather well. 'The white people have too many chiefs. They do not understand each other. They do not talk alike. . . . Such a Government has something wrong about it. I cannot understand why so many chiefs are allowed to talk so many different ways, and promise so many different things'. (Brady, 1904, pp. 72 & 73).

Gradually the full implications of the Treaty unfolded – the Sioux were expected to settle down to farming and they must not oppose the building of the railroad off defined limits of the reservation. This had a sting which surely no Sioux could have foreseen. When railroads were built, a five to forty mile depth of land was given as an inducement to the Construction Companies and some Indian communities were displaced. In later years the Blackfoot in Canada would also face problems due to the railroad – that of prairie fires caused by the Canadian Pacific Railway which ran along the northern boundary of their reserve. The People became alarmed: 'Strong men grow, weak men die. The uncivilized and barbarous tribes which will not accept civilization perish before its march. It is the law of the universe and you cannot check it by any constitutional or legislative enactment.' (Congressman Hurlbut, Congressional Record, 1876).

Appreciating the immense difficulty which the American Indian had on viewing the white man from any point of view other than his own, the government had early developed a policy of inviting prominent Indians to meet the Great White Father in Washington. Few returned unimpressed by the obvious power and potential of the white man and, considering the nature of things, it was

Little Raven, head chief of the Arapaho, 1871. It had early been a policy to invite Indian delegations to Washington. One of many was that led by Little Raven in the summer of 1871 to meet the 'Great Chief of the American Nation' and to have the boundaries of their reservation clearly defined. Little Raven returned home and told his people that he had seen the Great Father making money at the mint – so 'Washington' did not expect the Arapaho to raise corn since they had plenty of money to hire help for the Indian. Photographed for the Trustees of the Blackmore Museum, Salisbury. William Blackmore Collection, British Museum.

Right. Red Cloud, Oglala Sioux, c. 1870. This chief consistently opposed the oncoming white man and refused to sign any treaties which might endanger the hunting grounds of his people. In the 1860s he directed a war opposing the building of Forts along the Bozeman Trail. He won a complete victory for the Sioux and signed the treaty of 1868 only on the condition that the Forts were abandoned and burnt. He was born at the forks of the Platte River in Nebraska in 1822 and died at Pine Ridge, South Dakota, in December 1909. A member of a distinguished Oglala family, many of his descendants still live on the Pine Ridge reservation.
Frank Humphries Collection.

Above. Fort McKenzie site as it is today. Near Loma, Montana. Nothing now remains of the Fort. Brulé Flats, a well known area where the tribes pitched their tipis when they came to trade, is part farmland. It is still possible however to pick up numerous beads, broken clay pipe stems and an arrowhead and musket ball here and there and to discern the actual location of the fort. The bluffs across the Missouri – but a short distance away, for at this point the river is quite narrow – are now a little more rounded since Bodmer painted the scene nearly a century and a half ago and trees still grow at the same location.

perhaps the most subtle way of telling The People that they were members of a fast-vanishing race. From such visits we do fortunately have some of the earliest pictorial records – a historic bonus – of many of the most distinguished representatives of the Western Indians. An early method of recording was by the so-called Hawkins' Physiognotrace which enabled accurate silhouettes to be obtained of the Indian sitters within a few minutes. A number of these, including silhouettes of Pawnee Indians, are now in the Museum of History and Technology, Washington and date from 1805–1806. Then there were such official government painters as Charles Bird King and George Cooke and finally, particularly from 1860 onwards, the records of such photographers as Gardner, Shindler and Jackson, many working at the instigation of the Englishman, William Blackmore, a wealthy and influential entrepreneur with a deep interest in the North American Indian.

Indian delegations were usually treated rather well and often given the opportunity of publicly presenting their side of the picture. Newspaper reports generally gave sympathetic coverage of such events, pointing out the difficulties confronting both races.

Typical was the Cheyenne, Arapaho and Wichita delegation led by the head chief of the Arapaho, Ohnastie or Little Raven, who arrived early in the summer of 1871. Their main purpose was to meet the 'Great Chief of the American Nation' and to have their reservation boundary lines clearly defined. They were 'astonished by our cities; such a gathering of men all in one place . . . they do not understand our railways, telegraphs, etc. They know such things are done, but they cannot understand by what power, etc. . . . they have no words in their language to comprehend all they see'. (*New York Times*, 1 June 1871).

On Thursday evening, 1 June 1871, at the Cooper Institute in New York, a grand reception was held for the chiefs, who included not only Little Raven but Powder Face and Bird Chief of the same tribe, Little Robe and Stone Calf of the Cheyenne and Good Buffalo of the Wichita. The Leader for the influential *Boston Post* of Wednesday, 7 June 1871, welcomed the visit by the Indian chiefs, commenting that it 'is calculated to do us good, by opening our minds to a knowledge of the people they represent, by enlightening our consciences upon our obligations to them, and by arousing a sentiment of sympathy for their oppressed condition which may lead to a more active and just interest in their behalf'. Referring to the embarrassing and extremely difficult problems which confronted the solution to the 'Indian Question' it ventured the opinion that the policy of the Government towards the Indians had always 'nominally, been honest and just and wise and humane', blaming the mismanagement on the 'corruption, neglect in execution and demoralizing influence of private influences which had hindered government policy so as to render it practically oppressive'. The main

government fault was the failure 'to execute what has been devised, and its neglect ultimately to enforce the theories it has adopted'. Thus, the *Boston Post* predicted that with the election of President Grant the Administration would now for the first time be making an honest effort to live on terms of friendship and 'fair play with the race'.

William Blackmore who was present at the reception was evidently impressed by the historical occasion. Not only does his vast file of data contain press cuttings reporting the speeches but he personally arranged to have all these Indians photographed for the 'Trustees of The Blackmore Museum' in Salisbury, England.

The following year saw the visit of Red Cloud and a formidable delegation of Brulé and Oglala Sioux. This was the chief's second visit. The previous one in June 1870 had been somewhat spoilt, when on arrival he found that Spotted Tail of the Brulé was already there. Then too in Washington Red Cloud had been shown the gigantic guns in the arsenal – one was fired for him and he measured its length with his eagle wing fan. As much as he was a patriot to the cause of his people he must have realized the hopelessness of their situation. Little, in fact, was ever achieved by the Sioux on such visits other than to become progressively demoralized. Probably only their social engagements made the effort worthwhile.

Makhpiya-luta – Red Cloud – was an impressive man, just on fifty years of age. He had risen to prominence amongst the southern bands of Sioux by force of character, having no hereditary claim to chieftainship. As a warrior he stood first amongst his people and eighty coups were credited to his name. He held equal rank as a statesman and was generally recognized as an honest patriot. Whites who became well acquainted with him described him as a 'most courtly chief and a natural-born gentleman, with a bow as graceful as that of a Chesterfield'. (See Handbook, 1907–1910, p. 359).

This time, Red Cloud met William Blackmore, which made the occasion a memorable one for the visiting Sioux. Of this meeting Blackmore's nephew, seventeen-year-old Sidney Hamp from Bedford, England, has left a highly interesting personal record. On Saturday, 26 May 1872, he wrote in his diary: 'When I came down this morning I found Mr Moran and Professor Hayden in the room, and having breakfasted with them, we all (except Mr Moran) went to see some Indians. The first we saw was a chief named "Red Cloud" to whom Uncle gave a knife, and the chief shook hands and said how! how! which is the utmost extent of their English. We next saw two squaws to whom Aunt gave each a shawl, and some sham jewelry, they were very pleased and chattered in their own tongue like women! Then we saw 8 or 9 Indians of the Sioux in a room sitting on their beds, and we shook hands with them and said how! how! After dinner we went to the "Smithsonian Museum" and so did the Indians. Lots of people were there to see them, they were dressed in plain clothes, which did not look at all well. They are mostly big fellows, but they do not seem to be able to stand much fatigue.'

On 29 May an excursion 'down to the river' was organized for the Sioux and some of Blackmore's friends. Red Cloud expressed his approval of the excellent treatment they had received whilst in Washington and hoped that they would one day be able to return the hospitality.

Dinner was, at least to young Hamp, a hilarious event; he wrote: 'It was such a *lark* to see the Indians eat. One mixed strawberries and olives together, another plumbcake and pickled oysters. Some ate holding the things in their hands, and some ate ice cream, pine apple and fowl all at once, with a knife and fork. Together they managed very well.' Later Blackmore proposed a toast to the President, Queen Victoria and the Chiefs, and Red Cloud delivered an eloquent reply. A fine orator and an impressive figure, he added further weight to his effect by standing impassive and dignified during the intervals of translation. Then the Sioux gave Blackmore a finely beaded pipe bag and except for the fact that one Indian put his finger right into the mouth of a white woman in order to point out the gold in her teeth to his companions, everything seemed to go in an orderly fashion! 'Everyone, I think, enjoyed themselves very much.' (Brayer, 1946, pp. 261–262).

Later, Blackmore arranged to have the entire Sioux delegation photographed by Alexander Gardner. One was also taken with William Blackmore shaking the chief's hand. The series of photographs are now believed to be the first taken of Red Cloud and, as with the many other photographs commissioned by Blackmore, they were again published for the 'Trustees of the Blackmore Museum', Salisbury, England.

Smouldering apathy gave way to progressive discontent. An Act of Congress passed on 3 March 1871 ceased to recognize the tribes as independent nations with which the United States was obliged to solemnly enter into Treaty, replacing them by less exacting, simple agreements. Virtually unable to negotiate at the government level, except on the white man's terms, the Treaty chiefs were further undermined, as wily agents with an eye to the main chance did their bit. As one 'Major' reported: 'I have endeavoured to destroy the tribal relations as much as possible, and also to destroy the influence of certain chiefs. I have allowed relatives to band together and would appoint one of the number a chief or headman and suggest to him to take his people off to some good locality and make permanent houses. Of course, every band formed this way weakens the influence of some chief in proportion as it takes individuals from his band. Bands that at one time numbered over a hundred people, have been reduced this way to less than twenty. I have had many houses made this way by Indians who never worked before. The advantage to the man appointed by me was that he became

Sioux delegation, Washington, 1875. By the mid-seventies Red Cloud was engaged in a battle of words and led many delegations to Washington attempting to better the conditions on the Sioux reservations. The members of the delegations are, Front row: left to right, Sitting Bull, Swift Bear and Spotted Tail. Back row, Julius Mayer, an interpreter, and Red Cloud (the seated figure is not the famous Hunkpapa chief but an Oglala by the same name). Following the Custer disaster in June 1876 Red Cloud was suspected of secretly encouraging the hostilities and Spotted Tail was appointed chief at both the Red Cloud and Spotted Tail agencies. He negotiated the settlement by which his nephew Crazy Horse surrendered in the spring of 1877. Copied from an original print from the estate of General Hugh Scott in the Bureau of American Ethnology. Smithsonian Institution, National Anthropological Archives, Washington.

more prominent and controlled the funds derived from the sale of beef hides.' (Wissler, 1938, p. 37).

But the Plains Indians were not easily throttled. By 1873, the Treaty Sioux were becoming so aggressive towards their agents that troops were stationed at the Red Cloud and Spotted Tail Agencies – a violation of the 1868 Laramie Treaty.

When William Blackmore viewed the situation in the mid-70s, he was led to observe that it would be extremely difficult to find *any* Treaty entered into by the Government during the previous twenty years which had been 'strictly and honourably fulfilled' and added that frauds by Indian agents and encroachment on the reservations by the whites had been the cause of the Indian wars (Dodge, 1876, pp. XII and XV and Blackmore ms, 1868, Salisbury). This was no idle observation. Although at least a century ahead of his time by any standards, Blackmore himself was hardly an Indian lover. A land speculator of almost unbelievable magnitude (and questionable legality) he could count amongst his many friends and close acquaintances railroaders, army officers, politicians, and even Presidents.

The worsening conditions were universal. In 1874, Jesse W. Griest, U.S. Indian Agent at the Ottoe Agency, Nebraska, reported that his charges, who had left their agency in a desperate attempt to find buffalo, were found in such a destitute state that food had to be furnished in order

Shooting buffalo on the track of the Kansas Pacific Railway, 1871. The slaughter of the buffalo at this time was incredible and while Indians starved on the reservations professional hunters and wealthy sportsmen killed buffalo by the thousand, leaving the carcasses to rot on the prairie. One Indian agent pleaded that if the meat of the buffalo slaughtered on the frontier by white hunters merely for their hides could be transported to his reservation it would relieve the starvation facing his wards.

to enable them to reach home. Later, even their 'privilege' (?) of hunting buffalo was withdrawn and the continued depredations of the whites was 'rapidly stripping the reservation of its timber, and unless efficient means to prevent it are available, the most that is valuable will soon be gone'. (Griest, 1874, p. 205).

To the south, hide hunters were slaughtering buffalo in incredible numbers. As we have seen, the whole life style of the Plains Indians pivoted on buffalo; it provided them with food, clothing, shelter, virtually everything they needed or used and now this very life force was being destroyed before their eyes. As early as 1872, it had been estimated that the number of buffalo which were being slaughtered for their hides alone was at least 1,000,000 a year.

Professional hunters formed lines of camps along the banks of the Arkansas River and *continuously* shot buffalo, night and day as they came down to drink. In Dodge City, early in October 1873, William Blackmore spoke to one of the leading professional hunters about the slaughter '[he] was the proprietor of one of the best skinning outfits in Kansas, [and] he told me that he usually killed only about eighty per day, as he found that his three men could not well skin more'. When Blackmore enquired as to the largest number he had ever shot from one stand, a figure of 133 was quoted, adding that 'he had frequently killed all that he wanted for the days skinning from one stand'. Colonel Dodge, a friend of Blackmore's, quoted even more startling figures – he was able to give an instance of having personally counted 112 carcasses inside a semi-circle of some 200 yards radius, all of which had been killed by one man from the same spot in less than three-quarters of an hour. (Blackmore ms, 1902, London).

Although the greatest slaughter undoubtedly

came from these professional hide hunters, there were many others who hunted purely for diversion. Elaborate buffalo hunts were arranged for wealthy patrons, including such people as the Grand Duke Alexis of Russia, English lords and ladies, and even officers of the Grenadier Guards – and they were generally organized by U.S. Army officers such as George A. Custer and Colonel Richard Irving Dodge. The London *Times* ran an advertisement for hunts '50 guineas for a round trip to Wallace'. No doubt many coveted North American Indian ethnographical trophies, which turn up from time to time in the great houses of the landed gentry in England, can be traced to this period of the virtual extermination of the buffalo. Ladies who could not stand the rigours of horseback could conserve their energy by riding in a sedate 'ambulance' or even shoot the game from the safety of a locomotive carriage as the railroads, such as the Kansas Pacific, Atchison, Topeka, and Santa Fé, criss-crossed former Indian territory.

The wanton slaughter appalled the Indians, not least Sitting Bull, who later, whilst in Canada, said of his former homeland 'the country there is poisoned with blood – a poison that kills all the buffaloes or drives them away. It is strange that the Americans should complain that the Indians kill buffaloes. We kill buffaloes, as we kill other animals, for food and clothing, and to make our lodges warm. They kill buffaloes – for what? Go through [the] country. See the thousands of carcasses rotting on the Plains. Your young men shoot for pleasure. All they take from dead buffalo is his tail, or his head, or his horns, perhaps, to show they have killed a buffalo. What is this? Is it robbery? You call us savages. What are *they*?' (*New York Herald*, 16 November 1877).

In the same year as Blackmore spoke to the professional hide hunters in Kansas, the *Sioux City Journal* (Iowa) commented on the immense slaughter of other animals in the Upper Missouri region. In one year Durfee and Peck of Iowa, working for the Northwestern Transportation Company, shipped forty tons of antelope and deer skins; 'on an average these skins weigh two and a half pounds each which makes a total of 32,000 skins, worth at the least calculation $40,000'. They also shipped 2000 wolf, 1000 fox, 500 elk and 600 beaver skins at the estimated value of $15,000. It was a lucrative business and the report further commented that there were a score of other parties whose bounty had not been included in their estimates. A newspaper cartoon summed the situation up with grim humour – a live buffalo stripping off his very hide as a man takes off his overcoat crying to an astonished hunter 'Don't shoot! Take my robe, and let me go in peace'.

Soon there was little left but the bones, and bone picking outfits collected buffalo bones and sold them at $5 a ton. Most were shipped to Philadelphia and used as fertilizer 'for the soil enfeebled districts of the eastern and middle states'. But the less porous bone was turned into buttons, combs and knife-handles. Mixed with the great piles of bones awaiting shipment, one observer reported, were Indian skulls, legs and arms; and in some instances the skulls and vertebrae of women and children, adding 'An Indian skull is said to be worth a dollar and a quarter for combs, and the Indian thigh makes knife handles that are beautiful to behold.' (Blackmore ms, 1932, London).

It was a grim reflection that, as far as frontier people were concerned, there was little distinction between buffalo and Indian.

Tribes who had treated with the white man faced starvation and at least one agent pleaded 'if the meat of the buffalo that are slaughtered on the frontier by white hunters merely for their hides could be obtained on the line of the railroad and shipped in for food, it would be a means of relieving destitution here'. The pleadings did not go entirely unheeded. There were many philanthropic organizations which sprang up in the eastern cities which attempted to fight the Indians' cause or relieve their misery. From the Ottoe Agency in Nebraska, Indian Agent Griest acknowledged receipt of funds from the 'Friends of Philadelphia' for building purposes and materials despatched by the 'Society of Friends' to make clothing for the Indian children. Reports such as these remind one more of the modern day disaster funds such as those for Biafra or Ethiopia. Yet these 19th-century American Indians signed what were purported to be honourable treaties! I once examined in a large ethnographical collection a pair of Sioux moccasins which had been made during this turbulent reservation period and it struck me at the time the extent of The People's humiliation and poverty. Buckskin was beyond their means, so the uppers were made of stained and fraying canvas and the sole of tiny pieces of leather sewn neatly together. But all dignity was not lost, for in bold Sioux style they were partly embellished with tiny blue, white and red seed beads. I think those moccasins just about summed up the low ebb to which The People had been reduced.

But the Treaty Sioux still had Powder River country to which they could retreat. It was there that each spring and summer they could meet up with those groups who considered themselves non-Treaty people – Sitting Bull and Crazy Horse – and live the old life. But even those days were to be numbered. As game dwindled to the east and south a greedy eye was cast toward the remoter regions of Wyoming, Western Colorado and Montana and reports of that lush territory reached the eastern papers. The 12 September 1874 edition of the *New York Herald* ran a report from their correspondent accompanying the Hayden expedition. 'Game of all kinds abounds in great profusion in these mountains. You may, in fact, call the Rocky Mountains the hunters paradise. Elk, which have *superb antlers* and weigh from 400 to 700 pounds when dressed, are stupid in the presence of the hunter, generally following their leader regardless of the consequences. Mountain sheep are easy game to kill, and make delicious meat, as do the deer and fawn. About the middle of September the high mountain game are driven down into the valleys and on the plateaux by the approach of winter and then the slaughter of the hunter is at its height.' The article ended 'May many come and see for themselves in 1875.'

There were to be other problems. It had been rumoured for some years that gold and other minerals were to be found in abundance in the Black Hills. Thus, in the summer of 1874, the government sent an expedition to investigate. It was led by Lieutenant-Colonel George A. Custer from Fort Abraham Lincoln on the Upper Missouri. Although the Black Hills were on the Sioux reservation as recognized by the 1868 Laramie Treaty and, the expedition was bitterly opposed by the Sioux, it was ostensibly a scientific expedition. In fact, the few scientists were heavily guarded by a military escort comprising 'ten companies of the Seventh Cavalry, two companies of infantry, sixty Indian scouts, four Gatling guns and a very long wagon-train loaded with supplies'. (Dustin, 1958, p. 6). The formidable expedition met no opposition and in fact turned out to be a pleasant excursion for most of the participants. They found a little gold and news of their discovery reached Fort Laramie in August 1874. The discovery was widely reported and a second expedition under Lieutenant-Colonel R. I. Dodge, together with a distinguished mineralogist, Professor W. P. Jenney, was sent out in the spring of 1875 to evaluate more rigorously the gold deposits. Well before negotiations of any sort could be carried out with the

Weekly Ration Ticket, 1882. As the tribes faced starvation ration tickets were issued to each family head. On the Blackfoot reservation beef was butchered every Friday, and Saturday was ration day 'when the men stood in line and presented their tickets to be punched as they received their rations' (Ewers, 1968, p.173). Beef issues often fell short of amounts agreed in treaties and in the winter of 1884 more than one quarter of the Blackfoot in the United States died of starvation.

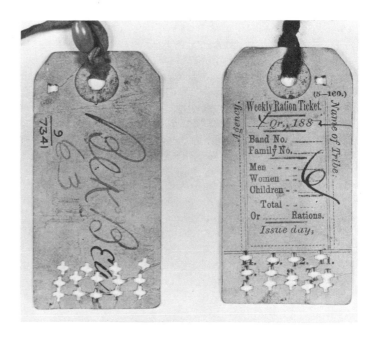

Sioux, a Gold Rush had started. This flagrant violation of the solemn promises made in the 1868 Treaty infuriated the Sioux and while, initially, the military attempted to keep the miners and others out by rounding up several of the leaders and imprisoning them at Fort Laramie, their resources just could not check the flood. Later, Senator Hurlbut commented: 'I say to you there is not power enough in this Government to stop the progress of this [our] conquering race to *any place they* may choose to go, and we may as well accept the fact. It is one of the evils of our special form of government that you cannot repress the conquering, predatory spirit, if you please, of the people of this country. *There is not power enough to do it....* And what is this government to do? I admit we ought to maintain treaties. [But] I abhor the idea altogether of treaties with Indians, because they are not nations. I hope we will try to keep good faith so far as we can. But you cannot stop it in any way of the world . . . if you increase your army to 50,000 men . . . there is not power enough to stop the migration of our people.' (Congressional Record, July, 1876).

The Government attempted to buy mining rights in the Black Hills from the Sioux; they refused. They offered to purchase outright for $6,000,000; the Sioux still refused. Red Cloud, by now an experienced negotiator and probably advised by the astute Spotted Tail, demanded $70,000,000 and further declared that the government must support the Sioux for seven generations to come. Since the government made the Indians live on reservations, had taken away their hunting grounds, it was only right they should foot the bill, he contended. Sitting Bull was even less compromising. He refused to sell at any price – even refused to parley. Said he, 'We want no white men here. The Black Hills belong to me. If the whites try to take them, I will fight.' (Vestal, 1957, p. 133).

The Sioux became increasingly restless. The government, as Senator Seelye of Massachusetts subsequently pointed out, had failed to make adequate appropriation for their subsistence. 'Instead of feeding them, we have been starving them.' (Congressional Record, July 1876).

Meantime, Sitting Bull and his non-treaties up in Powder River country and clear to the Canadian border, had *never* been brought under control, never made a Treaty, and this leader of the last free Warriors of the Plains 'who have been regarded as mists of the mountains or as myths' (Congressional Record, July, 1876), was now rapidly becoming unpopular. As early as 1866 he had clearly shown his attitude towards Peace Commissioners, who had attempted to parley with him on the bluffs at the mouth of the Yellowstone, opposite old Fort Union, Montana. The Territorial Delegate of Montana, Mr Maginnis, later reported the incident to the House of Representatives. 'He received the presents graciously, then wheedled the commissioners out of twenty kegs of powder and ball, and then broke up the Council, and went

for their scalps [laughter]. They escaped to the steamer, and under a shower of their own bullets got safe across to the fort. . . . That commission then dissolved. [Laughter].' (Congressional Record, July, 1876).

On 3 December 1875, at a direct request from Ulysses Grant, President of the United States, the Honourable Z. Chandler, Secretary of the Department of the Interior, wrote to the Honourable William Belknap, Secretary of War, 'I have this day directed the Commissioner of Indian Affairs to notify said Indians ['certain *hostile* Sioux Indians residing outside of their reservations'], that they must remove to a reservation before the 31st day of January next; that if they neglect or refuse so to remove, they will be reported to the War Department as hostile Indians, and that a military force will be sent to compel them to obey the orders of the Indian Office.' (Congressional Record, July, 1876).

It is important to appreciate the terms of the 1868 Laramie Treaty and how it affected the northern Sioux whom Sitting Bull championed. Article 11 in part says 'the tribes who are parties to this agreement'; further, Article 16 in terms as plain as the English language could possibly make it, left Powder River country (that land now occupied by Sitting Bull), a vast neutral territory excluding homesteaders, and stipulated that no white people should pass through it without the consent of the Indians.

The non-treaties were just that, and attempts to circumvent the true meaning of the 1868 Treaty, to imply that Sitting Bull's people were bound by its obligations, really does not stand up to examination. In fairness, it must be pointed out that few of the elected representatives probably had any grasp of the structure of the Sioux nation – that the Tetons, the dwellers of the Plains, were separated into distinct groups, Oglala, Brulé, Miniconjou, Sans Arcs, Sihasapa (Blackfoot), Hunkpapa, Oohenonpa (Two Kettles), and although linguistically related most saw themselves as distinct tribes. They shared a common territory but because of their migration history (extending back to the 18th century) the Oglala, Miniconjou and Brulé commonly roamed south and the Hunkpapa, Sans Arcs and Sihasapa north, in the Sioux domain.

The non-treaties viewed Sitting Bull much the way the Treaty Sioux had viewed Red Cloud in earlier days – as a twin spirit in fighting the cause of their people. The obvious, honest and fairest (and probably in the long run the most economic) solution would have been another Treaty, but there were to be no more treaties of the type made with Red Cloud, which at least one Congressman had described as 'a grave mistake, if not a national dishonour and a national disgrace'. (Congressional Record, July, 1876). Nor even a complete re-appraisal of the great patchwork of Indian policy. As one astute Congressman observed 'the whole Indian service should be systematized . . .

Ration Issue, Pine Ridge, c. 1880. With the virtual extermination of the buffalo in 1883 the Sioux and other tribes who were mainly meat eaters were issued with beef, which most Indians considered inferior to buffalo meat, supplemented by flour, coffee, sugar, dried beans and corn. Nomadic hunters probably consumed up to three pounds of meat per day. In 1881 the Blackfoot were theoretically allowed $1\frac{1}{2}$ lb a day; in practice, as with many tribes, the amount often fell far short of this figure. Denver Public Library Western Collection

we may not need so many of these pious agents who defraud both the government and the Indian. We may have, as they have in Canada, some *honest, fair and accountable* system. . . .' (Congressional Record, July, 1876).

It was a pity that Sitting Bull did not take the Congressional Record, for considering his subsequent actions and the way he viewed the North West Mounted Police he would have applauded such sentiments!

It is on record that more than once Sitting Bull had stated he was not adverse to honest traders in his country and to individual white men he was generally friendly. He avoided both fighting and killing white people whenever possible and it is probably true that he had never personally killed a white man. Although Sitting Bull represented a basically warlike people, slaughter on a large scale between the warring equestrian tribes was unusual and he disliked what the professional American soldier stood for. 'You come to fight me. *That's all* you soldiers are made for – *just* to fight', he once said in a personal interview with General Nelson A. Miles (Vestal, 1957, p. 196). As someone who got to know him well once wrote 'in his way I think Sitting Bull was a lover of humanity'. (De Cost Smith, 1949, p. 185).

Needless to say, Sitting Bull and his followers did not comply with the President's directive and on 1 February 1876, the Secretary of the Interior again wrote to the Department of War:

'Sir: on the 3rd December last I had the honour to address a communication to you relative to the hostile Sioux roaming in the Powder River country under the leadership of Sitting Bull, informing you that I had directed couriers to be sent from each of the Sioux agencies, informing that chief that he must come in with his followers to one of the Sioux agencies before the 31st ultimo, prepared to remain in peace near the agency, or he would be turned over to the War Department and the Army be directed to compel him to comply with the orders of this Department.

'The time given him in which to return to an agency having expired and the advices received at the Indian Office being to the effect that Sitting Bull still refuses to comply with the directions of the Commissioner, the said Indians are hereby turned over to the War Department for such action on the part of the Army as you may deem proper under the circumstances.

'I enclose copy of communication from the Commissioner of Indian Affairs, dated the 31st ultimo, recommending that hostilities be commenced.' (Congressional Record, July, 1876).

A new war with the Sioux was on.

Within a month of the issue of the order, Brigadier-General George Crook, Department Commander of the Platte, had ordered a concentration of ten cavalry companies at Fort Fetterman. On 1 March the column left Fort Fetterman,

Top. Custer Hill today. The markers which indicate approximately the positions where the soldiers fell are clustered around Custer Hill. The area, which encompasses both the Custer and Reno field is now a National Monument and a museum has been built a short distance from Custer Hill. Here one can view models of the entire terrain and follow in detail, from experienced guides, the whole course of the Little Big Horn affair.

Above. The Last of the Buffalo, from the painting by Albert Bierstadt. Whitney Gallery of Western Art, Cody, Wyoming.

with 883 officers and men commanded by Colonel Joseph J. Reynolds – Crook accompanying the column as an observer. This latter, somewhat unusual step, subsequently exonerated Crook of all direct responsibility for what turned out to be an abortive campaign and resulted in a court martial for Reynolds; perhaps Crook had anticipated the difficulties facing the force.

Winter campaigns against Plains Indians were generally the most successful – the Sand Creek and Washita encounters, which broke the spirit of the southern tribes, had been conducted in winter. At this time the nomadic tribes took on a sedentary mode of life, being virtually immobilized by the weather which was particularly severe on the central and northern Plains. Further, the number of 'hostile' Indians would probably be less since only in summer were their numbers augmented by others from the agencies who attempted to get the best of both worlds.

The Reynolds' column were moving into a largely unmapped area of some 90,000 square miles, with only forty days' rations (which were not supplemented with hot food), inadequate shelter and with temperatures often forty degrees below zero. Neither Crook nor Reynolds had any significant experience either of fighting Plains Indians or conducting operations under winter conditions. On 16 March an Indian trail was found by the scout Frank Grouard, and on the morning of the 17th a Northern Cheyenne village was located on the west side of the Powder River near present-day Moorhead, Montana. Reynolds attacked – and encountered severe resistance, losing four men and having six wounded. Only one Indian was killed although the abandoned village was captured and burnt. By now, more than sixty men were suffering from frost-bite and all were in an exhausted condition and so it was decided to draw the winter campaign to a close.

The subsequent summer campaign was to be even more disastrous. On 29 May, Lieutenant-General P. H. Sheridan wrote to General W. T. Sherman in Washington, outlining the plan of the three-pronged campaign under Terry and Crook:

'Headquarters, Military Division of the Missouri, Chicago, Ill.,

29 May, 1876

General: Brigadier-General Terry moved out of his command from Fort Abraham Lincoln in the direction of the mouth of Powder River on the 17th instant. The total strength of his column is about nine hundred men exclusive of a force of three companies in charge of the supply-camp at Glendive Creek, the old supply station on the Yellowstone.

Brigadier-General Crook will move from Fort Fetterman with a column about the same size.

Colonel John Gibbon is now moving down north of the Yellowstone and east of the mouth of the Big Horn with a force of about four hundred, all but four companies of which are infantry.

As no very accurate information can be obtained as to the location of the hostile Indians, and as there would be no telling how long they would stay in one place, if it was known, I have given no instructions to Generals Crook or Terry, preferring that they should do the best they can under the circumstances . . . as I think it would be unwise to make any combinations in such a country as they will have to operate in, as hostile Indians in any great numbers, cannot keep the field as a body for a week, or at the most ten days. I therefore consider – and so do Terry and Crook – that each column should be able to take care of itself, and to chastise the Indians, should it have the opportunity. . . .

I presume the following will occur: General Terry will drive the Indians towards the Big Horn valley and General Crook will drive them back towards Terry; Colonel Gibbon moving down on the north side of the Yellowstone, to intercept if possible such as may want to go north of the Missouri to Milk River. The result of the movement of these three columns may force many of the hostile Indians back to the agencies on the Missouri River and to Red Cloud and Spotted Tail agencies.

P. H. Sheridan,
Lieutenant-General'

Plains Indian tribes were seldom found concentrated in large numbers; the difficulties of obtaining a sufficient supply of fresh food, and of feeding the large pony herds worked against large communal organization. However, in their ancient history – as discussed in Chapter I – they did at times band together in very large numbers for pedestrian warfare. That they maintained the ability to work together is reflected in their effective camp organization during the period of the Sun Dance when many thousands came together, united by a common religious festival. By early June the 'hostiles' – Northern Cheyenne and representatives of all the Sioux bands – were drifting towards the Little Big Horn in present-day southern Montana, this time motivated by one major factor – the survival of their way of life.

Not one of the army commanders – and this included George A. Custer, one of the most experienced of Indian fighters – seriously anticipated either large concentrations of Indians or unified opposition. A factor in the army's favour was that they were warring against village communities, which the warriors of the Plains well knew the white soldiers would not hesitate to attack and destroy; thus there was obviously a marked reluctance by the warriors to leave a village unguarded and their wives and children ready prey to a close enemy. An effective strategy worked out by the army was to operate 'more than one column near the hostiles, so that if the fighting men left the village to attack one column there was always the threat of an attack by another column'. (Taunton, 1963, p. 7).

By 16 June, Gibbon with some 400 men was camped at the mouth of the Rosebud on the Yellowstone – the steamer *Far West* loaded with supplies was moored nearby. Gibbon was awaiting the arrival of the Terry–Custer column which had left Fort Abraham Lincoln on 17 May with some 925 men, including the entire Seventh United States Cavalry. The army camp was situated about seventy-five miles north of the 'hostile' Sioux village which unknown to the army commanders was now building up to one of the largest concentrations of Indians ever known on the Plains during the historic period. Strung for three miles along the Little Big Horn, within a further week it would contain more than 1500 tipis – perhaps housing between 12,000 to 15,000 Indians including 4000 to 5000 warriors. In May, Sitting Bull had sent a messenger to Crowfoot, a powerful chief of the Blackfoot in Canada, and invited him 'to join the Sioux against the Americans . . . after the Americans and Crow had been defeated the Sioux would come to Canada with the Blackfeet and exterminate the whites'. (Dempsey, 1972, p. 88). Crowfoot refused to join – a great tribute to the fair treatment by the Mounted Police.

The major leaders of the 'hostiles' in the United States, representing above all else the true ethos of the free Plains Indians, were Crazy Horse and Sitting Bull, a good combination of unsurpassed warrior ability and spiritual power.

Crook, with more than 1000 officers and men and some 260 Crow and Shoshone scouts, was now at the headwaters of the Rosebud about twenty-two miles south of the Sioux encampment. At 8.30 on the morning of 17 June, while Crook was in the middle of playing a game of cards and his men were having breakfast, Crazy Horse, leading a well-deployed force of Sioux, attacked the massive army camp, taking them completely by surprise. The engagement lasted for six hours and taught Crook a great deal about the fighting ability of the

Sioux. Some seventeen miles from their village on the Little Big Horn they could now afford to employ offensive tactics. By the end of the day the largest of the three-pronged movements against The People had been strategically defeated. With nearly one hundred dead and wounded and a severe depletion of their ammunition, Crook, who had fought with such success against the pedestrian Apache in Arizona, was now brought to a standstill (and effectively out of the summer campaign), as he waited at Goose Creek for reinforcements.

On the afternoon of 21 June, Custer and Gibbon joined Terry on board the *Far West*. Here 'a council of war was held and the most controversial campaign in American history then commenced'. (Taunton, 1963, p. 8).

On the same day, Gibbon's column proceeded up the Yellowstone. Their route was to be to the mouth of the Bighorn River and then south to the Little Bighorn. Gibbon himself was to take command after the *Far West* had overtaken the column. After the council it was agreed that Custer, leading the Seventh – which Terry considered as his most effective tactical force – would proceed up the Rosebud, the objective being to trap the Sioux between the two forces. Terry had planned that the Gibbon/Custer columns would attack on the morning of 26 June; however, on the afternoon of 24 June scouts reported that the Sioux encampment was probably to the west, in the Little Big Horn valley. Anxious that the Sioux might escape, Custer force-marched the column under cover of darkness. At about noon on 25 June, some ten miles from the Little Big Horn, Custer split this command into three battalions. And he, together with some 225 officers and men, rode into immortality.

When the Indians withdrew from the Custer battlefield on the afternoon of 26 June, they first moved north up the Little Bighorn valley and for just over a fortnight stayed together. Then the tribal camps split up east of the Powder River. Just before they crossed the river, another Cheyenne died of wounds received in the battle which, according to a Cheyenne woman informant (Kate Bighead), brought their loss up to seven warriors whilst the Sioux had lost twenty-four. Referring to the large number of suicides which the Indians said they witnessed amongst the exhausted soldiers, Kate said 'Many more Indians would have been killed if the Everywhere Spirit had not caused the white men to go crazy and turn their guns upon themselves.' (Marquis, 1933, p. 5). The Cheyenne afterwards set up their winter camp on a stream 'far up the Powder River on its west side close to the Bighorn mountains'. (Marquis, 1933, p. 8). By September 1876, most 'hostiles' had decided on the location of their winter encampment. Many being – in compliance with the stipulations of the 1868 Treaty – within the limits of the Great Sioux Reservation. Sitting Bull was with a 'thousand warriors in his camp near Twin Buttes on Grand

The Twilight of the Indian, from a painting by Frederick Remington. As part of annuity payments Indians were issued with a variety of merchandise – much of it worthless: chairs, tables and brass bedsteads did not fit well in a conical tipi. Not many Plains Indians took to the plough as shown here; for most, the transition from nomadism to a beef-eating sedentary existence was virtually impossible and most idled their time away dreaming of past days of glory. Originally published in 1891 by R. H. Russell, New York, 1891.

River' and was still accompanied by Crazy Horse. A few miles away was American Horse's camp on Slim Buttes. (See Vestal, 1957, p. 184). On 8 July 1876 in the House of Representatives in Washington Mr Maginnis, Territorial Delegate of Montana stated his view on Custer's defeat and the Indian problem:

'One repulse does not give enemies final victory, and the safety of the frontiers, the peace of all the other tribes, the blood of our soldiers demand that these Indians shall be pursued until they sue for peace and submit themselves to the authority of the nation which will oppress no one and wrong nobody, but which is bound to give peace, security, and law to all red men and white alike.' (Congressional Record, July, 1876).

On 5 August 1876 from Headquarters, Military Division of Missouri, Chicago, Lieutenant-General Phil Sheridan, Division Commander, sent a telegram to Commanding General W. T. Sherman, Washington. 'I beg you to see the military committee of the House, and urge on it the necessity of increasing the cavalry to one hundred to each company.

'General Crook's total strength is seventeen hundred and seventy four; Terry's is eighteen hundred and seventy three; and to give them this force I have *stripped every post* from the line of Manitoba to Texas. We want more mounted men. . . .'

By 11 August, Sherman had requested Congress to authorise an increase of 2500 cavalry, adding that if this were rejected then the President 'should be authorised to call out up to 5000 state and territorial volunteers from those territories nearest the Sioux country'. So serious was the situation considered to be that Congress approved *both proposals* although in fact the latter authorization was never implemented.

During the autumn of 1876 there was a rapid and massive increase in the strength of the cavalry regiments.

'The 7th received 500 recruits from Jefferson barracks, giving it 1205 enlisted men; the 2nd was increased to 966; the 3rd to 1022; and the 5th to 1073. The battalion of the 4th totalled 379.' (Taunton, 1963, p. 10). The commanders now had at their disposal well over 4000 troops, but so hurried was the build-up that many of these new *cavalry* recruits couldn't even ride a horse, let alone fight Indians. 'After the 7th had been sent to Standing Rock to disarm the hostiles it was learned that many of them were unable to ride.' (Taunton, 1963, p. 10). By late autumn 1876 'there were 657 officers and 8420 enlisted men in the Departments of the Platte and Dakota. Of these 261 officers and 3482 enlisted men were actively campaigning against the Sioux and Cheyenne.' (Report of the Secretary of War for 1876). Thus, there was at the disposal of the field commanders – for they could call on both the Departments of the Platte and Dakota – almost fifty per cent of the total officers and men of all arms in the United States Army for war against the last free warriors of the Plains. If, as one noted authority stated, the conflicts between whites and Indians were for the most part 'games of hide and seek' (Wissler, 1938, p. 22), the army took *that* war game seriously.

By the end of September 1876, Terry had disbanded the 'Dakota' column and what was left of the 7th cavalry and had returned to Fort Abraham Lincoln. Crook had remained longer in the field, having been reinforced by the 5th Cavalry in August, but eventually running desperately short of supplies, he too was forced to withdraw and returned to Fort Laramie. A two-pronged winter campaign against the Sioux and Cheyenne now started to take effect – war could now be more efficiently waged with the establishment of a cantonment – later to be called Fort Keogh – at the mouth of the Tongue River (and incidentally in violation of the 1868 Treaty, the conditions of which by this time had largely gone by the board). It was warfare which savagely destroyed the very soul of The People and the suffering was appalling. When Mackenzie wiped out Dull Knife's village south of the Big Horn Mountains on 25 November, for example, he destroyed both their tipis and their entire stock of winter supplies. That night, in sub-zero conditions, those tenacious Cheyenne who had survived the initial onslaught kept themselves from freezing by thrusting hands and feet into their disembowelled ponies. 'As it was, twelve

George Armstrong Custer, 1876. This picture shows Custer in the full dress uniform of lieutenant-colonel of the 7th Cavalry. It is a steelplate engraving, probably taken from his last photograph. Of this likeness Mrs Custer later wrote, 'I cannot say how pleased I am with the steel-plate engraving you sent me. It grows upon me and I think it gives the General's intellectual look better than any portrait I have.' Custer was only thirty-seven years old at the time of his death, on the Little Big Horn in June 1876. First published as the frontispiece of Whittaker's *A Complete Life of Gen. George A. Custer.* English Westerners' Society, London.

Sitting Bull, Canada 1878. This great spiritual leader of the 'Buffalo Indians' – last of the free Warriors of the Plains – rallied one of the largest gathering of Plains Indians ever seen on the North American continent in a desperate attempt to stop the flood of white invaders. Taken by T. G. Anderton of Fort Walsh, Canada. R.C.M.P. Winnipeg.

place.' (Congressional Record, July, 1876). But the warriors of the Plains had little intention of submitting docilely to their destiny. The main engagements and incidents of the next year are summarized in the following table:

Location Incident	Date	Engagement/	Comments
Slim Buttes	8 Sept. 1876	Mills and Crook attack American Horse & his Sioux.	Village captured and destroyed. American Horse killed. Crazy Horse greatly out-numbered and repulsed.
Red Cloud and other Sioux Agencies	Nov. 1876	Crook subdues Agency Indians by display of strength.	At this time, Crook deposed Red Cloud and put the 'progressive' Spotted Tail (a Brulé chief) in charge of the Agency Indians.
Willow Creek, south of the Big Horn Mountains	25 Nov. 1876	Mackenzie destroys Dull Knife's Cheyenne village.	Village & winter supplies of Cheyenne destroyed. Relics of Custer battle found in village. North and 100 of his Pawnee scouts accompanied Mackenzie. 7 troopers killed and 26 wounded. 30 Cheyenne warriors killed. 700 Cheyenne ponies captured.
Cedar Creek Yellowstone River	20 Oct. 1876	Parley and subsequent skirmish between Miles and Sitting Bull.	Sitting Bull demands peace on the old basis – 'He spoke like a conqueror & he looked like one' Miles wrote afterwards. Sitting Bull withdraws.
Wolf Mountains, Big Horn range.	8 Jan. 1877	Miles attacks Sioux under Crazy Horse.	Artillery guns employed. At the close of the battle combatants fighting in the midst of a blinding snow storm. Medicine Man Big Crow killed. Large portion of Indian camp equipment & supplies captured & their ammunition exhausted. Crazy Horse withdraws.
Lame Deer, west of Tongue River	7 May 1877	Miles attacks Miniconjou Sioux village.	Miles almost killed. Lame Deer and Iron Star killed. Village captured.
Red Cloud Agency	May 1877	Crazy Horse surrenders with 300 warriors.	Crazy Horse and Sitting Bull had discussed surrender a number of times but Sitting Bull said 'I don't wish to die yet.' (Vestal, 1957, p.182).
Wood Mountain, Saskatchewan, Canada	March 1877	Sitting Bull, with about 900 Sioux, retreats to Canada.	Indian Summer. 'That first year in the Grandmother's country was a spell of fine weather in Sitting Bull's troubled life. Now, for the first time in years, he could eat plenty, sleep soundly, and give himself to the pleasures of family life and friendship without fear.' (Vestal, 1957, p.207).
Fort Robinson, Nebraska	7 Sept. 1877	Crazy Horse to be imprisoned in Dry Tortugas, Florida.	Resists arrest, bayoneted by guard. 'My father, I am bad hurt. Tell The People it is no use to depend on me any more now.'

little Indian babies froze to death that night.' (Brady, 1904, p. 317).

The fall and winter campaignings caused many dispirited and broken hostiles to capitulate and surrender at the agencies.

'He knows no law but force. Give him force, but temper it with the spirit of Christianity and the rules of civilization. Use force, genial force if possible, harsh if necessary, but force nevertheless, and with that you will control the Indian, and at least prevent him from murdering white men. For three hundred years we have left him in self control and have prayed for his civilization. The whole system must be changed. Scatter them among the white men or sprinkle white men with them. Give him civilized rulers and make him obey civilized laws. If that cannot be done, then let him submit to destiny, a destiny as certain and as unerring as the decrees of fate. Let him go to the happy hunting grounds of his fathers, and let white men, or at least civilized men, take his

Crazy Horse was dead!

Dr Cyrus Townsend Brady, who took it on himself to document the Plains Indians wars and who was published around the turn of the century, described the death of Crazy Horse as follows. 'He was dissatisfied always, in spite of his surrender, and had been conspiring to take the warpath again. Believing that his intentions had become known and that he would be rigorously dealt with on account of the discovery, he started to *run amuck*, with a knife of which he had become possessed by some means in the guard house. When the fracas was over, he was found on the ground with a desperate wound in the abdomen. Whether the wound was given by the bayonet of the sentry at the door, whether the blow was delivered by some of the Indians who threw themselves upon him and with whom he struggled, is a matter which cannot be determined. However it was come by, it was enough, for from the effects he died in a short time.' (Brady, 1904, p. 333). Such was the reporting by one of the most popular writers of the period.

Another, more authoritative, version did not become available until much later – after many of the chief characters in the tragedy were dead. In 1929, Dr V. T. McGillycuddy's account of the episode was published. In 1877 McGillycuddy was Assistant Post Surgeon at Fort Robinson, and, after Crazy Horse's surrender in the spring of 1877 he became a close friend of the chief whose wife was suffering from tuberculosis. He visited the Sioux camp every few days. McGillycuddy was of the considered opinion that both the arrest and killing of the chief was 'unnecessary, uncalled-for and inexcusable. It was the result of jealousy, treachery and fear. . . . I saw him enter the guard-room next door, a prisoner, out of which he sprang without delay, with a drawn knife, to regain his freedom, and I was standing forty feet from him when one of the guard, a private of the Ninth Infantry, lunged his bayonet into the chiefs abdomen, and he fell to the ground.' (Brininstool, 1949, pp. 43 & 45).

So died one of the greatest chiefs the Sioux ever produced, recognized as war chief of the southern Sioux and leader of the hostile Oglala. It was probably Crazy Horse who so brilliantly and suddenly changed Sioux warfare tactics from the characteristic hit and run to a pitched battle, fighting Crook's thousand-plus soldiers (including fifteen troops of cavalry – some nine hundred men) at the Battle of the Rosebud on 17 June 1876, forcing him to a standstill and, more significantly, out of the summer operations against the Sioux.

No known pictorial record exists of Crazy Horse. Though photographs do turn up from time to time which purport to be of him, the famous frontier photographer, D. F. Barry, told E. A. Brininstool in 1926 that he had repeatedly tried to get the chief to sit for his photograph but 'the chief refused to be bribed' (Brininstool, 1949, p. 11). Captain John G. Bourke has, however, left us an interesting description based on personal observation. 'I saw before me a man who looked quite young, not over thirty years old, five feet eight inches high, lithe and sinewy, with a scar in the face. The expression on his countenance was one of quiet dignity, but morose, dogged, tenacious, and melancholy. He believed with stolidity, like a man who realized that he had to give in to Fate, but would do so as sullenly as possible.' (Bourke, 1892, p. 48).

Crazy Horse had a high reputation for personal courage among all Indians; even before he was twenty-six years of age he was regarded with great respect. When directing warriors towards the enemy he was always at the front and none were allowed to pass him. The Sioux considered that he was generous to a fault, never keeping anything for himself from the spoils of war. Little wonder, as Bourke wrote later, 'I never heard an Indian mention his name save in terms of respect.' (Bourke, 1892, p. 48).

The annihilation of Custer and the troubles in the United States against the Sioux and Cheyenne made many of Canada's Indians restless. In August 1876, Inspector Cecil Denny of the Royal North-West Mounted Police reported that the Blackfoot had been approached by the American Sioux in an effort to join an anti-white movement. The American Blackfoot, particularly the Piegan, had much to hate the white man for – long before buffalo had ceased to roam they had been circumvented by cattle ranchers, miners and homesteaders and as the tempo of civilized development in Montana gained momentum, a bewildering number of treaties were made with them 'which were often not ratified in Washington and remained mere scraps of paper' (Lewis, 1942, p. 67).

But the Alberta Plains in Canada tended to act as a great safety valve where the pressed tribes could hunt safely and retreat when the pressure became too great. Had they been pushed hard to the wall as with the Sioux and Cheyenne it is probable that the loosely-knit confederation would have consolidated and offered equally fierce resistance to white encroachment. The Canadian tribes so far had fared well, in comparison to their American brothers; firstly, much of western Canada was

Last stand of the Nez Percé, 5 October 1877.
After an incredible 2000 mile retreat pursued by General Howard the Nez Percé finally capitulated at the Bear Paw Mountains only 80 miles from the Canadian border. By then most of the prominent war chiefs had been killed (although a small group under White Bird did manage to reach Canada) and Chief Joseph, a peace loving man who had been forced into the disaster by circumstances over which he had no control, was left to negotiate the surrender terms. With him were 184 women, 147 children and only 87 warriors. The combined U.S. military force at that time numbered more than 800 men.
Col. Nelson A. Miles to whom Joseph surrendered attempted to comply with the promises he made at the time but he was overruled by his superiors. Few of these 'hostile' Nez Percé ever returned home and the remnants of these brave people now live on the Colville reservation in eastern Washington. From an old engraving in Leslie's Illustrated Weekly, November 1877.

never settled with the density of whites as in the United States and settlements were far more gradual. Most important was that on the advice of the remarkable Lieutenant W. F. Butler of the 69th Regiment, who had been on a fact-finding tour into 'The Saskatchewan' in 1870, the famous Royal North-West Mounted Police Force was founded in 1873. 'I would recommend . . . for consideration of your Excellency . . . the organization of a well-equipped force of from 100 to 150 men, one-third to be well mounted, specially recruited and engaged for service, in the Saskatchewan; enlisting for two or three years service, and at expiration of that period to become military settlers, receiving grants of land, but still remaining as a reserve force should their services be required.' (Butler, 1891, pp. 378–379).

The prompt and efficient action of these Mounted Police tended to spare the Canadian tribes the bitter experiences of their American brethren. The Royal North-West Mounted Police were scrupulously honest, fair-minded men; their straight talk and fearless action went right to the heart of the warriors of the Plains. As W. F. Cody (Buffalo Bill) once said 'The whole secret of treating with Indians is to be honest with them and do as you agree.' (Vestal, 1957, p. 251).

The Blackfoot chiefs had great faith in the goodwill of the Red Coats (as the R.N.W.M.P. were called), and there seemed to be respect and regard on both sides. In 1874, Assistant Commissioner Colonel MacLeod had parleyed with chiefs of the Blood, Piegan and Blackfoot. He reported that he found them 'very intelligent men', and was greatly impressed by the dignified way they conducted themselves. MacLeod attempted to explain the friendly intentions of the Canadian Government 'that the Police had come not to take the country from the Indians' and would 'soon send some of the great men of the country to deal with the Indians and make treaty agreements with them.' (Macbeth, 1931, p. 62).

Thus, on 16 September 1877, at the Blackfoot Crossing on the Bow River just under 100 miles from Fort McLeod, combined tribes of Blackfoot, Piegan, Assiniboin and Sarcee gathered to parley with Governor David Laird and Commissioner Colonel MacLeod of the Mounted Police. Typically, the independent Blood were late; not until the evening of 20 September did they arrive, headed by Red Crow, a powerful chief, who wielded great authority in council. Unlike Crowfoot, chief of the Blackfoot tribe (*not* nation – which comprised Blackfoot, Piegan and Blood, linguistically related groups but politically independent), he was less known to the whites. It was Crowfoot who on such occasions acted as the main spokesman. (Dempsey, 1972, p. 95).

Two days later, not without considerable misgivings, Treaty Number Seven was signed. A large measure of its success was due to the high regard that the Indians had for the Mounted Police. Said Crowfoot, head chief of the Blackfoot, 'The Mounted Police have protected us as the feathers of the bird protect it from the frosts of winter. I wish them all good and trust that all our hearts will increase in goodness from this time forward. I am satisfied, I will sign the treaty.' Recent research suggests that when Crowfoot was asked to 'touch the pen', as was customary when a treaty was signed, 'Crowfoot made a motion toward the pen and his mark was inscribed' but his hand purposely failed to touch the pen. 'Ah', said Crowfoot to a companion after the signing 'I did not touch it.' (Dempsey, 1972, p. 105). Said Red Crow, head chief of the Blood 'I entirely trust Stamix-oto-kan (Colonel MacLeod) and will leave everything to him. I will sign with Crowfoot.' (Macbeth, 1931, p. 74). Probably recalling his meeting with Sitting Bull earlier that year, the astute Crowfoot 'pleaded with the commissioners not to deceive him'. Like many chiefs he was eloquent and effective in his use of words. 'Great Father! Take pity on me with regard to my country, with regard to the mountains, the hills and the valleys; with regard to the prairies, the forests and the waters; with regard to all the animals that inhabit them, and do not take them from myself or my children for ever.' (Dempsey, 1972, p. 105).

The provisions were that the Blackfoot would confine themselves to one large reserve. In exchange, an annual allowance would be provided for schools, ammunition, cattle and agricultural implements. In addition the treaty 'provided a payment of $12 and an annuity of $5 for each man, woman and child; $25 for each chief and $15 for each minor chief'. (Lewis, 1942, p. 67). At the Indians' request, payments were made through the Mounted Police and this was carried out efficiently over the succeeding years. Although Crowfoot himself probably understood the provisions of the treaty, few if any of the other Indians did. It was virtually impossible for the Plains Indian mind to comprehend 'surrendering the things which were around them. To give up the land was akin to giving up the sky, the mountains, or the buffalo. . . . The interpreters were incapable of explaining the terms of the treaty and could not deal with such matters as land surrenders and reserves. At the same time, how could any interpreter explain to a nomadic Indian that 128 acres of the prairie would be his?' (Dempsey, 1972, pp. 105 & 106).

There is little doubt that the whole philosophy of handling the Plains Indians in Canada during this period was based on the way Canadian officials saw the tragic events which occurred south of them in the United States. As Lieutenant Butler commented in his 1871 Report. 'Another increasing source of Indian discontent is to be found in the policy pursued by the American Government in their settlement of the countries lying south of the Saskatchewan. Throughout the territories of Dakota and Montana a state of hostility has long existed between the Americans and the tribes of Sioux, Blackfeet, and Piegan Indians. This state of hostility has latterly degenerated, on the part of the Americans, into a war of extermination; and the policy of "clearing out" the red man has now become a recognized portion of Indian warfare. Some of these acts of extermination find their way into the public records, many of them never find publicity.' (Butler, 1891, p. 359).

In December 1876, some 2000 American Indians had retreated into Canada; with large numbers of horses and mules they camped at Wood Mountain just across the 'medicine line' (the 49th parallel) in present-day Saskatchewan. They told the Mounted Police who visited them that 'they had been driven out by the American and had come to look for peace; that they had been told by their grandfathers that they would find peace in the land of the British'. (Macbeth, 1931, p. 79). They referred to the case of their cousins the Santee, many of whom, after the 'Minnesota Massacre' of 1862, had sought refuge in Canada and eventually been given a reserve near Battleford.

In March 1877, Sitting Bull together with about 135 lodges – including chiefs Spotted Eagle (war chief of the Sans Arcs), Pretty Bear, Bear's Cap, The Eagle Sitting Down and the later to be famous Rain in the Face (who Longfellow has immortalized with his 'The Revenge of Rain-in-the-Face') – crossed the International line into Canada. Inspector J. M. Walsh of the Mounted Police (who was later to become a firm friend of Sitting Bull) rode out to meet the Sioux in company with a sergeant, two constables and an interpreter. Walsh asked Sitting Bull why he had come. Sitting Bull replied 'We are British Indians; our grandfathers were raised on British soil.' He showed the whites peace medals which had been given them by King George III as tokens of friendship and he astutely observed that he could not understand why the white mother had given *their* country to the Americans. Sitting Bull had struck a fundamentally debatable point – he was evidently referring to the establishment of the 49th parallel in 1818. Formerly the international boundary dipped well down into what is now North Dakota – the homeland of the northern sub-tribes of the Teton Sioux. In all fairness, the Canadian Government could do no more than allow them to stay, and they early adopted a policy of not placing undue pressure on Indians who 'sought asylum under the British flag'. (Macbeth, 1931, p. 83).

Sitting Bull promised to obey the laws of the Great Mother and joined the elderly chief Black Moon in the great refugee encampment near the Cypress Hills in present-day south-western Saskatchewan. This encampment now contained about 400 lodges of displaced American Indians. Later in the year, it would be swelled by some of Joseph's Nez Percé under White Bird after their epic 2000 mile retreat for freedom which ended so tragically at the Bear Paw Mountains (less than 100 miles from the Canadian border) on 4 October 1877.

The refugees were a great source of concern to the Canadian authorities and even though, as honestly as they could, they obeyed the law 'the

Winter quarters of Sitting Bull's band while it was imprisoned at Fort Randall, Dakota Territory, 1882. After spending four years in Canada, where he hoped to be granted a reservation, Sitting Bull finally surrendered at Fort Buford (in present day North Dakota) in July 1881, together with 186 followers. He was held a prisoner of war at Fort Randall until May 1883. The tipis appear to be made of canvas; by then buffalo was so scarce it was impossible to obtain sufficient hides to renew the covers. Smithsonian Institution, National Anthropological Archives, Washington.

very name of Sioux strikes terror into the hearts of many of the settlers' wrote Superintendent James Walker of the Mounted Police. (Macbeth, 1931, p. 86). In the spring of 1877, Sitting Bull met Crowfoot just north of the Cypress Hills. Although Crowfoot had earlier refused to join Sitting Bull in a united front against the white man, the two struck up an immediate friendship. 'The Blackfoot and Sioux held a friendship dance in the camp before the Sioux returned south later in the day.' (Dempsey, 1972, p. 92). The two chiefs obviously held one another in high regard – they were of one accord in fighting for The People. Later, Sitting Bull was to name his son in honour of the great Blackfoot chief. The unique standing that Sitting Bull had is exemplified by the fact that in any conferences which took place between the authorities and the Indians it was generally Sitting Bull who acted as the main spokesman. Assistant Commissioner A. G. Irvine was much impressed at their first meeting. 'I was particularly struck with Sitting Bull,' he wrote. 'He is a man of somewhat short stature, but with a pleasant face, a man showing great determination and a fine high forehead. When he smiled, which he often did, his face brightened up wonderfully. I should say he is a man of about forty-five years of age. When talking at the conference he spoke as a man who understands his subject well and who had thoroughly weighed it before speaking. He believes no one from the other side and said so. His speech showed him to be a man of wonderful capability.' (Macbeth, 1931, pp. 82–83). Similar descriptions of Sitting Bull have come down through history. Even his old antagonist, Colonel Nelson A. Miles, who met him face to face a few months after the Custer battle, described him as 'a strong, hardy, sturdy looking man' adding that 'his manner was cold, but dignified and courteous.' (Miles, 1896, p. 226).

Some eight months after Sitting Bull crossed the border, General Alfred H. Terry headed an impressive United States Commission to the Sioux. His message from the President of the United States, was that if the 'hostiles' returned to the United States they would be allowed to settle on the reservations in peace. They must surrender their guns and horses for which they would be given food, clothing and cattle, while stock and farm implements together with instructors were offered as an incentive to settle down to farming.

'They asked me today to give them my horses. I bought my horses, and they are mine. . . . They do *not* belong to the government; neither do the rifles. The rifles are also mine. I bought them; I paid for them. Why *I should* give them up *I do not know. I will not* give them up.' (Sitting Bull, Interview, 17 October 1877. In *New York Herald*, Friday, 16 November 1877).

The Red Coats' diplomacy and patience had been stretched to the limit in their efforts to persuade the Sioux to meet the Commission at Fort Walsh. 'There is no use in talking to these Americans; they are all liars, you cannot believe anything they say. No matter what terms they offer, we cannot accept them because we have no faith in their promises,' said Sitting Bull (Vestal, 1957, p. 215). To make matters worse, the day Inspector Walsh was in the Sioux encampment on his errand of persuasion, wounded and bleeding Nez Percé Indians limped in from the Bear Paw Mountains. They were from White Bird's band who had refused to capitulate with Joseph. Sitting Bull rode out to meet them and after bidding them welcome he said 'I am sorry indeed your skin is like mine, that your hair is like mine, and that every one around you is a pure red man like myself. *We too have lost our country* by falsehood and theft.' (The New Northwest, Montana, April, 1878).

Eventually, on 17 October, the conference was held in a room at Fort Walsh; Sitting Bull 'representing the Chiefs, entered and shook hands warmly with Colonel MacLeod, but passed the American commissioners with the utmost disdain'. (Macbeth, 1931, p. 84). The chiefs emphatically refused to leave Canada, Sitting Bull telling Terry: 'You are a bigger fool than I am if you think I believe you. This place, the home of the soldiers of the Grandmother is the Medicine House where the truth lives and you come here to tell us lies. When you go back to your country, take your lies with you.' (Howard, 1972, p. 9).

The mission was a complete failure; too long had these people been abused by unscrupulous agents, exploiters and badly co-ordinated Government policies. They must, too, have been aware of the bloody aftermath of the Custer Battle – of Slim Buttes, of the frightening show of troops at the agencies, the deposal of the tenacious Red Cloud, the destruction of Dull Knife's village and the freezing women and children, the death of Lame Deer, and the surrender of Crazy Horse and his bloody end – the whole of which was vividly underlined by the battered Nez Percé remnants who had sought refuge with the Sioux a few days before. Sitting Bull said, 'For sixty-four years you have

Sitting Bull, Fort Randall, 1882. Comparing this picture with that taken at Fort Walsh only four years before it can be seen that Sitting Bull has considerably aged. The loss of his freedom was a hard blow to his pride and he attempted to maintain a fierce independence. Basically a fine humanitarian he felt however that he could trust no American official. A man of unusual discernment he could forsee more than most the inevitable extermination of his race. Today so-called 'militant' American Indians attempting to find a clearly defined place in American society recognize the powerful message Sitting Bull attempted to convey and they have adopted much of his philosophy.

treated my people bad' [obviously referring to the War of 1812]. 'Over there we could go nowhere, so we have taken refuge here. I shake hands with these people' [the Police], 'you can go back home, that part of the country we came from belonged to us and you took it from us, now we live here.' (Macbeth, 1931, p. 85).

But the road ahead was to be particularly difficult for the Sioux. Sitting Bull's band wandered between Fort Walsh and Fort Qu'Appelle some 250 miles away and when game became particularly scarce they struck across the border to hunt buffalo. At Fort Qu'Appelle, Sitting Bull appealed to Superintendent S. B. Steele for a reserve to be set aside in Canada for him and his followers. Indian Commissioner Dewdney went to see Sitting Bull and explained that the Canadian Government would not give him one as there was already a reserve in the United States set aside for him. In fact, not until 1913 was a reserve set aside – a full quarter of a century after Sitting Bull's death. There are now seventy Dakota at Wood Mountain (Howard, 1972, p. 8). Dewdney, who was born in Devonshire, England, advised Sitting Bull to return to the United States. He was obviously in sympathy with the Sioux and took a great interest in Indians with whom he generally got on well. (Dewdney collected both Blackfoot and Hunkpapa Sioux costume and other regalia from these people and his collection has finally found its way into the Exeter Museum in Devonshire, England. It includes a fine horned headdress which is possibly Strong Heart Society regalia of which Sitting Bull was a leading member.)

The winter of 1880 was severe, food became scarce and people ill. The police weakened Sitting Bull's influence by persuading the lesser chiefs to return to the United States, so as the memories of their American conflicts became dulled by time, and life became progressively more difficult, even agency life began to look appealing and hundreds returned. But Sitting Bull refused to give up his freedom: 'The country there is poisoned with blood. . . . So long as there remains a gopher to eat, I *will not* go back.' He traded virtually everything he owned to live; even James Mooney, who could hardly be labelled as pro-Sitting Bull, later wrote 'To obtain subsistence while in Canada his people had been obliged to sell almost everything they possessed, including their fire-arms, so they returned to their homes in an impoverished condition.' (Mooney, 1896, p. 861).

At Wood Mountain, not far from present-day Moose Jaw, Saskatchewan, close to the border, he approached Inspector A. R. Macdonnell of the Royal North-West Mounted Police and in desperation asked for rations to feed his destitute people. The request was refused and with a show of anger – never before so strongly displayed towards the Red Coats whom he both admired and trusted – Sitting Bull threatened to take it by force. Now even Sitting Bull, the true leader of the last of the free warriors of the Plains, was being pressed

hard to the wall. The cool Macdonnell – who probably knew that Sitting Bull was bluffing anyway – replied to Sitting Bull's threat to the effect that he would 'ration the band with bullets if they tried that game'. (Macbeth, 1931, p. 87). In despair, the great chief threw up his arms and cried out: 'I am cast away!' (Vestal, 1957, p. 230 and Macbeth, 1931, p. 87).

At mid-day on 19 July 1881, Sitting Bull, leading 186 tired and hungry faithful followers, rode into the small United States military post of Fort Buford, but a short distance from the old fur trading post of happier days, Fort Union.

While the exhausted Sioux set up camp between the Fort and the boat landing, the officers came over to see them. One young officer W. H. C. Bowen, later described his impression of the famous Sioux chief. He 'did not appear to be a well man, showing in his face and figure the ravages of worry and hunger he had gone through. He was getting old. Since the sixties he had been the hero of his race. Giving in to the hated whites and the final surrender of his cherished independence was a hard blow to his pride, and he took it hard. He was much broken.' (Vestal, 1957, p. 232).

The next day the commanding officer, Major David H. Brotherton, accepted Sitting Bull's surrender on behalf of the United States Government. As a token of his submission, Sitting Bull directed his small son to take up his rifle and present it to the Major. That historic moment deserves precise documentation – just after 11 o'clock on the morning of Tuesday, 20 July 1881 at Fort Buford, latitude 48°, longitude 104° – for symbolically it was more than a surrender of 187 exhausted Sioux, it was the end of an era. 'Let me be a free man – free to travel, free to stop, free to work, free to trade, where I choose, free to choose my own teachers,

Dedication of the Standing Rock. Fort Yates, about 1885. This photograph shows Sitting Bull on the left and 'Major' James McLaughlin on the right. McLaughlin was the Indian agent on the Standing Rock reservation and it was he who ordered the arrest of Sitting Bull in December 1890. Indian agents were often in charge of Indian chiefs and headmen who were their superiors – morally, mentally and physically – and there was frequent conflict. The tenacious Red Cloud, even in his old age, never bowed to the demands of his agent and McLaughlin found it impossible to dominate Sitting Bull.

free to follow the religion of my fathers, free to think and talk and act for myself.' (Joseph, Nez Percé chief. In Brady, 1907, p. 74). Did those fine sentiments die that day?

Predictably, the promised reservation was not given to Sitting Bull and his followers and for nearly two years they were held as prisoners-of-war at Fort Randall. This was not, according to his biographer Stanley Vestal, an altogether unhappy period for Sitting Bull. The officers at Fort Randall 'liked and admired him', many of whom recognized some of the great wrongs done to the Indian. One wrote 'I marvelled at [their] patience and forebearance'. (In Vestal, 1957, p. 238).

Not until 10 May 1883 were Sitting Bull and his followers allowed to join the Hunkpapa at Standing Rock – to settle down to a 'monotonous beef eating [sedentary] existence' (Ewers, 1956, p. 21), on the Grand River not far from Sitting Bull's birthplace on Willow Creek just below the mouth of the Cheyenne River in present-day South Dakota. The site was located some twenty miles away from the agency headquarters at Fort Yates. Even today it is remote and almost inaccessible and when I visited the old encampment in the summer of 1966 I could not help but feel that Sitting Bull had attempted to keep well out of the way of Agent McLaughlin. But when he surrendered in 1881 Sitting Bull had attempted to make his position clear, and stated: 'If the Great Father gives me a reservation I do not want to be confined to any part of it. I want *no restraint.* I will keep on the reservation but I *want to go where I please.* I don't want a white man over me. I don't want an agent. I want to keep the white man with me but *not* to be my chief. I ask this because I want to do right by my people. I cannot trust anyone else to trade with them or talk to them.' (Johnson, 1962, p. 6). In fact, Tatan'ka-iyo'take was to maintain that fierce independence until the day he died.

By 1890, The People had reached a low ebb; there was deep distress of both mind and body. They had lost the entire system of values by which to interpret and organize their lives. In 1889, the Americans had broken up the Great Sioux Reservations into smaller units to give five smaller reservations for the seven Plains Sioux tribes. Sitting Bull had refused to be bought and had bitterly opposed the move but he was outrageously side-stepped and he took the situation very hard. After the lands had been signed away, someone asked him what the Indians thought about it. With a burst of passionate indignation he replied 'Indians! There are no Indians left now but me.' (Mooney, 1896, p. 861).

On no reservation was anything belonging to the past stable; the buffalo were gone, even many familiar landscapes which may have reminded The People of the past were in the hands of the white man. The power of most of the chiefs was broken and now vested almost entirely in the hands of questionably competent Indian Agents. The People were fast becoming strangers in the land where they had been born. Even such a hospitable and friendly tribe as the Omaha in Nebraska were being brutally betrayed. Only the timely intervention of that great ethnologist, Alice Fletcher, who championed their cause before congressional committees, church gatherings and meetings of leading citizens, and hence focussed attention on the Omaha's petition to the United States Government for full legal rights to be granted for 'their homes and to the land' prevented complete dispossession of their lands – something which had happened with their close neighbours, the Ponca, a short time before. (Fletcher and La Flesche, 1905–1906, p. 636).

All The People had now were their memories:

Once I was a warrior

iki´cize	a warrior
waön´kon	I have been
wana´	now
hena´la yelo´	it is all over
iyo´tiye kiya´	a hard time
waön´	I have

(1880 song of Sitting Bull, Densmore, 1918, p. 459).

There was a deeper message to this song than just the words, for when the ethnologist, Frances Densmore, who made a lifetime study of North American Indian music, analysed its melody she concluded that the wide and irregular intervals displayed at the opening were very characteristic of Sioux songs conveying sentiments of disappointment or distress. It was sung at a time when vast areas of Sioux territory were being ceded which boded ill for the whole future of the tribe. 'Sitting Bull, who was a man of unusual discernment, may have foreseen what must inevitably follow.' (Densmore, 1918, p. 462). He recognized that the sun was setting on the Indians of the Plains.

Over one thousand miles away near Pyramid Lake, Nevada, towards the end of 1888, a Paiute Indian by the name of Wovoka was attacked by a dangerous fever. During his illness, an eclipse of the sun spread great excitement amongst his tribesmen and in his delirious state Wovoka had a vision in which he received a direct revelation from the god of Indians. 'When the sun died, I went up to heaven and saw God and all the people who had died a long time ago. God told me to come back and tell my people they must be good and love one another, and not fight, or steal, or lie. He gave me this dance to give my people.'

Wovoka received instructions that he must go back to earth and preach goodness, industry and peace to the Indians. If they followed his instructions they would be reunited with their relatives and friends who had died. A new world would be created where there would be no more death, sickness or old age. Many of the doctrines combined Indian religion with the Christian faith. An important phase of the new faith was a new dance for the Indians. It came to be known as The Spirit or Ghost Dance.

The new religion spread rapidly. Delegations of

Sitting Bull and land speculators, 1888. The astute Sitting Bull constantly opposed the selling of Sioux land, only by deceit was he finally beaten when the great Sioux reservation was split up into five smaller reservations. When someone asked Sitting Bull what the Indians thought of it he burst out with passionate despair 'Indians? There are no Indians left now but me!' Smithsonian Institution, National Anthropological Archives, Washington.

Indians visited Wovoka to receive instruction. The southern Sioux sent Good Thunder, Flat Iron, Yellow Breast and Broken Arm from Pine Ridge; Short Bull and another Sioux from Rosebud and Kicking Bear from the Cheyenne River Agency. When they returned in March 1890 they were much impressed. Wovoka had gone to considerable trouble to give them precise instructions: 'Dance four nights and the last night keep up the dance until the morning of the fifth day when all must bathe in the river and then disperse to their homes. . . . You must all do it the same way. . . . When your friends die, you must not cry; you must not hurt anybody or do harm to anyone. . . . You must not fight. . . . Do right always. . . . When the earth shakes at the coming of the new world, do not be afraid; it will not hurt you.' (Mooney, 1896, p. 722).

The new religion gained enormous momentum. It was quickly adopted by many tribes east of the mountains, each tribe adding new facets, promises and obligations. Wovoka now became an Indian messiah. He would restore the dead to life, return the buffalo and other game to the famished people. The Son of God would punish the white man for his wickedness and brutal injustice towards the Indians and wipe them from the face of the earth. On 9 October 1890, Kicking Bear visited Standing Rock reservation and explained the doctrine to the Sioux in Sitting Bull's camp. Agent James McLaughlin sent an Indian police force to arrest Kicking Bear and remove him from the reservation 'but they returned without executing the order, both officers being in a dazed condition and fearing the power of Kicking Bear's "medicine".' (Mooney, 1896, p. 847).

At Pine Ridge, the situation caused the new agent, D. F. Royer, to send frantic telegrams to Washington. On 12 October 1890 he reported that over 3000 of his charges were dancing; that they were 'entirely beyond the control of the police' and suggested that the whole matter be put in the hands of the military. (Mooney, 1896, p. 848). Not until over a month later did the authorities take note of Royer, who the Sioux called 'Lakota-Kokipa-Koshkala' (Young-man-afraid-of-Indians).

In early November, McLaughlin left his agency at Fort Yates and visited Sitting Bull on the Grand River to point out the 'absurdity of their belief'. There is no doubt that Sitting Bull was too astute to accept much of the Ghost Dance predictions, and based as it was in part on the white man's religion, he was especially cautious. Diplomatically, he suggested to McLaughlin 'that they should both go with competent attendants to the country of the messiah and see and question him for themselves, and rest the truth or falsity of the new doctrine on the result'. (Mooney, 1896, p. 849). After all, Sitting Bull probably surmised, the white man claimed that they had once been visited by the Son of God and they had completely rejected him, why not now the red man, who after all had far stronger religious convictions? That fair and balanced suggestion was not accepted by McLaughlin. It is interesting to speculate just what the outcome would have been had he done so. Considering the make-up of Sitting Bull, it is probable he would have rejected Wovoka's teachings, but either way there would have been a dangerous recognition of his great leader's standing amongst The People, for as far afield as Lapwai, Idaho, even today, aged Nez Percé Indians describe Sitting Bull as 'a great man'.

By 13 November, the President of the United States had directed the Secretary of War to assume military responsibility for the situation and, as in 1876, there was a massive transfer of troops to Sioux country. The campaign was under the direction of General Nelson A. Miles (now elevated to the position of commander of the Division of the Missouri), who established his headquarters at Rapid City. By early December 1890, there were nearly 3000 troops virtually encircling the Pine Ridge and Rosebud Reservations.

The influx of so many soldiers alarmed the Sioux families. As soon as the troops reached the Rosebud Agency they became so frightened that some 800 Indians fled west towards Pine Ridge and they were joined by others (complete with 'a large portion of the agency beef herd!') from Pine Ridge itself, and within a short time over 3000 Sioux retreated to the Badlands fifty miles northwest of the agency; here at least they would be 'protected by the natural fortresses and difficulties of the country'. (Mooney, 1896, p. 851).

During all this trouble, Major McLaughlin had considered it unnecessary to have troops stationed at Standing Rock to subdue the Sioux in his charge. History concedes that the situation was rather seen by him, and many others, as a very good excuse to get rid of Sitting Bull, but the indecisions were incredible, with orders, counter-orders, recommendations and counter-recommendations oscillating between the War Department and the Indian Office. Even Buffalo Bill was involved: 'The whole affair was merely the last round of that long bout between the Indian Bureau and the War Department for control of the Indians. Sitting Bull was an innocent bystander, the football of bureaucratic politics.' (Vestal, 1957, p. 287).

Finally, on Sunday 14 December 1890, at 4.30 p.m., James McLaughlin, Agent for the United States Indian Service, issued his instructions to the Indian police. 'I believe that the time has arrived for the arrest of Sitting Bull . . . that it can be made by the Indian Police without much risk . . . make the arrest before daylight tomorrow. . . . The cavalry will leave here tonight . . . [and] will remain [at Oak Creek] until they hear from you. . . . P.S. *You must not let him escape under any circumstances.*' (Vestal, 1957, p. 283).

The Indian police at Fort Yates, a number of whom were Yanktonai Sioux, were probably amongst the best of the constabulary set up by the Indian Bureau during the reservation period. McLaughlin – Ma'-za Ka'-ga (The Iron Worker) as the Sioux called him – had much experience with Indians. In less than a decade he had built up a corps who effectively dealt with small scale crime on the reservation. To McLaughlin's credit

Standing Rock Agency. Red Tomahawk, who killed Sitting Bull on 15 December 1890. Acting under orders from Agent McLaughlin, who accused Sitting Bull of stirring up trouble during the Ghost Dance cult, the Indian constabulary attempted to arrest Sitting Bull at his camp on Grand River. In the ensuing melée Sitting Bull, a number of his followers and members of the Indian police were killed. Sitting Bull's horse, which had been given to him by an admiring Buffalo Bill, was one of the spoils of the victors – here Red Tomahawk is seen astride the horse outside the workshop buildings where Sitting Bull's body was taken for burial at Fort Yates. Minnesota Historical Society.

Sitting Bull's two wives and daughters photographed outside his cabin in January 1891, shortly after his death. The cabin stood on the Grand River about twenty miles from the agency headquarters at Fort Yates. Such habitations were only adopted by the Sioux after they were forced to abandon their nomadic life. This cabin was dismantled and shipped to the World's Fair in Chicago in 1893, where it was hoped it would be a star attraction—if the curious looked closely enough they were rewarded by the sight of a number of bullet holes in the logs. (The project was a financial disaster for the promoters). North Dakota State Historical Society.

he had maintained law and order amongst perhaps some of the most unprogressive conservative Sioux on the Plains. Five of the encampments strung along the banks of the Grand River under Chiefs Running Antelope, Sitting Bull, Pretty Bird, Spotted Horse and Thunder Hawk, contained warriors who had recently fought bitterly and successfully against white encroachment. Many of those who rode at daybreak into Sitting Bull's camp that bleak December morning must have been apprehensive and awed men, for beneath those dark blue uniforms, with the baggy trousers, brass buttons and black hats, were Sioux warriors, steeped in superstition. They were to test their medicine power against that of one of the greatest among them *and* with the Messiah cult thrown in for good measure.

They surrounded Sitting Bull's cabin. Lieutenant Bull Head, described by one recent historian as 'a fine specimen of Indian manhood, he was courageous, resourceful, and *completely devoted* to McLaughlin' (Utley, 1963, p. 150), Sergeants Red Tomahawk, Shave Head and others entered and woke the Chief. 'If you fight you will be killed here,' said Red Tomahawk. Sitting Bull agreed to go to the Agency. He instructed his wife to get his clothes while White Bird and Red Bear saddled his grey circus horse (the one presented to him by Buffalo Bill in 1885). As they left the cabin, they were confronted by a formidable array of Hunkpapa. The frightened policemen were now edging Sitting Bull towards his saddled horse. Either side of Sitting Bull were Shave Head, first sergeant, and Bull Head, Lieutenant of the Indian police; behind walked Sergeant Red Tomahawk. Ten to fifteen yards from the cabin, Tatan'ka-iyo-take

stopped and surveyed the scene. The situation was tense and critical. 'Everybody was standing still, and their steaming breath began to be visible in the graying dimness of that chill dawn.' (Vestal, 1957, pp. 298 & 299). Suddenly, amid the confusion, someone cried – possibly Sitting Bull himself – 'Shoot the two leaders; the rest will run away!' (Smith, 1949, p. 212). Rifles thundered, Shave Head and Bull Head crashed to the ground and with them went Sitting Bull – a bullet through his side from the mortally wounded Bull Head and another through the back of the head from the gun of Red Tomahawk.

A legend amongst the Sioux still prevalent today speaks of a ghostly horseman who appeared in the early morning mists of distant Teton camps and from a high butte proclaimed his death (See Turner, 1973, p. 260). Sitting Bull, the generous, Hunkeshnee – thoughtful one – great spiritual leader, the champion of the Plains Indians, was no more.

His old friend, James Morrow Walsh of the Royal North-West Mounted Police, now retired and in Winnipeg, wrote Tatan'ka-iyo'take's obituary on the 16th December.

> 'A nation against one man. On the U.S. side there were numbers; on Sitting Bull's side there was principle. The one man was murdered by the nation to destroy the principle he advocated – that no man against his will should be forced to be a beggar. Sitting Bull was the marked man of his people.'
> (In Turner, 1973, p. 263).

Fifteen days after Sitting Bull's death came the final reckoning – the last stand of The People – the Massacre at Wounded Knee.

The Battlefields Today

'Hear me, my chiefs, I am tired, my heart is sick and sad.
From where the sun now stands I will fight no more forever.'

Chief Joseph at the capitulation of the
Nez Percé. Bear Paw Mountains, October 1877

ON 9 AUGUST 1833, the German explorer Maximilian, Prince of Wied Neuweld together with a young Swiss artist named Carl Bodmer and their servant who had the improbable name of Dreidoppel arrived at Fort McKenzie which was situated almost 300 miles west of Fort Union on the Upper Missouri; it was then, and in fact still is, one of the remotest and least explored areas within the Great Plains region. Maximilian, who was on a scientific tour of the interior of North America with the major objective of studying Plains Indian tribes, was now in the very heart of Blackfoot country and had chosen his spot well for his detailed researches. Near the Fort, on what was later to be known as Brulé Flats, were usually camped large bands of Plains Indians who came to trade.

The most remote outpost of the American Fur Company, Fort McKenzie was small – about 150 feet on its longest side – and contained only twenty-seven engagés who together with their women and children brought the total number to fifty-three. Here the small community, surrounded by the unpredictable Blackfoot tribes who for nearly thirty years (since the unfortunate killing of the Piegan warrior, He-that-looks-at-the-Calf, by members of the Lewis and Clark expedition in July 1806) had remained hostile to Americans, carried on a trade the effects of which were felt as far west as Flathead and Nez Percé country and extending south to the Crow. It could be a lucrative business, but also very dangerous, and one had to be a master of Blackfoot psychology to remain alive.

As with most such trading posts Fort McKenzie consisted of an almost square blockade with cabins, warehouses and workshops around three walls. The main entrance consisted of a corridor gated at both ends and when Indians came to trade a few were let in at a time; then the outer gate was closed and the privileged party allowed to pass through into the inner quadrangle.

At this period, trade was mostly in buffalo robes, the demand for beaver having diminished due to the introduction of the silk hat which outmoded the once fashionable beaver-fur top hat. Some nine thousand buffalo robes were traded in the winter of 1834–1835 (Larpenteur, Vol. 1, 1898, p. 79), which kept the engagés busy pressing the furs for transportation by keel-boat down river to Fort Union (which could take a month or more of hard travel) and then on to St Louis.

Maximilian stayed at the Fort for more than a month and delighted in recording minute ethnological details of the Blackfoot tribes. It was an anthropologist's paradise; here at first hand could be observed the economy and life style of tribes who were still living in a sophisticated stone age. Maximilian was the first trained observer to describe the age-graded societies, each of which had its own regalia and most of whom took on the responsibility for maintaining camp order. He noted that their weapons were very similar to those of other tribes on the Missouri but that because there was no suitable wood available in their country for making bows they carried on a trade for 'yellow' wood which was brought from the area of the Arkansas river. For quivers, the Blackfoot preferred a cougar skin, for which they were willing to give a horse. The tail hung down from the quiver, he observed, and was 'trimmed with red cloth on the inner side, embroidered with white beads at the end or elsewhere, with strips of skin, like tassels' (Maximilian, 1843, p. 258). Few carried lances but most had shields of thick leather generally painted green and red 'and hung with feathers and other things to which some superstitious belief is attached'.

Having spent almost three weeks of scientific study amongst the Blackfoot, whose buffalo hide tipis he visited daily – and exhausted the able Bodmer with numerous requests to make pictorial records – the Prince's idyllic open laboratory was suddenly shattered.

At daybreak on 29 August the occupants were rudely awakened by the crack of a musket shot. An engagé burst into Maximilian's room crying 'Levez-vous, il faut nous battre!'

Hurriedly dressing and loading their muskets they entered the courtyard of the fort, the occupants of which were in a state of high excitement, many firing through the portholes or from the roofs of the fort into a mêlée outside. As he ascended to the stockade platform Maximilian was to witness at close hand the savage fury of full-scale inter-tribal warfare and subsequently Bodmer was to paint the action – a picture unsurpassed for vitality, and accuracy of detail.

The whole prairie was covered with Indians on horseback and on foot whilst other groups were forming on the surrounding hills. Some twenty tipis of Piegan, a Blackfoot tribe, pitched near the fort, 'the inmates of which had been singing and drinking the whole night' and fallen into a deep sleep towards morning, had been surprised by about 600 Assiniboin and Cree warriors. 'Four women and several children lay dead near the fort and many others were wounded. The men, about thirty in number, had partly fired their guns at the enemy, and then fled to the gates of the fort where they were admitted. They immediately hastened to the roofs, and began a well supported fire on the Assiniboins' (Maximilian, 1843, p. 273). The Assiniboin and Cree had cut through the tipis of the Piegan with knives and, taking the occupants completely by surprise, shot them down with arrows and bullets.

Because most of the engagés had sold their ammunition to the Indians they were quite unprepared to take care of themselves, and ball and shot had to be hurriedly furnished not only to the dismayed Piegan but also to the white occupants of the fort. The consternation of the Piegan was equally matched by the confusion of the whites, who had assumed that they were also targets for this surprise attack. As the interpreter, Jacob Berger, and chief clerk, David Mitchell, opened the doors of the fort to admit the surviving women and children they were informed otherwise. One hostile, with arrow ready, cried out 'White man, make room, I will shoot those enemies!' This exclamation was the first hint that the attack was not directed against the occupants of the fort but only against the small Piegan band. David Mitchell immediately gave orders to the engagés to cease firing but could not restrain the angered

Piegan. By now reinforcements were arriving from the main Piegan camp some eight miles away. They came 'galloping in groups, from three to twenty together, their horses covered with foam, and they themselves in their finest apparel, with all kinds of ornaments and arms, bows and quivers on their backs, guns in their hands, furnished with their medicines, with feathers on their heads; some had splendid crowns of black and white eagles' feathers, and a large hood of feathers hanging down behind – the upper part of their bodies partly naked – and carrying shields adorned with feathers and pieces of cloth'. Now virtually matching the Assiniboin and Cree man for man and helped by a dozen or so whites from the fort, the furious Piegan drove the enemy back as far as the Marias river and by evening the Assiniboin had retreated to the safety of the Bear Paw Mountains.

Ever the scientist, Maximilian attempted to get the skull of the one dead Assiniboin who had not been carried away by relatives and friends but by

Combined forces of Assiniboin and Cree attacking, a Blackfoot tracking party. Fort MacKenzie, Upper Missouri, 29 August, 1833. The battle was witnessed at daybreak by the German explorer Maximilian, Prince of Wied Neuwied, and his artist companion Carl Bodmer, when a combined force of Assiniboin and Cree numbering about 600 warriors attacked a small band of Piegan (one of the three tribes of the Blackfoot confederacy) consisting of twenty tipis who had come to the Fort to trade. The occupants of the Fort may be seen firing down into the melée attempting to give support to the Piegan who had been taken completely by surprise. At the left panic-stricken women are attempting to make their escape with their children and luggage while the men cover their retreat. From Maximilian's *Atlas*. Museum of Mankind, London.

the time he got to the corpse it had been scalped and 'so pierced and burnt as scarcely to retain any semblance of the human form'. (Maximilian, 1843, p. 276).

Now safe from further attack, the Piegan began to tend to the wounded and dead. The tipis had been ripped to shreds and dead and dying horses and dogs littered the ground. A number of the wounded men, women, and children were laid or placed against the walls, and others 'in their deplorable condition were pulled about by their relations, amid tears and lamentations'. White Buffalo, one of Maximilian's most interesting informants, had been wounded in the head 'they rattled the schischikue in his ears, that the evil spirit might not overcome him, and gave him brandy to drink. He himself, though stupified and intoxicated, sang without intermission and would not give himself up to the evil spirit'.

Otsequa-Stomik, an aged warrior, had been wounded in the knee by a musket ball 'which a woman cut out with a pen knife . . . during which operation he did not betray the least symptom of pain'. Maximilian helped Mitchell's men to treat some of the severely wounded and was gratified to hear that one chief felt that the reason no Assiniboin had hit him was the 'medicine' invoked when Bodmer painted his portrait the previous day.

The short encounter had been a bloody one, at least six Assiniboin and thirty Piegan being killed and a good many more wounded.

Ethnology, however, owes much to that engagement, for Maximilian's description and Bodmer's magnificent painting, give a rare and unsurpassed insight into one facet of Plains Indian warfare.

Like Maximilian, I visited Fort McKenzie – but with friends in an August nearly a century and a half later; nevertheless it proved to be one of the most rewarding experiences on our journey of rediscovery to some of the less explored historic sites on the Great Plains.

The area had changed little since the days of the fur trade; in fact that whole length of the Missouri, between the small town of Fort Benton and the Fort Peck Reservoir, nearly 200 miles down river, still retains most of the topographic and natural features which even as early as the days of Lewis and Clark, who passed this way in 1805, have commanded the admiration of every explorer and traveller. The canyon walls, the meadows, green lowlands, striking rock forms, the vegetation and much of the animal life still remain. Owls, hawks and eagles are numerous, especially along the river. Only the buffalo, grizzly, wolf and the wild free Indian are missing.

We approached the Fort McKenzie site from Fort Benton some eight miles up river. Fort Benton was established by Alexander Culbertson of the American Fur Company in 1846, the ultimate point of Missouri River navigation. The first steamer arrived here in 1860. It became a centre for the fur trade, with wagon trails radiating to the interior mountain towns. Only fragments of the adobe walls of the original Fort Benton survive but the old river bank where the steamers were once tied up still remains and much of historic interest is preserved there. We recalled the stirring tales of James Willard Shultz, author of *My life as an Indian, In the lodges of the Blackfeet* and other books on Plains Indians and who, as a young man fired with an ambition to see Indians and hunt buffalo, had arrived at Fort Benton in the summer of 1878. Shultz married into the Blackfoot tribe and warred with them against their enemies the Kutenai and Crow.

We found the now derelict I. G. Baker Trading Post where Shultz and his Indian friends came to trade and on one side wall we could still make out the companies old trading placard. 'Established 65 . . . Dry Goods, Groceries . . . light Harness and Wagons . . . cowboy saddles . . .'.

To the back of the small town are wide gently rising Plains where visiting Piegan, Blackfoot, Blood, Cree, Kutenai and Assiniboin camped when they came to trade at the adobe fort.

Fort Benton declined rapidly after the construction of the Northern Pacific and Great Northern railroads during the years following 1881 which destroyed the importance of the Missouri as the main artery of transport. Subsequent travel by modern highways have left large portions of the river in this area even more isolated than they were more than a century ago and Benton itself has a ghost town like atmosphere.

Ten miles east of Fort Benton we located the site of old Fort Piegan which was a temporary trading post built by James Kipp, a Canadian of German descent, in the winter of 1831. Although located at the confluence of the Marias and Missouri Rivers,

Site of old Fort Phil Kearny, Wyoming. Described as one of the finest forts ever built in the American West. It was constructed in July 1866 under the supervision of Colonel H. Carrington who drew up the plans and selected the site. Its construction violated existing treaties with the Sioux who were incensed at the audacity of its position – in the very heart of their hunting grounds – and under the direction of Red Cloud they constantly harassed its occupants. Many skirmishes and battles occurred in the vicinity, the most famous of which was the Fetterman Massacre of December 1866. Within two years the Fort was abandoned and burnt and the Bozeman Trail closed. Photograph by Sam Cahoon.

it was apparently unfavourably situated and abandoned the following year. We explored this area in detail and walked across the old Lewis and Clark camp-site, virtually unchanged since their stay between 3–11 June in 1805.

Five miles hard travel across a rough road finally brought us near the site of historic Fort McKenzie. The owner of the land was farmer Bob Lundy who pointed out old tipi rings on the prairie; these single circles of stones which were measured and found to range in diameter from 8 feet to 19 feet, and which were used to weigh down the edges of the tipi covers by nomadic warriors a century or so ago, were now embedded in the prairie.

Brulé Flats, a level area surrounding the site, was bordered on the south by the Missouri with high bluffs beyond and to the north – about three quarters of a mile away – were gently rising hills. Picture in hand of Bodmer's battle scene, we were able to locate the peaked bluffs and outcrop of trees and hence determine the precise location of the Fort, a conclusion which was confirmed by an abundance of trade beads, broken clay pipe stems, some arrow heads, and spent musket balls, some probably from guns fired on that historic morning of 28 August 1833.

Nearly a century and a quarter has passed since the Grattan Massacre of 19 August 1854. This conflict heralded the beginning of the wars with the Plains Indians and gave the young Red Cloud his first real experience of a bloody confrontation with the oncoming white man.

It is not easy, as it was at the Fort McKenzie site, to determine the exact positions taken by the participants on the battlefield. The main emigrant wagon road, along which the sore-footed cow was abandoned by the Mormons and which caused so much trouble, can be located; but land-levelling operations for irrigation purposes has tended to obliterate a number of historically identifiable landmarks. It is possible, however, to locate the site of James Bordeaux's trading post and also the hill on the west side of the wagon road from which Frank Salway, one of the interpreters, Charles Gareau, and a number of other whites observed the events which took place at the post and later in the Brulé camp.

Conquering Bear's lodge stood to the east of the camp, nearest to the Platte River, to the north of which about a half mile away were plum and willow thickets behind which the Sioux massed in readiness for battle. Although little of the foliage is left, the spot where Conquering Bear fell mortally wounded and where Grattan died a short while later – his body bristling with Sioux arrows – can be pin-pointed.

Although Grattan's body was taken to Fort Laramie for burial after the battle the bodies of the twenty-five privates and others were buried in a shallow grave on the battlefield and the site of the cairn erected over them can be located. For many years it could be seen from the old Oregon

Ridge at Fetterman Massacre Site, looking approximately south. On 21 December 1866 Fetterman and his entire command of eighty-one men were annihilated by the hostile Sioux. They had ridden some four miles from the Fort in pursuit of a Sioux war party and were ambushed by an overwhelming force of warriors. The ridge at the left of the picture with the gravelled road running along its spine is where Fetterman and forty-eight of the command made their stand. The main road at the right is Highway 87, which runs north to the Crow Indian Reservation in Montana. About halfway across the hill in the background beyond the road and to the left may be seen ruts which locate the line of the Bozeman Trail.

trail, a constant reminder of the beginning of a long and bitter struggle between Red and White.

A century had passed when we visited one of the most famous battle sites of the Plains Indian wars – that of the so called Fetterman disaster of 21 December 1866. On this field, no more than four miles from Fort Phil Kearny, Brevet Lieutenant Colonel Fetterman and his entire command of eighty-one officers, enlisted men and civilians, were killed by combined forces of Sioux, Cheyenne and Arapaho Indians who bitterly resented the building of the Fort (in July 1866) in the very heart of their domain.

We approached Fort Phil Kearny by way of Powder River Pass which cuts through the Big Horn Mountains in northern Wyoming. Little wonder the Sioux were so reluctant to relinquish this territory – the scenery is magnificent and the area still abounds with game. North of Buffalo we followed the route of the old Bozeman trail and just south of the little township of Story; after turning off east along a meandering and picturesque road, we finally reached the site of old Fort Phil Kearny. With the old Carrington map of the area we were able to identify most of the surrounding landmarks.

The Fort had been built on a small plateau between the north and south forks of the Piney Creek, distant bluffs overlook the site on three sides and some six miles west are the Big Horn Mountains. About half a mile to the north of the post are the Sullivant Hills beyond which, in the distance, can be seen the southern edge of Lodge Trail Ridge which reminded us of Carrington's parting words to Fetterman on that cold December morning long ago: 'Support the wood train; relieve it, and report to me. Do not engage or pursue Indians at its expense. Under no circumstances pursue over the ridge, viz, Lodge Trail Ridge, as per map in your possession.'

In 1913 the historian, E. A. Brininstool, visited

Location of Beecher Island. Arikaree Fork of Republican River, Colorado. The original island has been obliterated but this is virtually on the same site and shows the wide, almost dried up river bed with only a small amount of water either side – just as it was in September 1867 when Major George A. Forsyth and fifty men held off, for ten days, a large force of Cheyenne and Sioux under Roman Nose. Nearby are markers on 'Squaw Hill' where the women and children watched the progress of the battle and another marker on the high bluffs, one half mile to the south, locates 'Roman Nose Hill' from which he could direct his warriors. Photograph by Sam Cahoon.

this site and he found that where had been the old parade ground was now a fine alfalfa field. Scattered about were remnants of some of the old stoves and baking ovens used by the troops, and the east line of the old stockade was still discernible. Since that time part of the fort has been reconstructed, but it has few visitors. Here and there are fragments of wood, small pieces of broken glass and the line of the original stockade can still be determined since it virtually occupied the entire plateau. I was surprised at its size – about 600 by 800 feet. With its 400 odd officers and men (and some of their families) it must have acted as a sinister reminder to the Sioux and their allies of

Reno Crossing, looking west. Across this lowland and to the bluffs beyond Major Marcus A. Reno and three companies of cavalry retreated after attacking the 'hostile' Indian village on the Little Big Horn (25 June 1876) and being confronted by an immense combined force of Sioux and Cheyenne warriors who stood their ground to protect their women and children. The Reno command established defense lines on the hills east of the river and could give Custer, who shortly after the Reno retreat attacked the other end of the village, none of the planned support. Photograph by Sam Cahoon.

the immense resources of the United States.

It was not easy to decipher Carrington's map with respect to the actual location of Massacre ridge (shown A–B–C on the Carrington map), a major difficulty being the very rugged nature of the terrain.

I subsequently discovered that Carrington had foreshortened Lodge Trail Ridge, one half to the west having been omitted. It has, in recent years, been suggested that Carrington had done this deliberately 'so as to make it appear that the distance was short enough that Fetterman could have gotten to the west end of it in time to cut off the retreat of the Indians, thus sustaining his contention that Fetterman took that route'. (Vaughn, 1966, p. 59).

As we drove north it became apparent that 'Massacre Hill' was not so far northwest as shown; nevertheless the map was remarkable for the wealth of detail it gave. Surveys of the area, using aerial photographs and a metal detector, indicate that Carrington's map gives a good deal of accurate and reliable data.

The main position where Fetterman and his infantry took their stand is now accessible by a short road which runs along the spine of Massacre Hill; at the end of this road is a large rock monument with an inscription outlining the major details of the battle, much of which remains conjecture since there were no white survivors.

Forty-two years later, in July 1908, Colonel Carrington, then eighty-six years old, returned to Massacre Hill to attend a dedication ceremony. At that time he and other soldiers identified the precise spot where Fetterman's and Brown's bodies were found with forty-seven other soldiers. This group, as described in Chapter VI, were the first discovered by Captain Ten Eyck. Brown and Fetterman were found lying side by side each with a bullet wound in the left temple 'Their heads were burned and filled with powder around the wounds. Seeing that all was lost, they had evidently stood face to face, and each had shot the other dead with his revolver.' (Brady, 1904, p. 32).

Although the main battle position was well known, that where Lieutenant Grummond and his twenty-seven troopers of the Second Cavalry fell, and the spot where the civilians Wheatley and Fisher took their stand – imagining themselves invincible with their newly acquired Henry repeating rifles – were not so definitely located until a few years ago.

In 1960 the historian J. W. Vaughn and his friend L. C. Bishop went over the entire area with a metal detector and the actions of the two separate forces were carefully reconstructed 'in the light of known military standards of conduct under similar circumstances.' (Vaughn, 1966, p. 29).

At the point where Fetterman was found Vaughn located two steel lance points, uniform buttons and expended percussion caps 'of the type used with the muzzle-loading Springfields' carried by the infantry. The site is centred directly on the

Indians firing the grass. After Custer's destruction the gigantic Indian village, aware of the approach of another large force of soldiers under Generals Terry and Gibbon, began to break up. By morning of 26 June most bands were on the move (although some warriors remained to harass the entrenched Reno command). As a line of defence they fired the grass. Although the famous Battle of the Little Big Horn was a decided victory for the last of the free Plains Indians, it provoked the massive campaign on the part of the United States which aimed at subduing them forever. From a sketch by Frederick Remington entitled *Burning the Range*, originally published in Harpers Weekly, 17 September 1887.

Bozeman Trail and from the monument the ruts of the old road can be clearly seen running down the slope northeast of Lodge Trail Ridge.

North from the monument, at a distance of about half a mile, a number of expended Spencer cartridges were found together with lead bullets of about 0.52 calibre which were either mushroomed or flattened out and then doubled up 'which had obviously found their mark'. Since Grummond's men carried Spencer carbines the position where most of the cavalry detachment made their last stand was definitely located – some three and a half miles almost due north of the Fort. The Wheatley and Fisher site was not located with the certainty of the other two – as no 0.44 calibre Henry cartridges were found with the metal detectors, Vaughn and his companion concluded that most had been picked up as mementos probably years before when General Crook's army passed that way 'on two campaigns in 1876'.

Applying the time-versus-distance formula, Vaughn concluded that (contrary to the opinions of most modern students of the battle) only the cavalry rode as far ahead as Peno Creek, leaving the larger infantry group near, or on, the high crest running from Lodge Trail Ridge. The heavy firing which was first heard by the occupants of the fort about midday was probably that of the cavalry who were ambushed at the Creek and who then retreated back towards the Fort. Fetterman then possibly pushed forward to lend support but before the two groups could reunite they were separately destroyed by overwhelming numbers of Sioux, Cheyenne and Arapaho.

All three sites of the battle may now be seen from Highway 87 which runs due north from Buffalo past Lake De Smet and then just west of the battle ridge on to Sheridan and the Crow Reservation beyond.

About three miles south west of Massacre Hill we located the broad level plain where yet another bloody encounter took place on 2 August 1867; this time Indian losses were heavy, the soldiers having all been issued with breech-loading Springfield rifles. That encounter commonly referred to as the Wagon Box Fight is described in some detail in Chapter VII. The terrain of the battlefield matched closely the descriptions we had read of it, the defensive breastwork of wagon-boxes had been well placed since the surrounding country, unlike that of the Fetterman site, afforded little cover for the attacking Indians. At the centre of the field stands a high stone monument commemorating the battle, between an immense force of Sioux and Cheyenne led by Red Cloud and a small force of thirty-two officers and men of 'C' Company of the twenty-seventh infantry under Captain James Powell.

By August 1868 Red Cloud had won everything he had fought for and Fort Phil Kearny was abandoned. The Bozeman Trail was closed and for another ten years Powder River country remained in the hands of the warriors of the Plains.

Not until October 1888 did the soldiers who died during the occupation of Fort Phil Kearny reach their final resting place, when they were exhumed and reburied in the National Cemetery at the Custer Battlefield. Now they lie side by side with the war heroes of America possibly wondering, if ghosts can wonder, what it was really all about.

On 29 August 1868, Major George A. Forsyth, a brevet Colonel on General Sheridan's staff left Fort Hays, Kansas with fifty hand-picked Indian fighters; they were about equally divided between trappers and hunters and veterans of the Civil War. Lieutenant Frederick H. Beecher, of the Third Infantry, was second-in-command and the surgeon of the party was Dr John H. Mooers 'a highly-trained physician, who had come to the West in a spirit of restless adventure' (Brady, 1904, p. 77). The object was to scout for hostile Sioux, Cheyenne and Arapaho who, incensed by the building of the Kansas Pacific railroad across their territory, had started a campaign of terrorism against the Kansas settlers. 'In one month they cut off, killed, or captured eighty-four different settlers, including their wives and children. They swept the country bare. Again and again the different gangs of builders were wiped out, but the railroad went on.' (Brady, 1904, p. 75).

On 15 September the party reached the Arikaree Fork of the Republican River; Indian signs had been apparent and they were confident that they were within striking distance of a large encampment. The Arikaree River runs approximately southwest, passing through the most northwesterly portion of Kansas and into eastern Colorado.

Forsyth and his men, after a day of hard riding, camped at about 4 o'clock in the afternoon on the south bank of the river which at this point runs through a valley about two miles wide. The river was bordered with wild plum trees, willows and alders and was about 140 yards wide – in the middle was a small gravel island. As is typical of many Great Plains rivers in mid to late summer, most of the bed was dried up and water, about one foot deep, flowed for only about fifteen feet either side of the island.

At dawn on the 16th, a large combined force of about 700 Cheyenne and Sioux attacked the party, taking them completely by surprise. Their only possible chance was a retreat across to the island. For more than a week Forsyth and his men held the warriors at bay as they repeatedly assailed the island force. On the night of the 19th, Forsyth sent two volunteers with a message to Colonel Bankhead at Fort Wallace:

'I sent you two messengers on the night of the 17th inst., informing you of my critical condition. . . . I have eight badly wounded and ten slightly wounded men to take in. . . . Lieutenant Beecher is dead, and Acting Assistant Surgeon Mooers probably cannot live the night out. He was hit in the head Thursday, and has spoken but one rational word since. I am wounded in two places – in the right thigh, and my left leg is broken below the knee. . . . We are living on mule and horse meat, and are entirely out of rations. . . . I can hold out for six days longer if absolutely necessary, but please lose no time. . . .' (Brady, 1904, p. 93).

On the fourth day Forsyth was forced to cut the bullet out of his leg. 'He had his razor in his saddle bags and, while two men pressed the flesh back, he performed the operation successfully, to his immediate relief.' (Brady, 1904, p. 94).

By 21 September, the horse and mule meat had become putrid and unfit to eat and not until four days later did troops come to the rescue. Lieutenant Beecher was among those killed and the island was subsequently named in his honour. Dr Mooers died three days after being struck in the forehead by a bullet, two of the scouts had also been killed, and fifteen others wounded.

The Sioux and Cheyenne lost at least thirty-five men – amongst them their leader Roman Nose whose body was later discovered in a burial tipi on the other side of the valley.

Today, the shallow Arikaree Fork has shifted its course and only the general area of the Beecher's island can be located, the island itself having been completely obliterated. There is now a lot more foliage and the site is easily accessible along a modern highway. At the centre of the field stands a tall pointed obelisk with a plaque which outlines the main details of the encounter. Where a century ago Cheyenne and Sioux warriors under Roman Nose thundered forth on their war ponies, docile cows now graze in peaceful meadows.

On 21 June 1876, a Council of War was held aboard the steamer *Far West* (which was anchored on the Yellowstone River near the mouth of the Rosebud, in present-day Montana). The supreme commander of a gigantic U.S. military move against the last of the hostile 'Buffalo Indians' under Sitting Bull, was General Alfred H. Terry, Commander of the Department of the Dakota; using the *Far West* as headquarters, Terry hoped to outmanoeuvre the hard-to-catch tribes and crush them at the focus of three military columns (see Chapter VII).

Custer, with 31 officers, 586 soldiers, 33 Indian Scouts and 20 employees and citizens, marching at the rate of thirty miles a day, was to approach within co-ordinating distance of General Gibbon and, getting the Indians between the forces, compel them to fight.

When Custer said goodbye to Terry and Gibbon, the latter remarked: 'Now Custer, don't be greedy but wait for us,' Custer made the ambiguous reply: 'No, I will not.'

By 4.00 p.m. on 21 June, Custer's immediate command encamped on the Rosebud about ten miles from its mouth. Each man was armed with a single-shot U.S. Carbine, Model 1873 with 100 rounds of ammunition and a 0.45 calibre revolver with 24 rounds. Additionally, the pack train included 12 mules, each carrying 2000 extra rounds of carbine ammunition while some 160 mules carried 15 days' rations. Every man had 12 pounds of oats for his horse.

On 23 June, the march was resumed at 5.00 a.m. travelling thirty-three miles and although no hostiles were seen, three deserted Indian camps were passed. Custer had estimated that perhaps 1000 to 1500 Indians would eventually be found.

By 24 June, Custer's column was near the upper forks of Tullock's Creek some seventy miles from the mouth of the Rosebud and that night at 9.25 p.m. he called his officers together, telling them that scouts had reported a large Indian village in the Little Bighorn valley and that 'it would be necessary to cross over from the Rosebud at night

Monument to Chief Crazy Horse, Fort Robinson, Nebraska. In the spring of 1877, after severe harassment by United States soldiers, many bands finally capitulated –amongst them Crazy Horse, a great warrior and friend of Sitting Bull. By September 1877 Crazy Horse was dead–killed while resisting arrest. This monument is of native stone from the Black Hills–the sacred hunting grounds of the Sioux–and was erected in September 1934 on the site of the old guardhouse outside which Crazy Horse was killed. Thousands gathered at its unveiling in a three-day pageant and it was the first time in American history that a Plains Indian warrior had been so honoured through Government agencies. On the bronze plate it states 'A great chief of heroic character. He fought to the last to hold his native land for the Indian people.' Nebraska State History Society.

to avoid being discovered'. (Hammer, 1966, p. 3).

At 1.00 a.m. on 25 June, the march resumed towards the divide between the Rosebud and Little Bighorn, and at about 2.30 a.m. after a march of some eight miles, the column halted and unsaddled. From a high hill on the divide, from the famous landmark now known as Crow's Nest, scouts sent word that an Indian village had been sighted about '15 miles down in the Bighorn valley'. (Hammer, 1966, p. 3).

On the morning of 25 June Custer, using field-glasses, was unable to detect the village and expressed some doubt as to its location; by that time, however, hostile scouts had been seen observing the column and realising that the Indians would probably strike their tipis and escape, he made the decision to attack the village. At 12.05 he divided the regiment into four columns. Captain Frederick W. Benteen with 113 men was to proceed to the left, scout for about three miles, attack any Indians he found and report his findings to Custer. Major Marcus A. Reno, with 131 men was to parallel Custer's movements moving down the left of Sundance Creek towards the Little Bighorn. Custer, with Companies, C, E, F, I and L – in all 215 men – moved slightly ahead on the right of the Creek. Behind Reno rode Captain Thomas M. McDougall's Company B, escorting the valuable pack train.

At 2.15 some forty Sioux were seen in flight towards the river and Reno received further instructions from Custer ... 'move at as rapid a gait as you think prudent and to charge afterwards, and you will be supported by the whole outfit' (Hammer, 1966, p. 4). Reno rode forward at a fast trot, and by 2.30 was near the river; Custer was now behind Reno. Crossing Little Bighorn about four miles south of the Indian village, Reno advanced down the valley and 'swinging his force into line' he attacked the village at about 3.15. Sioux veterans later said: 'It was sure hard luck for Major Reno that he struck the Hunkpapa camp first' (Vestal, 1957, p. 162).

Instead of running, the Indians ahead multiplied until there was a solid front before the village. By 3.30 his men had dismounted and under heavy and sustained firing from the Indians were now pushed into a defensive position and attempted to withdraw into the timber along the river. The command was now being rapidly surrounded by Sioux and Cheyenne warriors and Reno ordered his men to mount; at that moment Bloody Knife, an Arikara Scout, a favourite of Custer's, was struck by a bullet and his brains were splattered into Reno's face; now unnerved, the shocked Major ordered his men to dismount and a few seconds later to mount again. The retreat now became a free-for-all, the panic-stricken cavalry dashing east across the Bighorn valley towards high bluffs the other side of the river. By the time they got there, one third of his immediate command were dead – it was now about 4.15.

The route which Custer took after he parted from Reno is conjectural; his experience with

Marker to Sitting Bull, Grand River. After confinement to the Standing Rock reservation in 1883, Sitting Bull lived on the Grand River some forty miles from Agency headquarters at Fort Yates. Although the inscription is written with some compassion it is surely inaccurate to describe Sitting Bull as 'misguided'. Photograph Floyd Ryan.

fighting Plains Indians probably led him to believe that at the first sign of attack they would attempt to escape. Knowing that Reno was attacking the southern end of the village, he possibly planned to attack it from the north. From a high point east of the Little Bighorn, as Reno engaged the Sioux, Custer was seen by some of the troops to wave his hat in encouragement – that was probably about 3.15. By 4.30 Custer was four miles farther up river from Reno, and probably now on the defensive. Crazy Horse, moving out from the Cheyenne camp-site which was located at the extremities of the Indian village (which stretched for four miles along the Little Bighorn) led his Oglala and others to attack the soldiers from the north while Gall attacked from the south, cutting off First Lieutenant James Calhoun's Company L. Crow King and his warriors stampeded the led horses and within minutes Company L had been annihilated. Before 5 o'clock, Custer was completely hemmed in and 'his doom was sealed' (Hammer, 1966, p. 5).

By 7 o'clock, Reno, now joined by Benteen's Battalion, had entrenched on a hill east of the river overlooking the Bighorn valley. Having by this time disposed of Custer and his immediate command, the Sioux and Cheyenne, many now armed with captured guns, renewed their attack. Crow King, a Hunkpapa Sioux, later said: 'We fired at them until the sun went down. We surrounded them and watched them all night and at daylight we fought them again. We killed many of them . . . then Sitting Bull gave this order. "This is not my doing, nor these men's. They are fighting because they were commanded to fight. We have killed their leader. Let them go. I will call the Great Spirit to witness what I say. We did not want to fight. Long Hair sent us word that he was coming to fight us, and we had to defend ourselves and our wives and children." If this command had not been given, we could have cut Reno's command to pieces, as we did Custer's.' (In *Leavenworth Weekly Times* – Thursday, 18 August 1881).

On the 25th, the troops of General Terry and Gibbon, in all about 450 men, were approaching the mouth of the Little Bighorn; the next day they met three Crow Indians who had been scouts with Custer. Conversing in signs, they told of Custer's destruction – news which was so incredible that it was not fully believed. 'Their story was not credited. It was supposed that some fighting, perhaps severe fighting had taken place; but it was not believed that disaster could have overtaken so large a force as twelve companies of cavalry.' General Terry, 27 June 1876. (In report of the Secretary of War, 1876).

As they approached the Little Bighorn, many Indians were sighted and that night the troops camped near the present site of the Crow Agency, Montana – less than ten miles from the Indian village.

Terry and Gibbon had attempted to send scouts through to what was supposed to be General Custer's position, but they were driven back by

large parties of Sioux and Cheyenne who hovered ahead of Gibbon's front; thus the approach of this further massive force of soldiers was well known to the occupants of the Indian village and they began to break camp: by 9.30 on 26 June, the gigantic village had dispersed. It had contained *at least* 10,000 Indians – probably one of the largest gatherings of Plains Indians ever assembled in the 19th century, a conservative estimate putting the number of warriors at not less than 3000.

On the morning of Tuesday the 27th, Lieutenant Bradley, sent with a detail to scout on the east side of the Little Big Horn, discovered Custer's slaughtered Command. A hasty survey of the battle gave a count of 197 bodies scattered in groups within an area less than half a square mile. One lone survivor, who had served under Custer's immediate command, was found amid the carnage on the battlefield – Captain Keogh's horse, Comanche. Wounded in seven places, the creature became a mascot of the Seventh and was subsequently paraded at every ceremony of the regiment.

By 10 a.m. Terry and his staff had reached the Reno position where immediate action was taken to care properly for the wounded and where, the news of Custer's fate was received with utter disbelief. There had been many heroics, both during the retreat to Reno Hill and the two day siege, and twenty-five Medals of Honour were subsequently awarded.

At 5.00 a.m. on the morning of the 28th, Reno and his command went over to the Custer battleground to bury the dead. Later, Edward S. Godfrey described the scene: 'The marble white bodies, the somber brown of the dead horses and dead ponies scattered all over the field, but thickest near

Call of the Bugle. Custer's Last Stand, 25 June 1876. While Reno's force was halted four miles downstream, Custer, attempting to attack Sitting Bull's village from the north, was himself surrounded by large forces of Sioux and Cheyenne under Crazy Horse, Gall, Crow King and others. Probably within less than one hour his entire immediate command was annihilated. Custer is seen near the top of the hill which now bears his name surrounded by those of his command who survived the initial repulse, and a bugler (centre) signals for help which will not be forthcoming. From a painting by J. K. Ralston based on detailed studies of the battle and field. Custer Battlefield National Monument Crow Agency, Montana.

Custer Hill, and the scattering tufts of reddish brown grass and almost ashy-white soil depicts a scene of loneliness and desolation, that bows down the heart in sorrow. I can never forget the sight; the early morning was bright, as we ascended to the top of the highest point whence the whole field came into view, with the sun to our backs. "What are those?" exclaimed several as they looked at what appeared to be white boulders. Nervously I took the field glasses and glanced at the objects; then, almost dropped them, and laconically said: "The dead!" Colonel Weir who was sitting near on his horse, exclaimed: "Oh how white they look!".' (Graham, 1953, pp. 364–365).

Reno ordered several company commanders each to take over a certain strip of terrain and advance in a skirmish line formation to cover the entire field. Moving across from the easternmost group below the end of the battle ridge to the south and working to the farthest group northward to where Custer fell, a grim story unfolded. In a cul-de-sac ravine to the south of Custer they found twenty-odd bodies of the Grey Horse troop (Captain Smith's Company 'E'); here the high banks had trapped the men as they fought a retreat from the onslaught of Gall's warriors. They could see where the troopers had passed down the edge and

The opening fight at Wounded Knee, December 1890. With the unrest created by the Ghost Dance, Big Foot, a Miniconjou Sioux chief, was requested by his Oglala relatives to travel to Pine Ridge to try and restore peace. The tragic death of Sitting Bull aggravated the situation and Big Foot's band, in flight now towards the Pine Ridge reservation, was intercepted by the Seventh Cavalry under Major Whitside. At Wounded Knee Creek abortive attempts were made to disarm the Sioux and at a signal from the medicine man, Yellow Bird, 6 young warriors suddenly threw aside their blankets and fired. The result was a most tragic encounter in which 200 Sioux–men women and children–died along with 25 soldiers. It is very unlikely that any of these warriors were wearing warbonnets. After a sketch by Frederick Remington originally published in Harpers Weekly, 24 January 1891

then attempted to scramble up on the other side, which was almost perpendicular.

'The marks were plain where they used their hands to get up, but the marks only extended half-way up the bank.' (Captain Myles Moylan, Reno Court of Inquiry, 1879).

There were very few tools in the command – perhaps a half-dozen spades and shovels, a couple of picks, a number of axes and hatchets; with these, knives and cups the dead were hastily buried.

View of Wounded Knee battlefield, New Year's Day 1891. Scattered across this field up to a distance of two miles from Big Foot's tent, were the remains of nearly two hundred Sioux. A snowstorm had covered many of the bodies and these were dug out and thrown in carts 'like so much cordwood' and buried in a mass grave–near the site of the Hotchkiss guns which had mowed them down or set light to their tipis so that they were burnt alive. Smithsonian Institution, National Anthropological Archives, Washington.

Custer and his brother were laid side by side in a shallow grave no more than eighteen inches deep, their bodies covered with pieces of blanket and canvas. Part of an Indian travois was placed over the mound and this was pinned to the ground with stakes and large stones. The burials of the others could however be hardly more than a symbolic gesture. Said Lieutenant Edward J. McClernand: 'As we had but a few spades, the burial of the dead was more of a pretense than a reality. A number were simply covered with sage brush. Yet we did our best.' (In *Cavalry Journal*, 1937).

In the valley where the tipi village had stood, Godfrey counted thirty-eight Indian burial scaffolds and Kill Eagle, a Blackfoot Sioux chief, later said that fourteen Indians had been killed on the field with Reno, thirty-nine on the Custer field and he knew of seven who died of wounds in the camp afterwards. (*New York Herald*, 6 October 1876).

Crow Agency – the tribal headquarters on the Crow Indian Reservation, Montana, is but three and a half miles from the Custer Battlefield. Camping with the Crow on the banks of the Little Big Horn creates the right atmosphere for the observation of local historic sites and tends to compel the enthusiast to daily travel to the battlefield and traverse the terrain in an attempt to bring a practical perspective to bear on the descriptions by countless writers who have studied the famous 'Custer's Last Stand', 'Custer Massacre' or 'Custer Tragedy' – depending on which Custer camp you belong to.

The battlefield – now a National Monument – can be reached from U.S. No. 87 or via the old Chicago, Burlington and Quincy railroad which runs to Crow Agency. Both routes run virtually parallel to Custer's original advance, that is approximately southeast from beyond Reno Hill to the northwest where the memorial now stands on the high hill overlooking the Little Big Horn.

The memorial stands over the remains of more than 200 men and is about six feet from the spot where Custer and his brother were found. It was erected in the spring and summer of 1881 by a party under the command of Lieutenant C. F. Roe of the Second Cavalry. (It replaced that made of cordwood and horse-bones erected by Captain C. Sanderson of the 11th U.S. Infantry in April 1879). The marker, on which are carved 261 names, consists of three granite blocks weighing approximately six tons apiece. They had been transported via the Big Horn river and then hauled by teams to their final destination; at this time, fully five years after the battle, most of the fallen were largely unburied, and wooden markers were driven into the ground where remains were found. Such markers were subsequently replaced by ones of stone. Thus, as you now stand on Custer Hill looking towards the Little Big Horn, you can see clusters of white markers scattered over the hillsides. Many markers, however, cannot be seen from Custer Hill, since they are concealed by the rolling contours of the slope down to the river. To the east may be seen the markers on Calhoun Hill where the men of companies I and L were annihilated and the horse, Comanche, was found.

Walking approximately southwest across the rugged terrain, we found scattered markers to the left and right; on reaching the Little Big Horn river the vegetation becomes lush and green – in contrast to the almost desert-like landscape of the battlefield itself, where in summer the earth is like brown sugar knitted together by the roots of dried buffalo grass and sage brush. Across the river could be seen the location of the old Cheyenne camp site – the most northern part of the Indian village. The original site is, however, best approached from the little community of Garryowen (named after the regimental battle song of the Seventh Cavalry) which consists of a farm, small store and post office adjacent to both the Reno battlefield and old Indian village site.

East across the river, one can see the high bluffs to which Reno retreated with such disastrous consequences after he was repulsed on the flats south of the village. The historically minded can walk across these flats and with careful observation of the topography locate the first and second skirmish line. From the latter it is then about two miles across farmland and the Little Big Horn to the Reno–Benteen entrenchment. In the fall of 1964, the historian, J. W. Vaughn, using a metal detector, commenced a systematic coverage of the Reno battlefield in the hope of finding tangible evidence of the location of the fighting. (Vaughn, 1966, p. 146). Planning his researches on the basis of the written records of participants, a map drawn up by Lieutenant Edward Maguire, and theories put forward by various students of the battle, his fascinating project led him to find long-lost cartridge cases, parts of uniforms and horse equipment. Their location has enabled him to reconstruct with considerable precision the various lines of attack and retreat across that green valley.

Today the motorists speed along Highway 87

The frozen body of Big Foot, Miniconjou chief. Suffering from pneumonia, the chief was supplied with a stove by the commanding officer Colonel Forsyth. As the firing commenced the chief ran out of his tent and was struck down. The tent caught fire and the stove, together with the remnants of the tent, can be seen in the background. Smithsonian Institution, National Anthropological Archives, Washington.

and past Garryowen, cutting right across the battlefield. Probably few of them realise the importance of this ground in the history of the Western frontier, or know that less than a century ago it witnessed not only the Custer defeat, but also one of the last great stands of the warriors of the Plains.

At the time of Sitting Bull's death on 15 December 1890, the Miniconjou Sioux Chief, Sitenka (Big Foot), and his band, were camped near Cherry Creek, some seventy miles south of the Grand River. Big Foot had by this time become somewhat disillusioned with the Ghost Dance, but many of his band, urged on by the medicine man, Yellow Bird, continued to participate in the ceremonies, in the frantic hope that the promises of a restoration of the old life would be fulfilled. It was in the direction of this encampment that some 250 of Sitting Bull's people fled after the Chief's death. About thirty miles from Big Foot's camp, they were met by Captain J. H. Hurst of the Seventh Infantry. The Sioux were exhausted and starving and they told Hurst that 'their great chief and friend Sitting Bull' had been killed at Standing Rock without cause and that they would never return. They could not find their friends and relatives and were undecided as to what to do; after much diplomatic parleying and promises of good treatment, Hurst persuaded the majority to surrender their guns. The next day they broke camp and were escorted to Fort Sully where they were held as prisoners of war.

Thirty-eight others of Sitting Bull's people, however, managed to join Big Foot's Miniconjou band, which was now considered potentially dangerous and the responsibility for keeping it under constant surveillance was assigned to Lieutenant-Colonel E. V. Sumner of the Eighth Cavalry. On 21 December Sumner met with Big Foot, telling him that the Miniconjou must return to their homes. At the same time he upbraided the Mini-

Marguerite Zitkala-noni, Wounded Knee survivor. As the burial party traversed the field they came across a baby girl wrapped up in a shawl. She was lying beside her dead mother who had been struck by two bullets. On the head of the child was a little buckskin cap upon which the American flag had been embroidered in beadwork. The Indian women in camp gave her the name of Zitkala-noni or 'Lost Bird' and she was adopted by General Colby, who commanded the Nebraska state troops. Lost Bird's father was never identified and was probably buried in the mass grave. In later years Marguerite sickened of white society but could find no peace amongst her people and she died destitute. From James Mooney's *The Ghost Dance Religion*, Washington, 1896.

conjou for harbouring the fugitive Hunkpapa, to which Big Foot retorted 'that they were his brothers and relations; that they had come to his people hungry, footsore, and almost naked; and that he had taken them in and fed them, and that no one with a heart could do any less'.

Surveying the scene, Sumner could hardly deny the truth of the Chief's statement.

By 22 December, some 330 men, women, and children, mostly Miniconjou but including the thirty-eight Hunkpapa, led by Big Foot and escorted by Colonel Sumner and his command of about 200 men, were making their slow way to Camp Cheyenne where Sumner planned to camp the Sioux and keep them under direct observation until the Ghost Dance troubles were resolved. Big Foot – forever the wise diplomat and compromiser – was both friendly and compliant with every order. By now Sumner, who 'had a genuine respect and sympathy for the Indian' (Utley, 1963, p. 174) appeared to have won Big Foot's confidence. He observed that Big Foot exerted unusual influence amongst his people. But the route to Camp Cheyenne passed the site of their home village. As the party approached, it became apparent that even Big Foot would be powerless to prevent the families from returning to their homes. Big Foot

rode over to Sumner and said 'I will go with you to your camp, but there will be trouble in trying to force these women and children, cold and hungry as they are, away from their homes. This is their home, where the Government has ordered them to stay, and none of my people have committed a single act requiring their removal by force.' (Utley, 1963, p. 181).

Before these events, even before the death of Sitting Bull, department headquarters at St Paul had telegrammed Sumner on 10 December indicating that they thought it desirable that Big Foot should be arrested and imprisoned at Fort Meade (located just northeast of present-day Deadwood City, South Dakota). Sumner, who recognized the peaceful influence of Big Foot on his band, had ignored this suggestion. Now he was in a dilemma, for he could see that the danger lay not so much with Big Foot himself but with the younger warriors who were becoming increasingly hostile; more than ever he needed to rely on the diplomatic Chief and his words needed weighing carefully.

Sumner agreed to allow the Sioux to stay on the promise that Big Foot, with the refugee Hunkpapa, would report next day to Camp Cheyenne for a council. To this Big Foot agreed, and thus Sumner and his command proceeded to Camp Cheyenne, arriving there in the early evening on 21 December. 'I concluded that one of two things must happen,' he later wrote. 'I must either consent to them going to their village or bring on a fight; and, if the latter, must be the aggressor and, if the aggressor, what possible reason could I produce for making an attack on peaceable, quiet Indians on their reservation and at their homes, killing perhaps many of them and offering, without any justification, the lives of many officers and enlisted men.' (Utley, 1963, p. 181).

By noon on 23 December, Big Foot had failed to report at Camp Cheyenne. Big Foot later explained that the refugee Hunkpapa had fled and that 'he did not want to face the Colonel until he had found them'. (Utley, 1963, p. 183). The situation was, however, more complex than this. According to the government ethnologist, James Mooney, who was to later make a detailed study of the entire Ghost Dance affair, there were by now almost 3000 troops in Sioux country. After exhaustive discussions, Big Foot and his headmen finally conceded to the majority demand which was for Big Foot to lead his people to their Oglala relatives at Pine Ridge who, two weeks previously, had sent Big Foot a message 'offering "the great compromiser" 100 ponies to come to Pine Ridge and restore tranquillity'. (Utley, 1963, p. 174).

On the morning of 24 December, Sumner received a message from the exhausted chief (he had by now begun to feel the effects of the onset of pneumonia): 'Tell Sumner, said Big Foot, that he, Big Foot, wanted to go to Bennett' (Fort Bennett near the Cheyenne River agency some miles north of present-day Pierre, South Dakota) 'but his people would not let him. They demanded that he lead them to Pine Ridge, and lead them he would.' (Utley, 1963, p. 185).

Perhaps, considering the nature of the fair minded Big Foot, it was as well he did not go to Sumner for on the same day the officer received a telegram from General Miles who had now set up his headquarters in Rapid City and assumed supreme command of all the units in Dakota: 'The attitude of Big Foot has been defiant and hostile and you are authorized to arrest him or any of his people. . . . The Standing Rock Indians (Hunkpapa) have no right to be there and should be arrested . . . if necessary round up the whole camp and disarm them, and take them to Fort Meade or Bennett.' (In Utley, 1963, p. 185).

The hunt for the Miniconjou was on!

On 28 December 1890, Major Whitside of the Seventh Cavalry finally managed to intercept Big Foot just west of the Badlands on the northern border of Pine Ridge Reservation. Big Foot requested a parley; Whitside refused and demanded an unconditional surrender which the frightened Indians immediately gave; by the time they reached Wounded Knee creek, a total force of 470 men – including eight troops of cavalry complete with four Hotchkiss guns – virtually encircled the 300 Miniconjou (200 of whom were women and children). As instructed, the Sioux pitched their tipis on a level open plain just west of the creek.

'In the centre of the camp the Indians had hoisted a white flag as a sign of peace and a guarantee of safety.' (Mooney, 1896, p. 115).

At about 8 a.m. on 29 December, preparations were made to disarm the Sioux. Colonel Forsyth, who had now taken over as commanding officer, walked towards Big Foot's tent. Here he explained that their arms must be surrendered and assured them 'that they were perfectly safe in the hands of *their old friends* the soldiers, and that starvation and other troubles were now happily at an end.' (Utley, 1963, p. 206).

Big Foot conferred with his warriors and finally he advised 'Give up the bad guns . . . keep the good ones.' During these parleys, children played in and around the tipis. Nobody anticipated a fight . . . but on a slight hill overlooking the crowded village were posted a battery of four Hotchkiss guns and they were 'trained directly on the Indian camp'. (Mooney, 1896, p. 115).

Twenty warriors were ordered to go to their tipis and bring out their guns – within minutes they returned, with two! Their reluctance precipitated sterner action and Forsyth ordered a detachment of troops to search the tipis. Versions vary widely as to the conduct of the troops and the reaction of the Sioux. Later, as he lay dying, Lieutenant Mann was to describe the scene that followed:

'We went through the tents searching for arms, and while this was going on, everyone seemed to be good natured, and we had no thought of trouble. The enlisted men were not allowed to go inside the tents and only took the arms as we [officers] handed

Burying the dead at Wounded Knee, January 1891. The bodies of the Sioux, stripped of Ghost Dance shirts, were thrown into a long deep trench on the hill overlooking Wounded Knee Creek. The tragedy brought to a sudden end the hopes of The People and finally drove home the impossibility of any escape from white dominance. West Point Museum Collection.

them out. The squaws were sitting on bundles concealing guns and other arms. We lifted them as tenderly and treated them as nicely as possible. Had they been the most refined ladies in the land, they could not have been treated with more consideration. The squaws made no resistance, and when we took the arms they seemed to be satisfied. Wallace (a tall, gaunt, fatherly looking man) played with the children chucking them under the chin and being as pleasant with them all as could be. He had picked up a stone war club, which he carried with him.' (In Utley, 1963, pp. 209–210).

James Mooney, however, related the incident another way:

'The search had consumed considerable time and created a good deal of excitement among the women and children, as the soldiers found it necessary in the process to overturn the beds and other furniture of the tipis and in some instances drove out the inmates. All this had its effect on their husbands and brothers, already wrought up to a high nervous tension and not knowing what might come next.' (Mooney, 1896, p. 115).

While the soldiers were searching for guns and the tension mounted, Yellow Bird, the medicine man, harangued the subdued warriors. He reminded them of the protective power of their Ghost Dance shirts; that the soldiers would become 'weak and powerless' and their bullets harmless and urged them to resist the insulting behaviour of the soldiers. The more mature warriors, forever aware of the close proximity of the women and children, ignored his suggestions, but the younger men became increasingly agitated. Largely frustrated by their attempts to locate firearms, Forsyth decided that the only effective course left was to search each warrior individually for weapons. As the first few were disarmed, Yellow Bird suddenly scooped a handful of dust from the ground and threw it into the air. An instant later,

Sioux camp near Wounded Knee. South Dakota, 1891. Finally driven into submission the survivors settle down to a sedentary existence. Already they are dependent on the products of the dominant race, using canvas for their tipis and wheeled carts, issued by the government, which have largely replaced the travois. It will be nearly half a century before anyone begins to care about them again.

five or six young warriors sprang from the ground, blankets now cast aside and guns levelled toward K troop; the warriors hesitated, rifles cocked:

'I thought, the pity of it! What can they be thinking of?' (Lieutenant Mann, in Utley, 1963, p. 212).

As the rifles of the six young men thundered into action, Lieutenant Mann shouted his command: 'Fire! Fire on them!'

In those first few seconds, the hundred carbines of troops K and J mowed down almost half of the able warriors – many of whom in fact had no guns. At the sound of the first volley, the Hotchkiss guns opened fire on the tipi village. The guns fired two pound explosive shells at the rate of almost fifty a minute 'mowing down everything alive'. (Mooney, 1896, p. 118). Many died within those first few tragic minutes and when the mopping up was over, almost 200 Sioux together with 25 soldiers were dead or dying on the battlefield.

The aged Eagle Elk later recalled one of many personal tragedies. He saw a Sioux woman holding a child under her blanket and she was crying. Not until she looked up did he recognize her as a young girl he had known in the Grandmother's land.

'"O Shonka' kan! Shonka' kan! They have killed him. They have killed him! . . ." I put her on my horse and led him, walking, and all the while she held the child close under her blanket, crying hard. It was a little boy and he was dead!' (Neihardt, 1953, p. 255).

By late afternoon Forsyth, with his wounded and dead, left the scene and made for Pine Ridge Agency. Within the space of a few hours – as if mother nature herself was sickened by the slaughter – a heavy snowstorm, followed by a blizzard, all but obliterated the carnage of that terrible confrontation of Red and White.

Three days later on New Year's Day, 1891, troops again returned to Wounded Knee; scattered for up to two miles from the scene of the encounter were the bodies of women and children who had attempted to escape. Some were found alive 'badly wounded or frozen, or both and most of them died after being brought in. Four babies were found alive under the snow . . . they were all badly frozen and only one lived . . . a baby girl of only three or four months was found under the snow, carefully wrapped under a shawl, beside her dead mother, whose body was pierced with two bullets. On her head was a little cap of buckskin, upon which the American flag was embroidered in bright beadwork.' (Mooney, 1896, pp. 127–132).

A deep trench was dug on the top of the hill overlooking Wounded Knee creek. Into this were piled the bodies of The People. Many of the bodies were stripped of the Ghost Dance shirts by souvenir-hunting whites. The bodies were stiff and frozen 'like so much cordwood'. The earth was heaped over them. Many cared, many mourned – red and some white – but it was too late; the sun had already set for the Warriors of the Plains.

Commenting on the event some forty years later, a Sioux remarked: 'After the Battle of Wounded Knee all ambition was taken out of us. We have never since been able to regain a foothold.' Social anthropologists, who made a special study of the Society and Personality development of the Pine Ridge Sioux thirty years ago, were led to comment that the tragedy brought to a sudden end the hopes of the Ghost Dancers, that Wounded Knee 'drove home the impossibility of escape from white subjugation' and that the battle had remained in the minds of many Pine Ridge people 'as a symbol of injustice and abuse at the hands of the white man'. (Macgregor, Hassrick and Henry, 1946, p. 33). When the ethnologist, James Mooney, visited the Wounded Knee site a year after the battle, he found that the Sioux had placed sticks in the ground to mark where the dead had fallen, and he was led to conclude that the first volley must have killed nearly half the warriors. Around the trench where at least 120 Sioux were buried, they had erected a wire fence and smeared the posts with sacred red medicine paint. He speculated too, that a ballad written by W. H. Panther, a coloured private of

Troop I of the Ninth Cavalry, which had become a favourite among the troops and with the scattered frontiersmen of Dakota and Nebraska during the campaign, was probably by this time 'a classic of the barracks' (Mooney, 1896, p. 136).

> 'The Red skins left their agency, the soldiers
>   left their Post,
> All on the strength of an Indian tale about
>   Messiah's ghost
> Got up by savage chieftains to lead their
>   tribes astray;
> But Uncle Sam wouldn't have it so, for he
>   ain't built that way.
> They swore that this Messiah came to them
>   in vision's sleep,
> And promised to restore their game and
>   Buffaloes a heap,
> So they must start a big ghost dance, then
>   all would join their band,
> And may be so we lead the way into the
>   great Bad Land.

Chorus:

> They claimed the shirt Messiah gave, no
>   bullet could go through,
> But when the soldiers fired at them they saw
>   that this was not true.
> The Medicine man supplied them with their
>   great Messiah's grace,
> And he, too, pulled his freight and swore the
>   7th hard to face.'

Running in all to five verses and described by Mooney as 'a good specimen of American ballad poetry', the song was published for distribution among the soldiers during the campaign; it is particularly interesting for it displays very well the prevalent frontier attitude towards the Sioux and underlined the immense difficulties facing the two races as the red man sought to adjust to his bleak future.

Today, the Wounded Knee site is located on the Pine Ridge (Oglala Sioux) Reservation in South Dakota. On our first visit to it, we drove down from the site where Sitting Bull had been killed near the Grand River on the Standing Rock Indian Reservation and on through the Cheyenne River Reservation, following the old Indian trail southward across Cherry Creek. We camped for the night in the Bad Lands, east of the Cheyenne River, near the small community of Scenic. Recalling that many Sioux families had retreated to this area during the Ghost Dance trouble of 1890, we marvelled at their ability to survive in such a hostile environment of grotesquely shaped stratified rock and drifting coloured sand. Temperatures soared during the day and plummeted to freezing point at night, even during the summer.

At Porcupine, just north of Wounded Knee, Sioux youngsters curious of the Union Jack which flapped from our car aerial seemed more interested in news of the Beatles than telling of the best route to Wounded Knee Creek, and seemed to know little of the affair there – although we were grati-

Site of Big Foot's tent. The church on the hill built near the mass grave has been the scene of 'Wounded Knee II'. Acting as headquarters and sanctuary for the hard-core activists of the American Indian Movement it was taken over in February 1972 to draw attention to the 'Trail of Broken Treaties'. Pointing to the greed, apathy and prejudice which dominates white society, some now justify violence to call attention to their condition. The basic message, however, of the new generation of North American Indians is summed up in the wise words of one of their heroes – Sitting Bull – 'Come, my brothers, let us see what kind of world we make for our children.'

fied to hear them conversing in their native tongue. (Proud grandparents on most of the large Reservations – Sioux, Cheyenne, Crow, especially – ensure that their grandchildren do not forget their native language).

The battlefield at Wounded Knee has not changed much since those grim winter days long ago. Running due west from the Wounded Knee Creek, one can still see the line of the ravine where, at the west bend, a number of Sioux took refuge during the onslaught. Markers clearly show the original location of troops, guns and Indians. A made-up road now cuts across the field to the north of which stood Big Foot's tent where he was shot down in the first few minutes of the battle. Where eighty-five years ago had stood four Hotchkiss guns trained down on the Sioux encampment, there is a small Roman Catholic Church standing on the hill which in its sombre way dominates the whole scene.

Behind the Church, now curbed with white stone and enclosing numerous faded plastic flowers (the real things die within minutes in the blazing sun), is the mass grave and alongside is a large stone marker engraved with the names of the fallen Sioux. As the cameras of gum-chewing tourists clicked around me, I thought of the new message printed on a Christmas card from a Sioux friend, that The People now offer:

> Maka akanl wicaśa iyuha el
>   (*Peace on earth*)
> Walakata na woawicin waśte
>   (*To men of good will*)

BIBLIOTHÈQUE DE BROSSARD

Bibliography

Bell W. *New Tracks in North America* 2 vols. London, 1869.

Benedict R. *Configurations of Culture in North America.* In American Anthropologist New Series Volume 34. No. 1. The American Anthropological Association. Menasha, Wisconsin, 1932.

Berlandier J. L. (Ed by J. C. Ewers). *The Indians of Texas in 1830.* Washington, 1969.

Blackmore W. *The North American Indians.* London, 1869

Blish H. H. *A Pictographic History of the Oglala Sioux.* Lincoln, Nebraska, 1967.

Bourke J. *On the Border with Crook.* New York, 1892.

Bowers A. W. *Mandan Social and Ceremonial Organization.* Chicago, 1950.

Brackenbridge H. M. *Journal of a Voyage up the River Missouri.* Reprinted in Thwaite's *Early Western Travels.* Vol 6. 1906.

Brady C. T. *Indian Fights and Fighters.* New York, 1904. *North Western Fights and Fighters.* New York, 1907.

Brininstool E. A. *Crazy Horse.* Los Angeles, 1949. *Fighting Indian Warriors.* Harrisburg, Pennsylvania, 1953.

Bushnell D. I. *Burials of the Algonquian, Sciouan and Caddoan Tribes West of the Mississippi.* Bulletin 83, Bureau of American Ethnology, Smithsonian Institution. Washington, 1927.

Catlin G. *The North American Indians.* London, 1841.

Clark W. P. *The Indian Sign Language.* Philadelphia, 1885.

Cocking M. *Matthew Cocking's Journal, 1772–1773* Vol 1. Proceedings and Transactions, Royal Society of Canada. Ottawa, 1907.

Congressional Record House of Representatives. Discussions of House Bill, No. 1335. 1876.

Culbertson T. (Ed. by J. F. McDermott). *Journal of an Expedition to the Mauvaises Terres and the Upper Missouri in 1850.* Bulletin 147. Bureau of American Ethnology, Smithsonian Institution. Washington, 1952.

Dempsey H. *Crowfoot: Chief of the Blackfeet.* University of Oklahoma Press, 1972.

Denig E. T. (Ed by J. N. B. Hewitt). *Indian Tribes of the Upper Missouri.* In 46th Annual Report of the Bureau of American Ethnology, Smithsonian Institution. Washington, 1930. (Ed by J. C. Ewers) *Five Indian Tribes of the Upper Missouri.* University of Oklahoma Press, 1961.

Densmore F. *Teton Sioux Music.* Bulletin 61, Bureau of American Ethnology, Smithsonian Institution. Washington, 1918. *Mandan and Hidatson Music.* Bulletin 80, Bureau of American Ethnology, Smithsonian Institution. Washington 1923. *A Collection of Specimens from the Teton Sioux.* Indian Notes and Monographs, Vol XI No. 3. Museum of the American Indian, Heye Foundation. New York, 1948.

Devereux G. *Reality and Dream. Psychotherapy of a Plains Indian.* New York, 1969.

Dodge R. I. *The Hunting Grounds of the Great West.* London, 1877.

Dorsey G. A. *The Arapaho Sun Dance.* Vol IV, Anthropological Series Publication 75. Chicago 1903. *The Cheyenne: The Sun Dance.* Vol IX, Anthropological Series Publication 103. Chicago, 1905.

Ewers J. C. *The Horse in Blackfoot Indian Culture.* Bulletin 159 Bureau of American Ethnology, Smithsonian Institution. Washington, 1955. Personal communication to the author, 1955. *George Catlin, Painter of Indians and the West.* In Smithsonian Report for 1955, pp. 483–528. Smithsonian Institution. Washington, 1956. *The Blackfoot.* University of Oklahoma Press, 1958. *Chiefs from the Missouri and Mississippi and Peale's Silhouettes of 1806.* In the Smithsonian Journal of History, Vol. I. Washington, 1966. *The White Man's Strongest Medicine.* Bulletin of Missouri Historical Society, 1967.

Farb P. *Man's Rise to Civilization.* London, 1969.

Flannery R. *The Gros Ventres of Montana.* The Catholic University of American Press. Washington D.C., 1953.

Fletcher A. C. and La Flesche. *The Omaha Tribe.* Twenty-seventh Annual Report, Bureau of American Ethnology, Smithsonian Institution, Washington, 1905–6.

Garretson J. *The American Buffalo.* New York, 1930.

Gilmore M. R. *Uses of Plants by the Indians of the Missouri River Region.* Thirty-third Annual Report of the Bureau of American Ethnology, Smithsonian Institution. Washington, 1919.

Graham W. A. *The Custer Myth.* Harrisburg, Pennsylvania, 1953.

Grinnell G. B. *The Story of the Indian.* London, 1896. *The Lodges of the Blackfeet.* In American Anthropologist, New Series Vol 3. New York, 1901. *The Fighting Cheyennes.* University of Oklahoma Press, 1956.

Hendry, Anthony. *York Factory to the Blackfoot Country; The Journal of Anthony Hendry 1754–1755.* Ed by Lawrence Burpee. Proceedings and Transactions of the Royal Society of Canada, 3rd Series, Vol 1. Ottawa, 1907.

Henry, Alexander and Thompson, David. *New Light on the Early History of the Greater Northwest.* The manuscript journals of Alexander Henry and David Thompson 1799–1814. Ed by Elliott Cowes. New York, 1897.

Hieb D. L. *Fort Laramie; National Monument Wyoming.* National Park Service Historical Handbook No. 20. Washington, 1954.

Hilger M. I. *Arapaho Child Life and its Cultural Background.* Bulletin 148. Bureau of American Ethnology, Smithsonian Institution. Washington, 1952.

Hodge F. W. (Ed.) *Handbook of American Indians North of Mexico.* Two volumes. Bureau of American Ethnology, Smithsonian Institution. Washington, 1907.

Howard J. H. *Dakota Winter counts as a Source of Plains History.* Anthropological Papers No. 61. In Bureau of American Ethnology Bulletin 173, Smithsonian Institution. Washington, 1960. *The Canadian Dakota.* Oklahoma, 1972.

Hyde G. *Red Cloud's Folk.* University of Oklahoma Press, 1937.

Innis H. A. *Peter Pond, Fur Trader and Adventurer.* Toronto, 1930.

Irving J. T. *Indian Sketches taken during an expedition to the Pawnee Tribes.* University of Oklahoma Press, 1955.

Jablow J. *The Cheyenne in Plains Indian Trade Relations 1795–1840.* Monograph 19, American Ethnological Society. University of Washington Press, 1950.

Johnson B. *Cheyennes in Court: An Aftermath of the Dull Knife Outbreak of 1878.* In English Westerners Brand Book Volume 4, No. 4. Publication No. 80. July 1962.

Kelsey H. *The Kelsey Papers.* Public Archives of Canada. Ottawa, 1929.

Kenton E. *Black Gown and Redskins.* London and Toronto, 1956.

Kurz R. (Ed by J. N. B. Hewitt). *Journal of Rudolph Frederick Kurz.* Bulletin 115, Bureau of American Ethnology, Smithsonian Institution. Washington, 1937.

Larocque F. *Journal of Larocque from the Assiniboine to the Yellowstone 1805.* Publications of the Canadian Archives, No. 3. Ottawa, 1909.

Laubin R. & G. *The Indian Tipi.* University of Oklahoma Press, 1957.

Lewis O. *The Effects of White Contact upon Blackfoot Culture.* Monograph 6. American Ethnological Society, University of Washington Press, 1942.

Lowie R. H. *Indians of the Plains.* The American Museum of Natural History. New York and London, 1954.

Maximilian, Prince of Wied Neuwied. *Travels in the Interior of North America.* Translated from the German by H. Evans Lloyd. Vol 3. Thwaites Edition, 1843.

Macbeth R. G. *Policing the Plains.* Toronto, 1931.

Mallery G. *Picture-Writing of the American Indians.* 10th Annual Report Bureau of American Ethnology, Smithsonian Institution. Washington, 1888–9.

Marquis T. B. *She Watched Custer's Last Battle.* Cactus Pony, Box 973, Scottsdale, Arizona, 1933. *Sitting Bull, Gall, The Warrior* Cactus Pony. Box 973 Scottsdale, Arizona, 1934.

MacEwan G. *Sitting Bull.* Edmonton, Alberta, 1973.

Macgregor G. *Warriors without Weapons.* University of Chicago Press, 1946.

McCann L. E. *The Grattan Massacre.* Nebraska History Volume XXXVII, Number 1, 1956.

McGillycuddy J. *McGillycuddy Agent.* Stanford University Press, 1941.

McClintock W. *The Old North Trail.* London, 1910.

Mooney J. *The Ghost Dance and Sioux Outbreak of 1890.* 14th Annual Report of the Bureau of American Ethnology, 1892–93, Part II. Washington, 1896.

McLaughlin J. *My Friend the Indian.* London, 1910.

Metcalf G. *Some Notes on an old Kiowa Shield and its History.* In the Great Plains Journal. Volume 8, No. 1. Lawton, Oklahoma, 1968.

Mishkin B. *Rank and Warfare among the Plains Indians.* Monograph 3. American Ethnological Society. University of Washington Press, 1940.

Miles N. A. *Personal Recollections and Observations of General Nelson A. Miles.* Chicago and New York, 1896.

Morgan L. H. *Lewis Henry Morgan: The Indian Journals 1859–62.* University of Michigan Press, 1959.

Neihardt J. G. *Eagle Voice: An Authentic Tale of the Sioux Indians.* London, 1953.

Pakes F. *The No-Flight Societies of the Plains Indians.* In the English Westerners Brand Book. Vol 10, No. 4. Publication No. 140, London, July, 1968.

Parkman F. *La Salle and the Discovery of the Great West.* Boston, 1883. *The Oregon Trail.* Boston, 1889.

Peterson H. L. *American Indian Tomahawks.* Museum of the American Indian, Contributors Vol XIX, 1965, Heye Foundation. New York, 1971.

Pfaller L. *Father De Smet in Dakota.* Assumption Abbey Press, Richardton, N. Dakota, 1962.

Pfefferkorn I. *Pfefferkorn's description of the Province of Sonora.* Coronado Cuarto Centennial Publication Vol 12. Albuquerque, New Mexico, 1949.

Powell P. J. *Sweet Medicine: The Continuing Role of the Sacred Arrows, The Sun Dance and the Sacred Buffalo Hut in Northern Cheyenne History.* 2 vols. University of Oklahoma Press, 1969.

Reynolds W. F. *Report on the Exploration of the Yellowstone and the Country Drained by that River.* Senate Executive Document 77, 40th Congress, 1st Session. Washington, 1868.

Robinson D. *A History of the Dakota or Sioux Indians.* South Dakota State Historical Society, 1904.

Schultz J. W. *My Life as an Indian: the Story of a Red Woman and a White Man in the Lodges of the Blackfeet.* New York, 1907.

Secoy F. R. *Changing Military Patterns on the Great Plains.* Monograph 21, American Ethnological Society. University of Washington Press, 1953.

Seton E. T. *Wild Animals at Home.* London, 1913.

Seymour E. W. *The Story of the Red man.* London, New York and Toronto, 1929.

Sheridan C. *Redskin Interlude.* London, 1938.

Shimkin D. B. *The Wind River Shoshone Sun Dance.* Anthropological Papers, No. 41. Bulletin 151, Bureau of American Ethnology, Smithsonian Institution. Washington, 1953.

Smith, De Cost. *Red Indian Experiences.* London, 1949.

Swanton J. R. *The Indian Tribes of North America.* Bulletin 145, Bureau of American Ethnology, Smithsonian Institution. Washington, 1952.

Taft R. *Photography and the American Scene.* New York, 1938.

Taunton F. *Army Failures against the Sioux in 1876.* In English Westerners Brand Book, Vol 5, No. 3. Publication No. 88. London, April 1963. *Treaty Obligations and the Sioux War of 1876.* In the English Westerners Brand Book. Vol 13, No. 3. London, April, 1971.

Taylor C. F. *The Plains Indians Leggings.* In the English Westerners Brand Book. Vol 3, No. 2. London, January, 1961. *Plains Indian Headgear.* In the English Westerners Brand Book. Vol 4, No. 3. London, April, 1962. *Early Plains Indian Quill Techniques in European Museum Collections.* In *Plains Anthropologist,* Journal of the Plains Conference. Vol 7, pp. 58–70. University of Nebraska, 1962. *Early Decorative Art of the Plains Indians.* In English Westerners Special Publication No. 1. 10th Anniversary Publication. London 1964. *The O-kee-pa and Four Bears: An Insight into Mandan Ethnology.* In the English Westerners Brand Book, Vol 15, No. 3. London, April, 1973.

Tomkins W. *Universal American Indian Sign Language.* San Diego, California, 1926.

Trenholm V. C. *The Arapahoes.* University of Oklahoma Press, 1970.

Turner C. F. *Across the Medicine Line.* Toronto, 1973.

Twaites R. G. *The Original Journals of the Lewis and Clark Expedition 1804–1806.* New York, 1904.

Umfreville E. *The Present State of Hudson's Bay.* London, 1790.

Utley R. M. *The Last Days of the Sioux Nation.* Yale University Press, 1963. *Frontiersmen in Blue: The United States Army and the Indian.* New York, 1967.

Vaughn J. W. *Indian Fights; New Facts on Seven Encounters.* University of Oklahoma Press, 1966.

Vestal S. *Sitting Bull: Champion of the Sioux.* University of Oklahoma Press, 1957.

Wallace E. and Hoebel E. *The Comanches.* University of Oklahoma Press, 1952.

Webb W. P. *The Great Plains.* New York and London, 1931.

Wedel W. R. *Prehistoric Man on the Great Plains.* University of Oklahoma Press, 1961.

Whitman M. *The Journal and Correspondence of Mrs Marcus Whitman.* In the Transactions of the Nineteenth Annual Reunion of the Oregon Pioneer Association for 1891. Portland, Oregon, 1893.

Wildscut W. (Ed by J. C. Ewers). *Crow Indian Medicine Bundles.* Museum of the American Indian, Contributors Vol XVII, Heye Foundation. New York, 1960.

Wilson G. L. *The Horse and the Dog in Hidatsan Culture.* Anthropological Papers, American Museum of Natural History, Vol 15, Part II. New York, 1924.

Wilson T. *Arrow Wounds.* In American Anthropologist, New Series, Vol 3. New York, 1901.

Winship G. P. *The Coronado Expedition, 1540–42.* Annual Reports of the Bureau of American Ethnology, Vol 14, Part I. Washington, 1892–3.

Wissler C. *Some Protective Designs of the Dakota.* Anthropological Papers, Vol 1, Part II. American Museum of Natural History. New York, 1908. *Material Culture of the Blackfoot Indians.* Vol 5. Anthropological Papers, American Museum of Natural History. New York, 1910. *The Social Life of the Blackfoot Indians.* American Museum of Natural History. Anthropological Papers. Vol VII, Part I. New York, 1911. *North American Indians of the Plains.* Handbook series No. 1. New York, 1920. *Indian Cavalcade.* New York, 1938.

Wood W. R. *An Interpretation of Mandan Culture and History.* Bulletin 198. Bureau of American Ethnology, Smithsonian Institution. Washington, 1967.

Acknowledgments

The publishers would like to thank the following for providing the illustrations indicated:

Black and white

Amon Carter Museum, Fort Worth, Texas 77; Bernisches Historisches Museen 5 top, 14 top, 14 bottom, 31, 51, 57, 69; Birmingham Reference Library 81 bottom right, 86 left, 86 right; British Museum 103; Chandler-Pohrt Collection 54; Custer Battlefield Historical and Museum Association, Inc. 135; Danish National Museum, Copenhagen 27; J. R. Datlen Collection 39 bottom left; Denver Public Library, Western Collection 111; Field Museum of Natural History, Chicago, 73 bottom; Glasgow Museums and Art Galleries 19 bottom right; Glenbow-Alberta Institute, Calgary 29; Hamlyn Group-Hawkley Studio Associates Ltd, 6, 13 top left, 17, 22, 24, 46, 63, 76 bottom left, 81 top left, 127; Bill Holm 56; Hudson's Bay Company 55 top, 55 bottom; Joslyn Art Museum, Northern Natural Gas Company Collection, Omaha, Nebraska 9 top right, 12,

42, 52, 59, 78, 87; Library of Congress, Washington 89 top; The Mansell Collection, London 108; Minnesota Historical Society 124; Montana Historical Society, Helena 5 bottom; Musée de l'Homme, Paris 21 top right, 43, 75 top left, 79 top left; Museen für Völkerkunde, Berlin 11; Museum of The American Indian, Heye Foundation, 9 bottom left, 39 top right, 39 bottom right, 45, 109; Museum of Archaeology and Ethnology, Cambridge University 76 top right; Museum of Ethnology, Harvard University 7; National Archives, Washington 83; Nebraska State Historical Society 47 top right, 133; Paul Dyck Collection, Paul Dyck Research Foundation 15, 71, 91 bottom right; Peabody Museum, Harvard University 32, 73 top; Royal Ontario Museum, Toronto 20, 28; Floyd T. Ryan 134; Smithsonian Institution, National Anthropological Archives, Washington, D.C. 13 bottom right, 23, 36, 60, 72, 79 bottom right 91 top left 99, 107, 119, 120, 136 bottom, 137, 140; State Historical Society of Colorado 90; State Historical Society of North Dakota 84, 121, 125; Thomas

Gilcrease Institute of American History and Art, Tulsa, Oklahoma 16, 93, 98, 101; Walters Art Gallery, Baltimore 85; West Point Museum Collections 139; Whitney Gallery of Western Art, Cody, Wyoming 67.

Colour

Bernisches Historisches Museen 48 bottom; British Museum 37 left, 37 right; Sam Cahoon 97 top; Chandler-Pohrt Collection 40 inset, 41; H. Frank Humphris 104; Musée de l'Homme, Paris 48 top; Public Archives of Canada 97 bottom; Whitney Gallery of Western Art, Cody, Wyoming 40, 112 bottom.

The author supplied the illustrations on the following pages: 8, 19 top left, 21 bottom left, 34, 35, 38, 47 bottom left, 53, 58, 61 top, 61 bottom, 64, 66, 70, 74, 75 bottom right, 89 bottom, 105, 112 top, 114, 115, 116, 117, 123, 128 top left, 128 bottom right, 129, 130 top, 130 bottom, 131, 136 top, 138, 141.

Index

PLAINS INDIAN TRIBES
DURING THE PERIOD 1800-1860

The broken line encloses the true high Plains Indian culture, c. 1820, generally defined as the nomadic-horse-buffalo culture. To the east were the semi-sedentary groups, and a detached group (Mandan, Hidatsa, Arikara) on the upper Missouri.

Note. During this period a number of tribes were moved from the east and relocated in this area. Principally the Kickapoo, Shawnee, and Delaware from the north-east and the Cherokee, Creek, Chickasaw, Seminole, and Chocotaw from the south-east. *Adapted from the original map by M. G. Johnson, Walsall.*

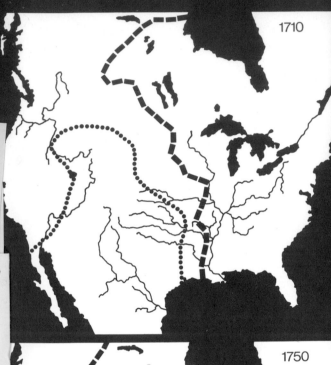

1710

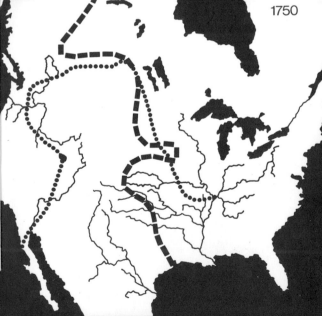

1750

■■■ Gun Frontier   ●●●●●●● Horse Frontier

The horse frontier moved north, and opened out — finally encompassing the whole west. The gun frontier moved west, inexorably. *Top*, North America in 1710 and, *bottom*, in 1750. *Based on information in F. R. Secoy: CHANGING MILITARY PATTERNS ON THE GREAT PLAINS. University of Washington Press, 1953.*